PROPERTY OF
ERAU PRESCOTT
LIBRARY

D1617129

Geologic Time Scale

EON	ERA	GEOLOGIC TIME (in millions of years)			DEVELOPMENT OF PLANTS AND ANIMALS
		PERIOD	EPOCH		
Phanerozoic	Cenozoic	Quaternary	Holocene	0.008	Humans develop
			Pleistocene	1.8	Ice Ages
		Tertiary	Pliocene	5.3	
			Miocene	23.8	
			Oligocene	33.7	"Age of Mammals"
			Eocene	55.5	
			Paleocene	65.0	
	Mesozoic	Cretaceous	145	"Age of Reptiles"	Extinction of dinosaurs and many other species
		Jurassic	213		First flowering plants
		Triassic	248		First birds
					Dinosaurs dominant
	Paleozoic	Permian	286	"Age of Amphibians"	Extinction of trilobites and many other marine animals
		Pennsylvanian	325		First reptiles
		Mississippian	360		Coal swamps
					Amphibians abundant
		Devonian	410	"Age of Fishes"	First insect fossils
		Silurian	440		Fishes dominant
					First land plants
		Ordovician	505	"Age of Invertebrates"	First fishes
		Cambrian	544		Trilobites dominant
					First organisms with shells
Proterozoic		Precambrian (makes up about 85% of the geologic time scale)			First multi-celled organisms
	2500				
Archean	3800				First one-celled organisms
Hadean	4500				Age of oldest rocks

Hiking

ARIZONA'S GEOLOGY

IVO LUCCHITTA

THE
MOUNTAINEERS
BOOKS

Published by
The Mountaineers Books
1001 SW Klickitat Way, Suite 201
Seattle, WA 98134

© 2001 by Ivo Lucchitta

All rights reserved

First edition, 2001

No part of this book may be reproduced in any form, or by any electronic, mechanical, or other means, without permission in writing from the publisher.

Published simultaneously in Great Britain by Cordee, 3a DeMontfort Street, Leicester, England, LE1 7HD

Manufactured in the United States of America

Acquiring Editor: Margaret Foster
Project Editor: Christine Ummel Hosler
Copy Editor: Kathy Walker
Production Coordinator: Dottie Martin
Series Cover and Book Design: The Mountaineers Books
Layout Artist: Jennifer LaRock Shontz
Cartographer and Illustrator: Jennifer LaRock Shontz
All photographs by the author unless otherwise noted

Cover photograph: *Antelope Canyon, Arizona* © Jenny Hager/Adventure Photo
Frontispiece: *In the basin and range country.* Photo by Ivo Lucchitta

Library of Congress Cataloging-in-Publication Data
    Lucchitta, Ivo.
      Hiking Arizona's geology / Ivo Lucchitta; [photographer, Ivo
    Lucchitta].— 1st ed.
          p. cm.
    Includes bibliographical references and index.
      ISBN 0-89886-730-4
      1. Hiking—Arizona—Guidebooks. 2. Geology—Arizona—Guidebooks. 3.
    Arizona—Guidebooks. I. Title.
      GV199.42.A7 L83 2001
      557.91—dc21
                                        2001003068

♻ Printed on recycled paper

Contents

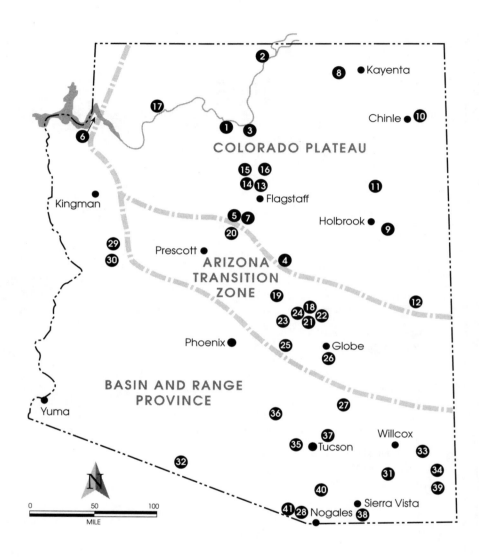

COLORADO PLATEAU

ARIZONA TRANSITION ZONE

BASIN AND RANGE PROVINCE

Kayenta

Chinle

Kingman

Flagstaff

Holbrook

Prescott

Phoenix

Globe

Yuma

Willcox

Tucson

Sierra Vista

Nogales

N

0   50   100
MILE

Preface

I have been a hiker all my life, disguised a good part of the time as a field geologist. All this hiking and walking has taught me a number of things. First, it beats the dismal rule that what is fun is bad for you, so this is a chance to have fun without paying some sinister penalty. Second, walking is the form of locomotion that best allows us to actually see and observe (there is a difference) and to hear what is around us. After all, we have evolved to interact with our surroundings at this kind of pace, which makes it possible to actually smell the flowers, the damp earth, the resin of the pines, and the sharp clean smell of the desert after a winter rain. All of which is more than can be claimed when careening about in or on some mechanical contraption.

Finally, the pleasure of hiking is enormously enhanced when the eyes are primed to observe and the brain is in gear, so that the natural surroundings begin to talk and display their inner workings, shyly at first, then almost exuberantly. This is what leads to inward cries of "Eureka!," flashes of understanding whereby the mind's eye discovers how the Earth today is the product of untold processes that came before. How today's parched desert, for example, may have been a warm shallow sea 600 million years ago, when life was busy inventing itself and exploding into an endless array of remarkable experiments. At that point, Earth, the underpinning of life, begins to talk.

This book, then, is aimed at those who like to have fun and who believe that walking is, in fact, great fun. It is also designed for those who know that the fun is greatly enhanced by having eyes and ears with which to see and hear the wonderful stories the Earth has to tell.

The mouth of the Grand Canyon

The Lees Ferry area

Acknowledgments

This is the place where it is customary to list all the people "without whose help this book would have never been possible." I find it difficult to do it this way. Each of us, at any given time, is connected with and indebted to so many people that it becomes almost capricious to single out some at the expense of others. So I will try another tack–that of tracing the conceptual lineage of this book, from those spiritual forebears who long ago opened my eyes to the world of geology, to those who have had a direct impact on the book itself.

Robert P. Sharp, extraordinary teacher at Caltech, suddenly and forcefully introduced the world of geology into my consciousness at a time when I was preoccupied with physics. Sharp's lectures and field trips made the world around me speak with clarity and elegance, revealing things that were never before imagined. There was no turning back.

Richard H. Jahns, my thesis professor, introduced me to the sheer delight to be found in craftsmanship and in asking the right questions, seeking the answers to these questions through careful observations in the field, and recording the results on those infinitely enticing pieces of paper called geologic maps.

Paul D. Krynine, endlessly eccentric and inscrutable to us graduate students, brought forth with relentless clarity the great Apollonian precept hidden under the clichés "separating the wheat from the chaff" and "not losing the forest for the trees." This man taught us how to think.

Edwin D. McKee, the spirit of the Grand Canyon, showed me how to tackle large research projects, got me started in Grand Canyon research, and kindled a fascinated love for that amazing place that will last as long as I do.

Rowland Tabor brought about the meeting between The Mountaineers Books and me, leading to the interesting tango between publisher and author that is at the heart of any book.

Kevin Horstman helped in a great many ways, not forgetting the great hospitality that he and Cori Hoag gave to weary travelers.

Achim Gottwald's help during the final stages of proofreading was essential; without him, the job would not have been done on time.

My wife Baerbel, formidable geologist whose interests range from Antarctica to Mars, has been my companion on most of the hikes logged in this book, making observations, shoring up my flimsy memory, and generally acting as a nonsense filter. She has been indispensable.

Finally, Yuri, our polite and amiable but fiercely independent Siberian husky, has encouraged me to go when I would rather have stayed, even humoring me with great patience when I lingered entirely too long over some rock totally devoid of interesting smells.

In spite of this splendid help, responsibility for errors and omissions that may have crept into this book is mine alone.

View from Estes Canyon–Bull Pasture Trail, looking south into Mexico; tuff breccia can be seen on the right.

Introduction

The foundation upon which this book rests is the notion that walking is a good thing and that understanding what is being walked through makes the good thing even better. The particular understanding at issue here is that of geology, a subject that does not come readily to the mind of many. Yet geology is the rocky foundation on which all life developed and—in the form of landscape—the stage on which it has played out its long and complex history. This is no less true for that peculiar variety of life called *Homo*, including its pretentious branch that is amusingly pleased to call itself *sapiens*.

Geology is a branch of science that has a certain grand simplicity about it, but this simplicity is not obvious when viewed from the perspective of human experience. Hills are not eternal. Hard rock can and often does flow like tar. The Earth is more like a ball of jello than a comfortingly rigid sphere. Everything is in motion. The top of Mount Everest is made of marine limestone. The landscape that you see and stand on today is probably young and bears no resemblance whatever to landscapes that preceded it. A million years is a short time for Earth yet an unfathomably long time for living things, including us. Clearly, common sense is a treacherous guide in these shoals, and a little knowledge can be a misleading thing indeed.

This book comes to the rescue by providing a brief primer to geology at the very beginning—no previous knowledge is assumed or expected of the reader. Reading this stuff really does help. Just settle into a comfortable armchair and have at it—it's not that long. Technical jargon is kept to a minimum but cannot be eliminated entirely because it is a shorthand designed to convey much information with economy. Technical terms are printed in *italics,* are usually explained in capsule form right after they are encountered, and are included in the glossary at the end of the book. At the front of the book you will find a diagram of the geologic time scale. Buying a good introductory textbook on geology will help you; the Suggested Reading list at the back of the book suggests a few.

Arizona is a large state, just a bit smaller than the country of Italy. Not surprisingly, it has a great many trails. It also has a complex geology. So, out of so many trails, how were these relatively few trails selected for inclusion here? One factor is that they all have scenic merit. Second, the trails illustrate the various aspects of Arizona geology. Third, they are distributed as evenly as possible throughout the state. Fourth, some kind of trail or route is available and accessible. Parts of the state, especially the southwest, even though geologically and scenically interesting, have no trails and are excessively remote. Others are inaccessible because of military reserves or Indian reservations. Finally, quite a few places of great geologic and scenic interest happen to be in private hands, which means that entering is vigorously discouraged. The results of these circumstances are twofold: the distribution of hikes is not even, and nearly all accessible trails (and most of those logged here) are on public lands. This discovery has led me to appreciate again the importance of these lands, underscoring the need to demand of our elected representatives that public lands be properly supported and decently funded. They are not the place to pinch pennies.

The geology and landscape of Arizona are complex. The Colorado Plateau occupies the northeastern part of the state; the Basin and Range Province occupies the southwestern part; and the Arizona Transition Zone—intermediate in geology and topography between the two—is a belt in between. These provinces differ from one another, so the hikes in this book have been selected to provide a good feel for the geologic characteristics and scenery of each.

Arizona is a hiker's paradise. The range in scenery is vast—desert ranges, saguaro-studded hills, volcanoes, great cliffs or "rims," and even the greatest canyon of them all, the Grand. But there is more. The three zones correspond to different elevations above sea level and thus have different climates. This might be seen as a disadvantage. For example, the southern deserts are inhospitable to hiking during the fiery summer months. However, the northern mountains are welcoming and cool in that season. The deserts are delightful in winter, when the mountains sleep under a thick cover of snow. The in-between zone is fine in the in-between seasons, fall and spring, and can give pleasurable hiking all year round. Distances between zones are not so great that the enthusiastic hiker cannot find an interesting and pleasant place to walk any time of the year. In addition, the different climatic zones make for a great range of vegetation types in the state, from hot desert scrub to tundra, passing on the way through desert riparian habitat, saguaro-paloverde desert, oak grassland, pinyon-juniper pigmy forest, ponderosa forest, aspen glades, and boreal forest of spruce, fir, and pine, each type with its own complement of flowers and birds. Could you ask for more?

HOW TO USE THIS BOOK

The information block at the head of each hike includes the hike's length, access, difficulty, maps, sources of information, and precautions about climate and weather. All this should help the reader know what to expect, decide where to go, and then enjoy a pleasant and safe trip. Most hikes listed are intended as day walks, because that is what most people prefer and because complexity increases greatly with overnight stays. However, some of the hikes are quite demanding, so could well be done in more than one day if desired. Stay alert to alternative routes and extensions of the hikes described here. Always consult your topographic map.

A NOTE ABOUT SAFETY

Safety is an important concern in all outdoor activities. No guidebook can alert you to every hazard or anticipate the limitations of every reader. Therefore, the descriptions of roads, trails, routes, and natural features in this book are not representations that a particular place or excursion will be safe for your party. When you follow any of the routes described in this book, you assume responsibility for your own safety. Under normal conditions, such excursions require the usual attention to traffic, road and trail conditions, weather, terrain, the capabilities of your party, and other factors. Keeping informed on current conditions and exercising common sense are the keys to a safe, enjoyable outing.

The Mountaineers Books

Proterozoic rocks between 1400 and 1800 million years old can be seen in the depths of the Grand Canyon's Inner Gorge (Hike 1).

The Art of Geology

Several branches of science have to do with dimensions that are entirely out of the field of human experience—astronomy, with its immense distances and seemingly infinite numbers of stars and galaxies, or particle physics, dealing with minuscule entities whose size and behavior are essentially incomprehensible in nonmathematical terms. Geology fits into this group because it deals with configurations of the Earth that have vanished, and with enormous spans of time.

The history of the Earth began some 4500 million years ago, when—it is thought—matter condensing out of dust clouds under the influence of gravitational attraction formed the solar system, consisting of the Sun and its attendant planets. For some planets or satellites—the Moon is a good example—history all but stopped shortly after it started, because these planets have neither internal activity nor surface processes that can bring about any significant change. Thus it is that the Moon displays mountains, lava flows, and impact craters that go back to its very beginning. Only the ceaseless rain of objects hurtling in from space and striking the Moon has modified its surface.

Earth is different. Earth is restless, driven by internal heat that causes great plates to move, collide, crumple, slide under each other, split apart. Earth has a substantial, water-rich atmosphere from which rain condenses and falls on the ground, gradually wearing away even the highest mountains. Earth has oceans of water, in which rocks are formed and in which life has evolved.

Understanding these processes of change is vital to understanding our planet, and so this book pays much heed to them, especially as recorded in landscapes. But landscapes are only the last link in a chain of events. The first is rocks and the minerals that compose them. So we must begin our journey with the fields of geology known as *mineralogy* (the study of minerals), *petrology* (the study of rocks), and *stratigraphy* (the study of rock layers). Once the rocks are in place, we can explore the processes by which they are bent, broken, and otherwise deformed; this is the field of *structure*. Only as a last step are we ready to tackle the processes of erosion that create landscapes. This is the domain of *geomorphology*, perhaps the most fun of all because it says something about the landscape that we see and on which we move.

In the mind of the geologist, two worlds must exist simultaneously. One is the three-dimensional world we observe all around us. The other, which the

17

THE ART OF GEOLOGY

mind reconstructs on the basis of what is seen today, is a long-vanished world that existed millions, or even billions, of years ago. So geology has a strong component of history. And reconstructing history demands skills that may seem almost intuitive, even though in reality they are based on observation and experience. For this reason geology is sometimes viewed as an art as much as a science. What's more, its historical aspect means that to understand geology we must first understand geologic time.

GEOLOGIC TIME

No understanding of Earth history is possible without some grasp of geologic time, which is so vast that we cannot understand it physically or intuitively. It can be done only by analogy. For example, let's look at *faults*, breaks of the earth's crust along which the two opposing sides move past one another. A rate of movement of 1 cm (this distance: _____) per year is not uncommon on faults. Consider a fault such as the San Andreas of California, where the movement is horizontal. Two points originally next to each other would be 10 km (6 miles) apart after 1 million years. Considering instead a fault on which the movement is vertical, the movement would create a mountain 10,000 meters (33,000 feet) high, higher than Mount Everest.

Not long after the birth of geology as a science, its practitioners discovered that *sedimentary* rocks (those deposited layer by layer, mostly in water) contain fossils of animals and plants that lived and died long ago. This is especially true of *marine* rocks (those deposited in the sea). The scientists further discovered that the fossil assemblage, or *fauna,* at the base of a thick stack of sedimentary rocks differs from faunas higher up the stack. Not only that, but the same fauna can be found at corresponding levels within sedimentary sequences in many different places.

Scientists then reasoned that each fauna marks a specific interval of geologic time, called a *period*. They gave each period a name derived from the name of the place where rocks with that assemblage of fossils were first discovered or are best exposed. For example, *Cambria,* the Roman name for Wales, gave its name to the Cambrian Period, the oldest period in the Paleozoic Era. Before long, it was discovered that rocks containing the fauna characteristic of the Cambrian strata of Wales were in fact widespread throughout the world. It became possible to define all strata containing that assemblage as Cambrian, whether they were exposed in Russia or in South Africa, and to consider them of equivalent age. Because faunas change over time, the result was an orderly sequence of periods, each with its unique and distinctive assemblage of fossils.

Once the various periods were studied and defined, it became clear that the geologic record showed major groupings of faunas, which in due course were formalized into a set of "umbrella" units. Rocks older than Cambrian contained few fossils; these rocks were first called *Precambrian* (before the Cambrian) and then later *Proterozoic* (having to do with first life), *Archean*, and *Hadean*. Overlying rocks, ranging from Cambrian at the base to Permian at the top, were grouped into the *Paleozoic* Era (having to do with ancient life), characterized by the explosion of marine life, although plants and amphibians did make it onto the land in the later part of this interval. Younger strata yet, ranging from Triassic to Cretaceous, were included in the *Mesozoic* Era (having to do with middle life). This was a time when the action shifted on land, which was populated not only by plants, but also by reptiles, including the dinosaurs. The youngest era is the *Cenozoic* (having to do with recent life), which includes the Tertiary and Quaternary Periods. This is the time of mammals, including at the very end those strange bipedal primates, humans. Collectively, this is called the stratigraphic system. It was a major achievement because it brought order to individual and local observations and allowed scientists to correlate rocks all across the world.

This, however, was only a relative time scale: one period was *younger* or *older* than another one. Nobody could tell, for example, just how many million years ago the mighty dinosaurs had ruled the world. That had to wait until the combined work of physicists, chemists, and geologists established an *absolute time scale* that could assign specific numerical ages to geologic events. This time scale is based on the observation that radioactive elements, the "parents," decay into other elements, the "daughters," at a fixed and unchangeable rate. The decay provided a means for measuring time.

First, scientists would measure precisely the amount of parent and daughter elements in the rock. Then they would use these numbers, together with the rate of decay, to determine how old the rock was. The resulting absolute age could be used to build the age framework of the stratigraphic system.

For example, suppose that somewhere in the world we find a datable material, perhaps a lava flow, near the base of Cambrian rocks, whose assignment to that period is based on their fossils. Once this flow is dated, we know that Cambrian time began at about the age given by the flow. By applying this method to other units of the stratigraphic record, we can gradually calibrate the entire record and establish a time (or *geochronologic*) framework. This has now been done, and the results are compiled in the geologic time scale shown near the front of this book.

The most impressive aspect of the time scale is that geologic time is so enormous, providing plenty of opportunities for the often slow processes that form minerals and assemble them into the rocks that collectively make up Earth's stony skeleton.

ROCKS AND MINERALS—
THE EARTH'S STONY SKELETON

People who study rocks and the minerals that form them recognize a daunting number of different types, many with complex and strange names. Fortunately, we can make do with a simple classification based on features readily seen in the field.

MINERALS

Minerals are inorganic substances made up of an orderly and characteristic arrangement of atoms of specific elements such as carbon or oxygen. The elements determine the mineral's chemical composition. For example, one atom of the element calcium combined with one atom of carbon and three atoms of oxygen produces calcium carbonate, written as $CaCO_3$, the composition of limestone. The chemical composition, together with its arrangement of atoms, determines the mineral's physical properties, such as hardness, and crystal form, such as the cube shape of sodium chloride (NaCl), or salt.

Although the number of minerals is very large, most of the rocks on earth are composed of a group of minerals which are called *silicates* because they contain *silica* (silicon dioxide or SiO_2) in combination with metals such as iron, magnesium, and aluminum. Of the seven minerals that are the most common constituents of rocks, six are silicates. The most common of these six are *feldspar*, an aluminum-bearing silicate, and *quartz*, which is pure silica. Both are usually light-colored. The other four are *olivine, pyroxene, amphibole,* and *biotite.* These contain iron and magnesium and are dark-colored (typically black, dark green, or dark brown), so they are called the dark minerals. Many of these common minerals are found in the well-known rock *granite,* in which dark minerals are scattered as specks within the light-colored bulk of the rock, composed of quartz and feldspar. Under a hand lens, the quartz grains look glassy but seldom show flat faces that flash in the sun. The feldspars, in contrast, do show faces that flash, are opaque, and are milky white or salmon-pink, depending on the kind of feldspar.

The last of the common minerals is a *carbonate*, specifically calcium carbonate, $CaCO_3$. The mineral with this composition is called *calcite*. The rock *limestone* is composed principally of calcite. A less common carbonate is the mineral *dolomite*, which contains magnesium and calcium.

The physical properties of minerals depend on the chemical composition and, in turn, have a major influence on the characteristics of rocks formed by the minerals. For example, the iron- and magnesium-rich dark minerals generally melt at a higher temperature than do the light-colored ones; dark minerals also tend to form hot, fluid *magmas* when molten. A consequence is that dark igneous rocks such as *basalt* are very hot and can flow far and fast when molten, whereas light-colored rocks such as *rhyolite* (with few dark minerals but much silica) are relatively cool and viscous in the molten state, so they flow little and with difficulty. These properties have a great influence on the behavior of volcanoes. Those that erupt silica-poor rocks form cones with gentle slopes, such as those in Hawaii, and seldom explode in a violent way. In contrast, volcanoes such as Vesuvius in Italy and Mount St. Helens in Washington state that erupt silica-rich rocks tend to have their throats plugged up by viscous lava. As a consequence, gas pressures within the volcano rise and rise until the plug is blown out in a catastrophic explosion.

ROCKS AND THEIR CLASSIFICATION

Rocks are composed of minerals and are divided into three groups based on their *genesis,* or how the rocks formed. *Igneous* rock has solidified from molten underground magma or from lava. *Sedimentary* rock is the result of the consolidation of loose sediment such as clay, silt, sand, or gravel that has accumulated in layers. *Metamorphic* rock is a preexisting rock that is altered without melting through changes in temperature, pressure, stress, or chemical environment. These three groups are discussed in greater detail later in this section.

Rocks are further divided on the basis of their chemical composition. This is especially important in classifying igneous and metamorphic rocks because these rocks are derived from a single source—either a mass of molten rock or a preexisting rock that has been heated and altered. These sources therefore constitute a well-defined chemical system. The chief chemical criterion used for classifying such rocks is the amount of silica present, which generally correlates inversely with the amount of iron and magnesium.

Each kind of igneous rock has a distinct chemical composition which determines what minerals one can expect to find in it. One of the consequences is that certain minerals cannot coexist in the same rock. For example, the silica-rich mineral quartz

The walls of Mount Ajo are composed mainly of rhyolite, a light-colored rock that has much silica but few dark minerals (Hike 32).

cannot exist in basalt, which has little silica, but the silica-poor mineral olivine can. These two minerals are not likely to be found in the same rock. This property can be very useful in identifying rocks in the field.

Sedimentary rocks are composed of fragments eroded from older rocks, so chemistry is not as important. The minerals in the rock come from many sources and are brought together by happenstance instead of being the product of a single original chemical system. Nevertheless, even these rocks are classified in part on the basis of the minerals they contain. For example, a kind of sandstone rich in grains of feldspar is called an *arkose*.

A further type of classification is based on the rock's physical characteristics. The use of modifier terms provides even more information by adding only a word or two.

Let's see how the classification works. A *granite* is a light-colored, silica-rich, dark-mineral-poor, coarse-grained igneous rock that cooled slowly at depth. A *biotite granite* is the same thing, but with substantial amounts of the mineral biotite. A *rhyolite* is a light-colored, silica-rich, dark-mineral-poor, fine-grained igneous rock that cooled rapidly at the surface. It might contain needles of the dark mineral *hornblende*, in which case it would be a *hornblende rhyolite*. A *gabbro* is a dark-colored, coarse-grained, iron- and magnesium-rich, silica-poor plutonic rock that cooled slowly at depth. A *basalt* is the same thing, but fine-grained because it cooled quickly at the surface. A basalt with notable amounts of the mineral *olivine* is an *olivine basalt*. A salt-and-pepper coarse-grained, banded rock containing flakes of transparent mica is a *muscovite* (the mica) gneiss, a metamorphic rock.

It is fun to look at a rock closely in the field, determine its characteristics and principal minerals, then give it a name on the basis of what you have determined. This will impress your friends, but it would be wise to learn something about the three main groups of rocks (based on genesis) before launching into this novel career.

Igneous Rocks

Igneous rocks are derived from hot, molten magma. As shown in the classification chart (see figure 1), they are subdivided into two main categories, depending on where the magma cooled and solidified. They are further subdivided on the basis of chemical composition.

Plutonic Rocks

Plutonic rocks are those that formed from a mass of hot, liquid magma that cooled slowly at depth—hence they are named after Pluto, the Roman god of the underworld. The magma originally forced its way into, or *intruded*, the surrounding rock that was there at the time, so *plutons* are intrusive masses

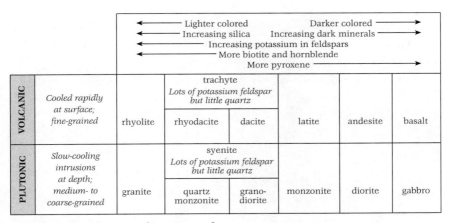

			trachyte				
			Lots of potassium feldspar but little quartz				
VOLCANIC	*Cooled rapidly at surface; fine-grained*	rhyolite	rhyodacite	dacite	latite	andesite	basalt
			syenite				
			Lots of potassium feldspar but little quartz				
PLUTONIC	*Slow-cooling intrusions at depth; medium- to coarse-grained*	granite	quartz monzonite	grano-diorite	monzonite	diorite	gabbro

Lighter colored ⟵ ⟶ Darker colored
⟵ Increasing silica Increasing dark minerals ⟶
⟵ Increasing potassium in feldspars
⟵ More biotite and hornblende
More pyroxene ⟶

Figure 1. Classification of igneous rocks

composed of plutonic rocks. Plutons larger than about 40 square miles in area are called *batholiths*, whereas smaller ones are *stocks*. Some intrusive rocks form *tabular* bodies, meaning they are table- or sheet-like. A *dike* is such a mass that cuts across the layering of the rocks it intrudes. Most dikes are vertical or nearly so. *Sills* are intruded parallel to the layering and tend to be horizontal.

Volcanic Rocks

Volcanic rocks are the product of hot, liquid magma that reached the surface of the earth, where it cooled rapidly. The products of volcanism reflect the chemistry of the magma and the amount of gas that was present.

When large amounts of very fluid basalt are erupted from the same vent with only minor amounts of gas, the resulting volcanic cone can be large and have gentle slopes. These are the *shield volcanoes*. Mauna Loa and Mauna Kea in Hawaii are fine examples of shield volcanoes, as is Arizona's Mount Baldy.

Short-lived eruptions of basalt rich in gas produce *cinder cones*. During these eruptions, blobs of magma are ejected into the air where they break up and freeze in flight. Smaller particles produced this way are called *volcanic ash*, whereas larger ones are *cinders*. *Bombs* can be several feet across. These materials fall mostly near the vent, gradually producing a *cone* that surrounds it. Some cinder cone eruptions also produce basalt flows, which usually emerge near the base of the cone. Arizona's SP Mountain has such a flow. Cinder cones are common in Arizona; the San Francisco and Springerville volcanic fields consist primarily of cinder cones.

Eruptions of magma with intermediate silica content, such as andesite and dacite, produce *composite volcanoes*, which are relatively steep sided. Mount Fuji, in Japan, is a classic composite volcano. Dacite and rhyolite *domes* are a common feature of these volcanoes. They are produced when viscous magma

Welded bombs, lapilli, and ash form the rim of a crater (Hike 16).

forces its way, or is *extruded*, to the surface but does not flow far from the vent, which often gets buried and plugged, trapping the high-pressure gases of the magma. The result can be catastrophic explosions that remove a good part of the volcanic cone. This is what happened to Mount St. Helens in Washington and to Mount Mazama, whose explosion created Crater Lake in Oregon. The truncated shape of the San Francisco Peaks in Arizona is also testimony to such events.

Another feature of composite volcanoes are *lahars*, hot mudflows that are formed when loose volcanic debris on the slopes of the volcano becomes mixed with water, forming a slurry that flows downhill at great speed. Lahars have taken many lives in the Andes and in the volcanic islands of the western Pacific.

Eruptions of dacite and silica-rich rhyolite commonly produce small domes with short, stubby flows. If the magma contains a lot of gas during the eruption, blobs of magma are thrown into the air, where they cool and solidify, then settle to the ground as layers of *ash*. Eventually, the ash solidifies into a rock known as *air-fall tuff*.

Sometimes the supply of magma and gas are both great. The result is the most violent and catastrophic volcanic events known. Many cubic miles of hot, gas-charged, frothy magma can be ejected almost instantaneously. This incandescent froth flows at great speed and covers large areas. The froth is so hot that the lower parts of the flows often become welded once movement has stopped. The result is a rock called *welded tuff*.

24

In many cases, the volume of material removed from below the surface is so great that the roof of the *magma chamber*, in which the magma resided before the eruption, is no longer supported and collapses downward, creating a steep-walled semi-circular depression as much as several miles in diameter. This is called a *caldera*. Eruptions of this type were common in Arizona's past and their products now give the state some of its most distinctive scenery. The Chiricahua and Superstition Mountains are composed largely of welded tuff and contain calderas.

Sedimentary Rocks

Many sedimentary rocks result from the *induration* (bonding together and hardening) of loose sediment that has accumulated, usually in layers, in water. The sediment is eroded from preexisting rocks and transported as debris from its source to the place of accumulation. Such sedimentary rocks are known as *clastic* rocks. An example is *sandstone*, a rock made up of grains of sand that are bound together by minerals in between the grains. These minerals *cement* the grains together.

Chemical Rocks

Chemical rocks consist of compounds such as rock salt (NaCl) and calcium carbonate ($CaCO_3$) that are dissolved from rocks in one place, then are brought out of solution, or *precipitated,* and deposited in another. In many instances, the precipitation—especially of calcium carbonate—comes about through organisms that remove the carbonate from the water in which they live, then concentrate it in their shells or skeletons. As the organisms die, the shells and skeletons slowly accumulate in seas and lakes, giving rise to layers of limestone. This kind of limestone is often *fossiliferous* because it contains the remains of the organisms that lived in the place where the limestone was accumulating.

Clastic Rocks

The sediment that forms clastic rocks is transported by water (rivers, streams, and washes), by ice (glaciers), or by wind. In some cases, the agent of transport is the force of gravity: rocks fall off cliffs and roll or slide down slopes, accumulating at the foot of the slopes as *scree* or *talus*.

The transporting medium and the length of transport leave their mark on the shape of the grains being carried along—that is, their degree of *rounding*. The energy and density of the transporting medium leave their mark on the *size* and *sorting* of the material transported. The manner in which sediment is deposited determines the *bedding characteristics* of the rock into which the sediment is later transformed. The history of the sediment after deposition determines its hardening into rock, or *induration*. Finally, the kind of minerals and rock fragments that are assembled into a sedimentary rock determine its *composition*. All these characteristics are important in working out the environment in which a sediment was formed and the processes that were involved.

Rounding. Particles that are transported by water or wind have their sharp corners removed by collision with other particles or with bedrock. As a result, they become *well rounded*. Rounding is less good when the transport has been short. These particles are *subrounded*. Other transporting media achieve little rounding (glaciers) or none at all (rock falls), giving rise to *subangular* and *angular* particles.

Size. Fast-moving water, such as a mountain torrent in flood, has lots of energy and can move boulders, whereas a slow-moving stream may only be able to move silt. Mud slurries, such as in debris flows, can move huge boulders because of their high density and high velocity. Conversely, air moves mostly silt and very fine sand because of its low density. Ice can move objects of any size because objects rest on top of the ice and are carried along as the ice flows.

Particles in a sediment have different names that depend on their size. Going from small to large, these are *clay, silt, sand, gravel*, and *boulder gravel*. The rocks derived from these sediments are called *claystone, siltstone, sandstone,* and *conglomerate* (or *breccia*), respectively. *Mudstone* is a nice earthy term for hardened mud composed of clay, silt, and fine sand. For rocks coarser than sandstone, things get a little complicated because the space between the *clasts* (pebbles and cobbles) gets filled in with finer material called a *matrix,* made up of clay, silt, and sand. A rock containing rounded clasts is a *conglomerate*, but one containing sharp angular clasts is a *breccia*.

Sorting. The property of sediments called *sorting* can tell much about the environment in which the material was deposited.

A *well-sorted* sediment is one in which the particles are all roughly the same size. This indicates that the energy of the transporting medium or the depositional environment was nearly constant. For example, wind can carry only the lightest of materials: silt and fine sand. The result is well-sorted deposits: *loess,* consisting of silt, and *dunes*, composed of fine, well-rounded, well-sorted sand.

Another process that produces good sorting is a river entering a body of water such as a lake. River water carries material because moving water has much energy. Finer material is carried in suspension in the water, and coarser material is dragged along the bottom of the river. As a river enters a lake, the velocity and energy of the water decrease, so material can no longer be carried. The first material to drop out and settle to the bottom, right where the river enters the lake, are pebbles, which need considerable current to be kept in motion. The next material to settle out a little farther into the lake, is sand.

Then comes silt, and finally clay, which is so fine that it settles out very slowly. Even the small amount of energy provided by wind ripples can keep clay suspended, so eventually clay is distributed and deposited throughout the lake.

A *poorly sorted* deposit contains particles in a range of sizes. Such a deposit signals rapid deposition, when sorting processes do not have much chance to do their work. An *unsorted* deposit is produced when material accumulates in the absence of a process that favors one size over others. A glacier can carry anything that falls on it, so *till*, the material deposited by glaciers, is unsorted and can contain material of all sizes, including house-size boulders. Similarly, dense and fast-flowing *debris flows* can carry material of any size. The most easily visualized material that is unsorted is *talus*, the jumble of rocks on a slope composed of whatever happens to fall from the cliffs above.

Bedding. *Bedding* is the layering of sediments and sedimentary rocks. Beds represent uninterrupted depositional events, and range in thickness from fractions of an inch, if the deposition rate was slow, to many feet, if it was fast.

Most beds are initially horizontal and parallel. *Cross beds* are an interesting and picturesque exception. They are hard to describe but easy to recognize in the field once you have developed an eye for them (see figure 12). In cross beds, the bedding planes are at an angle to the horizontal that ranges from a few degrees to more then 30°. There are two main kinds of cross beds. Low-angle *festoon-* or scoop-shaped ones are typical of river and beach deposits. High-angle parallel cross beds are characteristic of wind-deposited sandstone, where they represent the slip face (downwind side) of ancient sand dunes. This useful characteristic gives you the chance to play detective and figure out what former landscapes looked like—an ancient Sahara-like desert or the bed of some long-vanished river.

Induration. *Induration* is the degree to which particles of a sediment have been bonded together causing the sediment to harden into rock. The bonding material is called *cement* and is usually composed of calcite (calcium carbonate) or quartz (silica). Loose beach sand is an example of an *unindurated* sediment, whereas *quartzite*, composed of quartz grains bonded by quartz cement, is an example of a *highly indurated* or very durable rock.

Metamorphic Rocks

During their long history, many rocks are subjected to high temperatures, high pressures, or both. This changes the rocks into a new kind called *metamorphic rocks*. Among the many ways in which this can happen are proximity to a mass of magma, deep burial, or exposure to the pressures generated by tectonic plate collision. Metamorphic rocks contain minerals and arrangements of minerals that are characteristic of this type of rocks.

Metamorphic Minerals

Minerals are sensitive to temperature and pressure. As a rock is heated, its constituent minerals become unstable and change into forms that are stable at the new higher temperatures. A similar change occurs when the pressure is increased. A good illustration of this is the conversion of the element carbon from the familiar soft, black form of coal, to the mineral graphite, and finally, when the pressure is high indeed, to brilliant transparent diamond, the hardest substance on Earth. Of course, these unimaginable pressures occur only deep in the Earth or briefly in tiny containers in the laboratory.

Many minerals form only at a specific temperature and pressure. Geologists use such minerals to estimate the conditions under which a metamorphic rock was formed. Most metamorphic minerals are hard to identify in the field. An easy one is *garnet,* which is blood-red to brown-red, has good crystal faces, and forms compact crystals.

Textures

In most cases, rocks that are metamorphosed are heated and also squeezed and pushed around, that is, *deformed.* Think of an igneous pluton intruding into the surrounding rock. The pluton heats the rock but it also has to make space for itself, so it shoulders aside the preexisting rock. This squeezing produces features that collectively go under the name of *metamorphic texture,* the arrangement of grains within a rock.

A common arrangement of minerals is into bands or sheets, known as *foliation*. In the variety called *gneissic* foliation, minerals typical of granite are arranged

In the rock gneiss, *light-colored minerals (such as quartz and feldspar) and dark-colored minerals (such as black mica and hornblende) are segregated into separate bands, giving the rock a striped appearance (Hike 37).*

in contorted bands. The light-colored minerals (quartz and feldspar) and the dark minerals (mostly black mica and hornblende) tend to be segregated into separate bands, giving the rock a striped appearance. This is characteristic of the rock *gneiss*, which looks like a banded granite.

When platy minerals such as mica are abundant, the rock acquires a platy appearance because of the many planes within it that shine with mica. This is called *schistosity*, which is typical of *schist*, a shiny metamorphic rock much used for decorative purposes.

Classification

Textural terms can be used to designate a metamorphic rock, such as gneiss, schist, or slate. A more complete name results from combining a textural term such as "gneiss" with the name of a mineral that is abundant in the rock. For example, a *biotite gneiss* is a gneiss that contains substantial amounts of the mineral biotite. Rocks that do not fall into such a classification include *quartzite*, a very hard rock made up of silica—quartz grains cemented by silica—and *marble*, which is calcium carbonate (limestone) that has recrystallized into a coarse-grained metamorphic rock.

STRUCTURE—DEFORMING THE CRUST

Because the Earth is a geologically restless place, rocks seldom remain undisturbed for long and are bent or broken by the many events that constantly affect the Earth's crust. The study of such deformation is called *structural geology*. The aim of structural geology is to describe and document this deformation, then infer the forces and processes that caused it.

Tectonics is the name used for structural studies involving great forces or large regions of the Earth. *Plate tectonics* is the study of the great plates whose movements shape the surface of the Earth.

To describe deformation, one needs a reference from which to measure the orientation in space of the feature being examined. A horizontal plane is a useful reference because most sedimentary beds are horizontal when they are deposited, so their present-day inclination tells us how much they have been disturbed since being laid down. The other reference is north, which has become the universal reference, such as when setting a compass course or bearing.

STRIKE AND DIP

Many geologic features are planes, including bedding and faults. To describe the orientation of planes, we use two quantities derived from old mining practice: strike and dip.

Strike is the bearing (or direction) of a horizontal line drawn on the plane. Imagine a tilted plate of glass partially immersed in a pool of water. The strike of this plate is given by the "shoreline" of the water on the plate (see figure 2). The bearing of this line is read clockwise in degrees from north which is zero. For example, "030" means N 30° E, which is a strike that bears 30° away from due north toward the northeast.

Dip is the steepest slope on a plane. This maximum slope (the dip) is at 90° to the horizontal line, the strike. In our example, it is the direction in which water splashed on the glass plate would flow down the plate. Dips range from 0° (horizontal) to 90° (vertical).

STRUCTURAL FEATURES

The three principal kinds of structural features are faults, joints, and folds.

Faults

Faults are approximately planar fractures of the earth's crust along which there has been movement (see figure 3). On some faults, the movement is

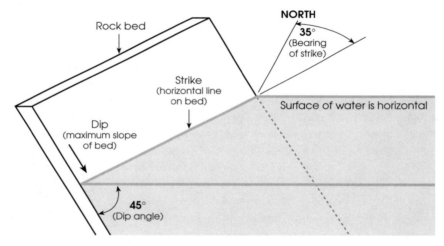

Figure 2. Strike and dip are used by geologists to describe the position, or attitude, of a planar feature such as a bed or fault. Visualize a plate of glass (representing the rock bed) immersed in a pool of water (representing horizontal). Since the surface of the standing water is horizontal, the "shoreline" of the water on the glass is also horizontal. This is the strike. Its bearing is given in degrees from north, measured clockwise. The dip of a bed is its maximum slope, always perpendicular to the strike. It is the direction in which a ball would roll down. The dip angle is measured in degrees from the horizontal to the bed. In this example, the bed strikes 35° clockwise of north, so the strike is N 35° E (about northeast). The dip direction is perpendicular to the strike (about southeast) and the dip angle is 45°.

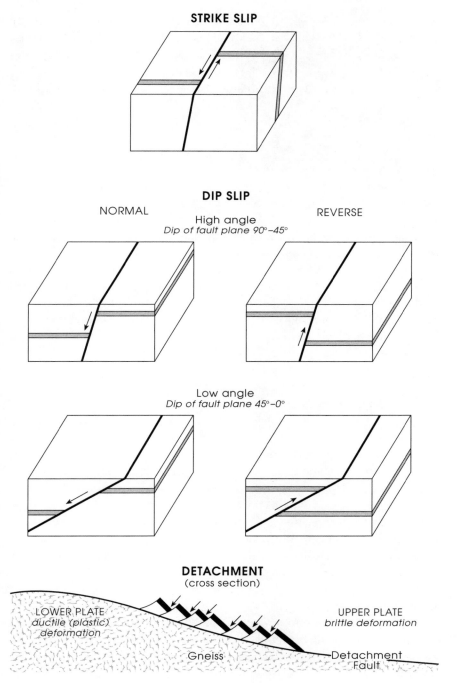

Figure 3. Types of faults

Layers of light-colored rock in the north wall of Barnhardt Canyon make it easy to see folds *caused by tectonic stresses (Hike 19).*

horizontal (parallel to the strike of the fault plane). These are *strike-slip* faults, of which California's San Andreas is a good example. *Dip-slip* faults are those in which movement is up or down, parallel to the dip. These faults form mountain ranges and basins such as Death Valley. Dip-slip faults are further subdivided on the basis of their angle with the horizontal—*vertical, high angle, low angle*— and on their direction of movement—*normal, reverse, thrust.* For example, when the block above the inclined fault plane has slid down the plane, as you would expect it to, you have a "normal" situation and thus a normal fault. If the block has slid up the plane, which is the reverse of what you would expect, the fault is reverse. When the fault has a low dip and the block above it has been pushed, or thrust, up the plane, then you have a thrust fault.

Joints

Joints are planar fractures in rocks. What distinguishes joints from faults is that there is no movement along joints, as along faults, except maybe a slight separation of the walls of the joint. Joints are typically part of a set of many joints with similar orientation. You may be able to see several sets in a single outcrop. This is conspicuous in certain types of volcanic rocks. For example, the welded tuff in Chiricahua National Monument is cut by several sets of vertical joints which together produce the impressive rock columns for which the monument is famous.

Folds

Folds result mainly from compression of the crust and are best seen in layers such as bedding or quartz veins. When the layers are bent into an arch, the fold is called an *anticline* (see figure 4). When they are bent down into a trough, the fold is a *syncline*. A *monocline* is a simple bend resulting from an anticline and a syncline in close proximity (see figure 5).

32

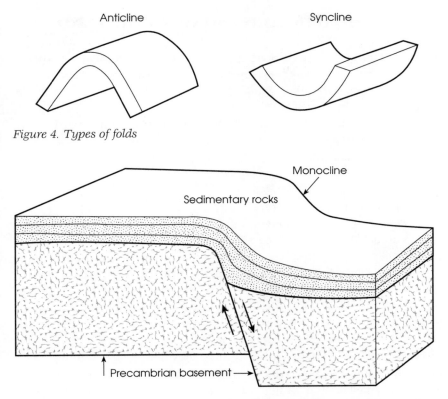

Figure 4. Types of folds

Figure 5. *Monoclines are made up of an anticline and a syncline next to each other. These structural folds are common on the Colorado Plateau. Many are formed by the draping of beds over a fault at depth.*

STRUCTURAL FEATURES VS. TOPOGRAPHY

Many people have trouble making the distinction between a structural feature such as an anticline and the surface of the land, or the topography. Usually, anticlines do not form hills and synclines do not form valleys, as you might think. Structural features are bends in rocks, which are below the Earth's surface. For example, you might see a syncline in rocks exposed in a roadcut, but the topography would be the surface of the hill into which the cut is made. The shape of this surface is generally not influenced by the structure of the underlying rocks.

In a few instances, structure and topography do coincide. This usually happens where the strata are hard to erode. If the strata are bowed up into an anticline, the topographic surface formed on the hard layer would form a dome-shaped hill. Northern Arizona has fine examples of this. The Kaibab Plateau is underlain by a big anticline, and the plateau itself has the shape of a big dome.

GEOMORPHOLOGY — SHAPING THE LAND

Certain processes create rocks, while others wear them down. Processes that operate on the surface of the Earth give it its ever-evolving shape. Earth has an atmosphere rich in water vapor, which condenses and falls on the surface, where it does its work of erosion and transportation. This work can also be done by wind—the atmosphere set in motion.

All this is the subject of *geomorphology*, the study of the Earth's surface and landscape. Landscape is what we admire and what we walk on; it is where we live. It has played a large role in our evolution as a species and in the history of our civilizations.

WATER AND ICE EROSION

Water does its work in a variety of ways. In its frozen form, it helps dislodge masses of rock from cliff faces because water expands as it freezes. When this happens in joints, the ice serves as an irresistible wedge that pries rocks apart. These rocks then fall off the cliff and accumulate on the slope below as talus.

Glaciers are formed when snow accumulates over the years and compacts into ice. Glaciers move downslope and are powerful agents of erosion on the floor and sides of valleys down which they flow. The result are the U-shaped valleys that are characteristic of glaciated terrain. Glaciers are also good at carrying material that falls on them or that they have plucked from the bedrock of the valley. This material accumulates along the sides and at the snout of the glacier, where the ice melts, leaving the rock load behind. The results are *moraines*, typically ridge-shaped masses of sedimentary debris that range in size from clay to house-sized boulders.

Most of the work done by water is in its liquid form. In desert parts of Arizona, many cloudbursts fall on mountain ranges. The resulting local floods produce surfaces that are cut into bedrock and slope gently from the foot of the mountains down to the adjacent basins. These extensive surfaces, the hallmark of desert country, are called *pediments*. They provide a means of transporting sediment efficiently from its source in the mountains to nearby valleys and basins. In contrast, *alluvial fans* are cone-shaped accumulations of sediment dumped into a valley or basin where a stream emerges from a mountain range. The debris in a fan can reach considerable thicknesses, whereas that of a pediment is thin. Material deposited on slopes without the aid of a stream is *colluvium*, which mantles the contours of a slope.

In due course, water falling on the land is concentrated in streams, washes, and rivers, where it flows downslope under the influence of gravity and carries out its work of deepening and widening the valleys, as well as transporting material toward the sea. Material carried and deposited directly by rivers and streams is called *alluvium*.

To move material, water needs energy. The amount of this energy depends on the quantity of water that is moving in the river (*discharge*) and on the speed (*velocity*) at which the water flows. Since the velocity of water flowing in a river increases as the discharge increases, the energy available to a river increases very rapidly as the discharge increases. The result is that rivers do most of their work of erosion and transportation in the flood stage. This explains how desert washes, which rarely contain flowing water, get their work done: they do their eroding and transporting when in flood.

Along the Blue Mesa Trail in Petrified Forest National Park, rills are abundant in a soft layer of clay. Every year these clay slopes lose inches to erosion (Hike 9).

The velocity of the water in a stream depends on its slope, or *gradient*. A river with a steeper gradient erodes more and carries more and bigger material than a similar river of lower gradient. That is why a youthful mountain torrent is much more vigorous than a sluggish mature stream meandering in a coastal plain. The gradient also explains why some rivers are busy cutting down their bed, while others are building it up.

DOWNCUTTING AND AGGRADING

Rivers are just as capable of *aggrading* (raising their beds) as they are of *downcutting* (lowering them). This can be explained by looking at the sediment supplied to a river by its tributaries. If the river has enough energy to carry this load, nothing happens: all the load is transported to the sea and the bed of the river remains unchanged. But suppose that the tributaries start supplying more material than the river can carry. This might happen because of increased erosion in the river's drainage basin due to deforestation or because a glacier upstream is dumping more debris into the river system, or a host of other causes. Since this material cannot be carried away, it stays in the channel, which it builds up. The river is aggrading. But there is an interesting consequence: the bed of the river has been raised, but its mouth is still at the same elevation—the gradient has increased. Thus, the velocity and the energy increase until the river once again has enough energy to carry the new load. The river goes back into equilibrium.

What about the opposite situation, when a river cuts down? Suppose the supply of sediment is decreased, maybe by reforestation. The river now has an excess of energy, which it puts to good use by cutting down. This time, the bed is lowered, and the gradient and energy decrease until the reduced energy is in balance with the reduced load. In this way, rivers are self-regulating.

What about the canyons that Arizona so proudly displays? Armed with the knowledge just gained, you might think they are cutting downward, and you are right. But why? The main reason is that the Colorado Plateau has been lifted up relatively recently in geologic time. Since the mouths of rivers such as the Colorado have remained at sea level, the result has been an increase in gradient, which brings an increase in energy and thus downcutting.

Rivers sometimes tell stories about what they have done in the past. Rivers flow in valleys, so at one time they must have cut down, maybe when they were more youthful and vigorous. But then something happened, and they built up their beds for a while, filling the channel with alluvium. When a river resumes cutting down through this material, it leaves behind *terraces* whose flat tops represent the former floodplain of the river.

WIND

The atmosphere can change the landscape directly by means of wind. Air is much less dense than water, so it is not nearly as powerful at moving material, generally carrying only sand and silt. But the volume of air that moves in a wind is enormous, far greater than any river, and wind is not restricted to channels, but can move freely over the land. This means that wind can move staggering amounts of material. Just think of the Sahara Desert. This process has been very active in the past, as witnessed by the petrified dunes now preserved in many parts of Arizona, where they form some of the most spectacular scenery of the Colorado Plateau.

What about wind as an agent of erosion? Wind that is carrying sand is effective because it operates through a process of sandblasting. Places that have lots of wind and much loose sand often show strangely sculptured rock formations. These are long ridges with one end rounded and blunt, the other thin. The blunt end points into the prevailing wind. These are *yardangs*, streamlined shapes produced by the incessant action of sand-charged wind. If you keep your eyes open, you can see these in the windswept steppe country of the Navajo Reservation in northeastern Arizona.

The Grand Canyon is the most famous of the many canyons carved into the Colorado Plateau.

The Making of Arizona

Arizona is a land whose concrete reality departs greatly from the common image of vast desert plains dotted with cacti, populated by rattlesnakes, stirred by dusty whirlwinds, and consumed by blazing heat. This kind of country is indeed present, but the first-time visitor, at times shivering in the thin air of high altitudes, often confronts with amazement the lofty mountains, vast forests, grassy plateaus extending to the horizon, and the great canyons that make up a good part of the state.

The reason for such great diversity is found in the varied geologic underpinnings of the state. These determine the types of rocks that are exposed at the surface and the structural features that disturb the rocks. These, in turn, control the topography and thereby the flora, fauna, and even the human history of the state.

Geologists recognize three *geologic provinces* in Arizona, a province being an area of relatively uniform geologic characteristics that are different from those of other provinces. These provinces extend well beyond the boundaries of the state, but they are especially well displayed in Arizona. From north to south, they are the *Colorado Plateau*, the *Arizona Transition Zone*, and the *Basin and Range Province,* all separated from one another by boundaries aligned approximately northwest.

Arizona's provinces are strikingly different, yet they came into being relatively recently in Arizona's long geologic history, which spans more than one-third of Earth's age.

This history began about 1800 million years ago, when the edge of the continent, busy building itself outward from its ancient core in Canada, reached the area that now is Arizona. The continent kept expanding toward the south for another 50 to 100 million years as volcanism created new *island arcs,* like today's Japan, and the forces of erosion carried sediments to the margins of the continent. Between 1800 and 1700 million years ago, the stately dance of the great tectonic plates that form the crust of the Earth changed, and plates began colliding with the continent. The resulting compression of the crust manifested itself in two ways. One was that rocks were metamorphosed over wide areas, producing, for example, the dark schist so well displayed in the Inner Gorge of the Grand Canyon. The other was that rocks were crumpled and shoved in great thrust sheets on top of one another and inward from the margins of the continent toward its interior. One place where these thrust sheets can be seen today are in the Mazatzal Mountains.

Then about 1400 million years ago, large granitic batholiths invaded the crust in many parts of the state. The lack of foliation (banding) in the granite shows that little deformation was going on at the time. A long period of erosion followed, after which the region was subjected to pull-apart forces, or *rifting*, perhaps associated with the initial opening of the Pacific Ocean. (The Pacific Ocean has not always been there, but came into being probably about 1200 million years ago when a continental mass split apart, and the two pieces drifted away in opposite directions.) This rifting created basins in Arizona in which were deposited thick layers of shallow-water sediments, as well as remarkable sills of dark *diabase*—a coarse-grained intrusive equivalent of basalt. These layers are well exposed in Salt River Canyon, Grand Canyon, and the Sierra Ancha. Deposition continued until less than 800 million years ago and was followed by deformation in places. Next came a long period of erosion that ushered in the Paleozoic Era, which started about 600 million years ago.

During most of Paleozoic time, Arizona was a *continental shelf,* which is the nearly flat area at the margin of a continent that is close to sea level. When sea level was high, the shelf was occupied by a shallow sea and received sediments. When sea level was low, the area was above water, so it received no sediment and was subject to erosion.

Big changes happened about 250 million years ago, the start of Mesozoic time. This was a period of geologic unrest, when the area was generally above sea level. To the west, the crust below the Pacific Ocean was thrust eastward under the continental crust of North America in a process called *subduction*. This crashing together of plates caused *orogenies*—mountain-building events. At the same time, rocks of the oceanic crust were taken to great depth under the continent, where they melted into magma. Some of the magma then rose into the upper crust, forming plutons, while some rose all the way to the surface, forming volcanoes much like those of the present Cascades (see figure 6).

The most intense of several orogenies was the *Laramide orogeny,* which occurred roughly 60 million years ago, at the end of Cretaceous time and spilling over into the beginning of the Tertiary. This mountain-building event was accompanied by widespread intrusion of igneous rock and the mineralization that has given Arizona most of its great mines.

The Laramide orogeny defined what is now the Colorado Plateau. At the conclusion of the orogeny, the plateau had the shape of a gigantic low-lying saucer rimmed by mountains. Arizona occupied the southern part of the saucer, where the rim consisted of the Central Arizona Highlands (or Mogollon Highlands), a belt of mountains that now has been transformed into another province, the Arizona Transition Zone. Streams flowed northward from these highlands onto the

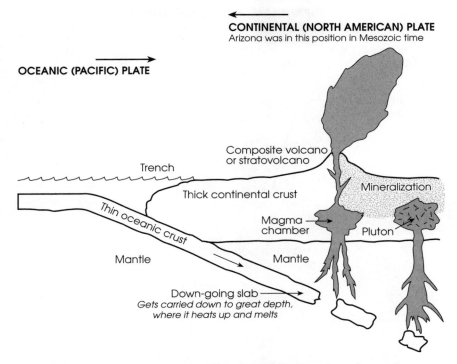

Figure 6. Plate-tectonic cross section showing subduction along the southwest coast of the North American continent during the Mesozoic era. At this time, the margin of the continent was near Arizona.

Colorado Plateau, depositing an apron of gravel and sand on the plains north of the mountains. To visualize this arrangement, it is helpful to think of the Rocky Mountains near Denver, along with the nearby High Plains.

Subduction continued into the first part of the Tertiary Period, creating more great volcanoes. But these were different from the earlier ones, producing calderas and enormous amounts of *welded tuff* such as those of the Chiricahua and Superstition Mountains.

Later in the Tertiary, some 27 million years ago, a change in the interactions of plates to the west brought about *extension* (pulling apart) not only in Arizona but throughout much of the western United States as well. The first phase lasted until about 17 million years ago. It was distinguished by extreme extension along low-angle faults and is best manifested in *metamorphic core complexes*, enigmatic geologic features well displayed in the Santa Catalina Mountains near Tucson and common in the desert country of western and southern Arizona.

The second phase involved *block faulting*—movement along high-angle

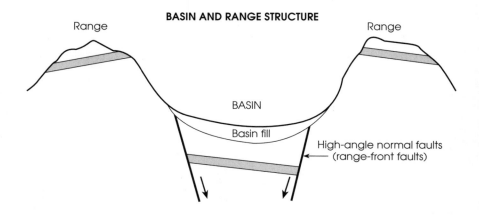

BASIN AND RANGE STRUCTURE

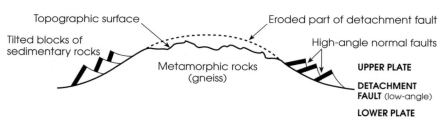

METAMORPHIC CORE COMPLEX STRUCTURE
Blister-like upwarp of detachment fault

Mountain composed of metamorphic "core" surrounded by sedimentary rocks

Figure 7. (Top) Cross section of basin and range structure, showing how ranges and basins are formed by range-front high-angle normal faults, which are usually buried by basin fill. (Bottom) Cross section of a metamorphic core complex, in which the horizontal detachment fault is bowed up into a blister-like uplift, at the core of which the fault has been eroded away, exposing metamorphic rocks of the "lower plate."

normal faults that created mountain ranges and the basins that separate them (see figure 7). This faulting, still going on in places, has produced the landscape visible today in the Basin and Range Province. It was during this phase that the mountainous belt of the Central Arizona Highlands "foundered" (broke apart and was dropped down) and stopped contributing sediment northward to the Colorado Plateau.

The Basin and Range Province is typical of the southern part of Arizona, but this rugged country also occupies substantial parts of California, Nevada, and Utah. The other two provinces of Arizona are defined by the amount of block faulting they have experienced: the Colorado Plateau has almost none, whereas the Arizona Transition Zone has an amount intermediate between the Plateau and the Basin and Range, so forms a transitional belt between the two.

COLORADO PLATEAU

The Colorado Plateau is truly a remarkable and unique place. Mountains, even impressive mountains, are not uncommon in the world. But vast steppe plains stretching far away into the distance, broken here and there by great scarps and sharp-edged mesas—this is a landscape not easily matched anywhere else on Earth. And all this cut unexpectedly by immense canyons and revealing in many places the rocky foundations in the form of *slickrock*—bare rock carved into monumental shapes and colored red, yellow, green, and purple by iron in various stages of oxidation. No wonder that the Hopi and Navajo are fiercely attached to the hard but beautiful land in which they have lived for centuries.

This impressive landscape comes directly from the geologic characteristics of the Colorado Plateau: horizontal strata, a high average elevation of about 5000 feet above sea level, a general lack of deformation, and an abundance of brightly colored and readily carved sandstone and shale.

The high elevation results in a harsh climate, marked by hot summers, cold winters, little rain, and ample wind. This combination yields a patchy vegetation that does little to hide the wonderful rocky skeleton of the land. It also does little to withstand the fierce downpours so characteristic of this region. Unchecked, these torrential rains carve and fret the land into an arroyo here, a rocky spine there, a canyon deep in violet shadow. The rains also produce the catastrophic mud and debris flows that play a major role in shaping this austere land.

Deep river-carved canyons can be produced only where the elevation of the land is high, because rivers cannot cut below the level of their mouths into the sea. This means that the bottom of a canyon must be above sea level, and the rim at least as high above sea level as the walls of the canyon are high. Rivers need a gradient to flow and erode. Since the gradient is related to the difference in elevation between the headwaters of a river and its mouth at the sea, it follows that the higher the headwaters, the steeper the gradient, the faster the flow, and the more vigorous the erosion. Thus, for these canyons to have been carved, the Colorado Plateau must have been uplifted to its present position before the canyons were cut. But when and how did this happen?

THE UPLIFT OF THE COLORADO PLATEAU

At the end of Mesozoic time, the area of the Colorado Plateau was at sea level and mostly occupied by an inland sea. Today, it has an average elevation of more than 5000 feet, which would be closer to 10,000 feet if all the eroded strata were still present. When did this enormous uplift of about 2 miles take place? Opinions differ. Early geologists were impressed by the erosion so characteristic of the plateau and believed that it must have been going on for a long time. Since it is uplift that gives erosion its start, they placed the uplift early in the Tertiary, about 60 million years ago. In contrast, many contemporary geologists believe that much of the uplift is quite young, in keeping with the rugged, *youthful* nature of the canyons. In this view, the Grand Canyon is only a few million years old rather than several tens of millions.

HOW WAS THE PLATEAU RAISED?

There is another reason why geologists are interested in when the Colorado Plateau was raised. In contrast to the uplift of deformed areas such as mountain ranges, which can be explained by thickening of the crust through crumpling under compressive forces, the uplift of undeformed areas such as plateaus is a geologic puzzle because no crumpling is involved. Solving this puzzle is greatly helped by knowing the timing of the uplift because the timing places constraints on mechanisms that might explain the uplift.

Continents have a crust composed of silica-rich rocks whose density is relatively low. This crust essentially floats on more dense and less rigid rocks of the upper mantle, much like an iceberg floats in water. So what mechanism would cause the crust of an area as large as the Colorado Plateau to "float" up higher than its surroundings? One possibility is that the crust beneath the plateau was thickened in some way. Another is that the density of the crust was decreased, most likely by heating. The third is that the density of the mantle was increased, probably by conversion of the mantle material into a more dense form. Which of these is responsible for its uplift is not yet known, but the subject is being studied with vigor. Regional events that have been proposed as being associated with the uplift include the great plate collision and mountain-building event at the end of the Mesozoic Era, Tertiary volcanism, and Tertiary plate interaction associated with extension in the Basin and Range Province west of the plateau.

LACK OF DEFORMATION

The Colorado Plateau is little deformed and has remained stable for a long time, in stark contrast to the intense and oft-repeated deformation in all surrounding areas. Overall, the plateau has the shape of a gigantic saucer, with high rims and a depressed center. In Arizona, the strata dip gently northeast, toward the center. This simple arrangement is broken by great folds of Laramide age, including monoclines, the characteristic folds of this province (see figure 5). Monoclines, well expressed along the Echo Cliffs and Gray Mountain, are the surface manifestation of faults at depth. In places, monoclines facing in opposite directions define a dome, such as the Kaibab Plateau. Faults of any significance are few. The most impressive are the Toroweap, Hurricane, and Grand Wash faults, all near the western edge of the plateau. The Grand Wash fault is the sharp boundary between the Colorado Plateau and the Basin and Range Province to the west.

Evidence is mounting that the long tranquillity of the Colorado Plateau is coming to an end. The edges of the plateau are apparently being eaten away by extension. The young volcanic fields clustered along the southern margin show that the crust here is heating up, a common precursor to extension. Furthermore, the magma resulting from the heating can find easy routes to the surface along faults, which are produced by extension. Also, several extensional faults are active because they are the sites of earthquakes. The conclusion is that extension and the accompanying volcanism are gradually eating their way into the plateau. The geologic prediction is that the Arizona Transition Zone (described below) will gradually become Basin and Range, which may be the ultimate fate of the plateau as well. The mechanisms by which this process is happening are not yet clear.

ROCKS AND LANDSCAPE OF THE PLATEAU

Most rocks exposed on the Colorado Plateau are Mesozoic sandstone and shale, with a sprinkling of Cenozoic volcanic rocks, mostly basalt, in the many volcanic fields. However, the southwest corner is underlain by Paleozoic rocks, which are well exposed along the plateau's south and west margins, in the Grand Canyon, and in a few uplifted areas. The even older Precambrian rocks are also exposed here. These places show us what lies beneath the surface in the rest of the plateau.

The Mesozoic section that forms the surface over much of the plateau includes several soft layers capped by relatively hard ones. Each produces a scarp. Given the northeast dip of strata, the scarps are aligned approximately northwest, parallel to the strike of the strata. From erosion, over time they retreat northeastward, down the dip of the strata. These scarps are characteristic of the plateau and have had a major effect on the drainage of the region. Good examples are the Echo Cliffs, Vermilion Cliffs, and battlements of Black Mesa. The Grand Staircase of southern Utah also consists of such scarps. The Mogollon Rim is a very prominent scarp that forms the southern edge of the Colorado Plateau. The origin of this scarp is complex and not well understood.

Among the most interesting features of the plateau are its volcanoes, which give rise to a variety of spectacular landscapes, and which are concentrated chiefly along the southern margin and to a lesser extent in the Four Corners region.

In Part 1, we examine in detail the geologic regions found on the Colorado

Plateau. These include the *canyons,* carved like intruders into the open landscape; the great *rims,* which form the southern and western borders; the scarps, mesas, and open valleys of the *tablelands;* and the shield and composite volcanoes, cinder cones, lava flows, necks, and diatremes of the *volcanic fields.*

ARIZONA TRANSITION ZONE

The Arizona Transition Zone is a northwest-trending belt in the middle of Arizona that includes some of the most rugged and inaccessible country in the state. The general configuration of this strikingly mountainous region is one of long valleys, such as Verde Valley and Tonto Basin, which are aligned northwestward and separate mountainous areas such as the Black Mountains, the Mazatzal Mountains, and the Sierra Ancha. Some of these look rather like plateaus but are much smaller than the Colorado Plateau. Others, together with the nearby linear valleys, remind you of those in the Basin and Range Province, but are less well developed. Overall, the characteristics are intermediate, or transitional, between those of the other two provinces, hence the name. This is easy to see on satellite images of the state.

At the end of Mesozoic time, this area was uplifted and mountainous, a consequence of the Laramide orogeny. The mountains shed sedimentary

The Arizona Transition Zone contains long mountainous areas such as the Sierra Ancha (foreground) and the Mazatzal Mountains (skyline).

debris northward onto the Colorado Plateau, which then was at a lower elevation than now. Later in Tertiary time, the mountainous area was pulled apart (rifted) along a system of faults and dropped down from its former lofty position. This stopped the transport of sediments onto the plateau.

In spite of the foundering, many of the mountains are high, so the Arizona Transition Zone remains topographically high. It also remains structurally high, as shown by the presence at the surface of ancient Precambrian rocks. Normally, these rocks are deep below the surface, being covered by younger strata. The Laramide orogeny lifted them up, and they have remained higher than in surrounding areas in spite of the Tertiary foundering.

The Precambrian sedimentary rocks include a picturesque sequence known as the Apache Group, similar in age and characteristics to the Grand Canyon Supergroup, which is exposed in the bottom of the Grand Canyon.

Volcanic rocks of Tertiary age, especially basalt, are abundant in the Arizona Transition Zone, where they are cut by faults but not steeply tilted. These rocks tend to be older than those on the nearby Colorado Plateau, supporting the idea that volcanism and extension are both progressing from the Basin and Range Province onto the plateau with time.

BASIN AND RANGE PROVINCE

Few who have flown over or driven across the Great Basin of Nevada have failed to be impressed by the immense linear basins and snow-capped ranges that collectively give the impression of giant caterpillars marching determinedly northward on some urgent quest. This is the home country of the Basin and Range Province, which here reaches its most spectacular form.

BASIN AND RANGE TYPE STRUCTURE

The linear ranges with intervening basins are formed by pull-apart forces, or extension. As the crust is stretched, great blocks slide downward between high-angle faults. The parts that do not slide down form other blocks that are left standing high as ranges, with abrupt margins near the faults (see figure 7). The process by which this happens is *block faulting,* and the result is basin and range type structure (having to do with the faults), and basin and range topography (having to do with the shape of the land's surface).

In Arizona, the basins and ranges tend to be less long, the basins wider, and the ranges lower than those in the Great Basin. This is partly because the faults responsible for forming this landscape are older here and partly because early extension in Arizona took place mostly along enormous low-angle faults, so the amount of pull-apart was greater. Because of the extension, the Pacific coast is considerably farther away from the Rocky Mountains now than it was in middle Tertiary time.

47

In Nevada, many faults are still active today, pushing up ranges and dropping basins. In Arizona, this is absent from the Basin and Range Province, where the faulting occurred mostly during the Miocene, giving the Arizona ranges an older, more worn-down look. But this is only relative, as the ranges remain high and rugged enough to satisfy even the most demanding hiker.

METAMORPHIC CORE COMPLEXES

Metamorphic core complexes are some of the most fascinating and poorly understood features in geology. They are so abundant in Arizona's Basin and Range Province that they can be regarded as "signature features" of the state.

In its simplest form, a *metamorphic core complex* consists of three parts, hence the name "complex" (see figure 7). At the top is a layer of the crust that has been broken apart into relatively small blocks by parallel faults. The blocks are tilted by the faults, and all dip in the same direction over substantial areas. This layer is called the *upper plate* (not the same as the plate tectonics feature). When you walk around in upper plate country, you are likely to see many ridges that are parallel and in which the strata dip the same way. Each ridge corresponds to a tilted block.

The faults and tilted blocks show that the upper plate was pulled apart and broken in brittle fashion, the way that glass breaks into pieces. There was no plastic deformation like that in taffy or tar. In places, the stretching was extreme, maybe as much as 100 percent. This means that two points once 10 miles apart would now be 20 miles apart.

The second part of a core complex is exposed where erosion has cut down all the way through the upper plate. What you see here is a big fault that has an unexpected orientation. We tend to think of faults as being nearly vertical, but this *detachment fault* is close to horizontal. Given good bedrock exposures, you can see that the faults and rotated blocks of the upper plate end against the detachment fault.

Below the detachment fault is a different world, one composed of metamorphic rocks such as gneiss. This is the *lower plate* of a metamorphic core complex. It was stretched just like the upper plate, but responded by deforming in plastic fashion, like taffy. The abrupt transition from lower to upper plate is the reason why we call the intervening fault a detachment fault. Rocks above the fault behaved differently and independently from those below it. The two plates are detached.

In places, the detachment faults are bowed up gently into huge domes. These domes often correspond to mountains, such as the Catalinas near Tucson. Erosion is active on mountains, so it has cut down through the upper plate, which was once present, exposing lower plate metamorphic rocks in the core of the mountain. The detachment fault and upper plate rocks are exposed on the flanks of the mountain around this metamorphic core.

ROCKS OF THE RANGES

The rocks exposed in the ranges of the Basin and Range Province are a compendium of the state's 1.8 billion years of geologic history, including as they do early Proterozoic igneous and metamorphic rocks, middle Proterozoic sedimentary and igneous rocks, Paleozoic and Mesozoic strata of various kinds, and spectacular volcanic rocks of Cenozoic age. You also find Laramide age rocks and associated mineral deposits that are responsible for Arizona's many mines.

Anyone familiar with Arizona's desert ranges knows that they have a distinctive look, both rugged and colorful. This is generally produced by Tertiary volcanic rocks ranging in composition from rhyolite (high in silica content) to basalt (low in silica content).

Volcanic tuffs and flows give many mountains in the Basin and Range Province their distinctive appearance.

Rhyolite, which tends to be light-colored—yellow, tan, and pink—forms small- to medium-sized but rugged mountains in many parts of the desert. Rhyolite can be present as irregular masses that intrude other rocks or as thick lumpy flows. Air-fall tuffs, a common feature of rhyolite volcanoes, form well-layered deposits. Good examples of such volcanoes are the Aubrey and Castaneda Hills near the Bill Williams River in west-central Arizona and the Ajo Mountains near Organ Pipe National Monument.

Rhyolite volcanoes take on an impressive form where they produced enormous volumes of *ash-flow tuffs*. These tuffs form thick, extensive sheets and are distinguished by their tendency to weather into picturesque columns and pinnacles. In many cases, emission of the tuffs left the core of the volcano unsupported, resulting in the formation of a caldera. The Chiricahua Mountains of southeastern Arizona and the Superstition Mountains near Phoenix are good examples of this.

Basalt flows are also common in the Basin and Range Province. In many cases, the lava erupted from vents in or near basins and flowed down into the low spots of the basins. Later, the floors of the basins were lowered by erosion, but the areas covered by the basalt were shielded by the protective cap of hard basalt, and were left as higher erosional remnants above the basin floors. Many such remnants are called "Black Mountain" or "Black Mesa." A particularly fine example is Fortification Hill northeast of Hoover Dam, at the downstream end of Lake Mead.

DESERT GEOMORPHOLOGY

The combination of basin and range topography and desert climate has given rise to interesting landforms that are the essence of the Southwest. Anyone who has spent time in saguaro, paloverde, and creosote country has traveled over these landforms, perhaps without even knowing it. Many landforms in the Southwest have interesting Spanish names given to them by early Mexican miners and ranchers, who were the first non-Native American settlers of the region.

In most places, steep mountain fronts give way abruptly to inclined alluvial surfaces that extend with ever-decreasing slope toward the center of the basin. The surfaces themselves have a variety of origins.

A *bajada* is a surface composed of coalescing *alluvial fans*, cones of sedimentary debris that issue from a gully or canyon cut into the range. Bajadas are surfaces of deposition; the alluvial deposits under them can reach thicknesses of hundreds or even thousands of feet. Bajadas are broadly undulating, with the high points at the apex of individual fans.

Pediments resemble bajadas, but are a little smoother. However, their origin is different because debris does not accumulate on pediments but is rather transported over them from the range into the basin. Consequently, only a few feet to tens of feet of alluvial deposits cover bedrock on a pediment. In the desert, pediments are more common than bajadas.

In Arizona, many bajadas and pediments slope toward valleys traversed by a low-gradient wash or river that flows through the valley to some distant lake or the sea. Examples are the valleys of the San Pedro and Santa Cruz Rivers and the desert part of the Gila River. Other basins, however, are closed sumps, with no through-flowing drainage. These are called *bolsons*, or basins of interior drainage, commonly abbreviated as *interior basins*. Many have ephemeral lakes, or *playas*. Good examples are Sulphur Springs Valley and Wilcox Playa.

Arroyos are the steep-sided gullies typical of desert country. Dry most of the time, they can be the sites of flash floods during the summer thunderstorm season.

The through-flowing drainage in much of Arizona's Basin and Range Province is an indication that basin and range faulting here is old. This type of faulting commonly produces bolsons, but these are integrated over time by streams that work their way into one bolson after another, eventually linking them into a continuous drainage system that empties into the sea. In Arizona, enough time has elapsed since the faulting for this process to have taken place. In contrast, this has not happened in the Great Basin, where active faulting continues to lower the basins and no organized drainage system exists.

A hiker atop Mount Wrightson consults his geologic map.

Preparing To Hike

When planning a hike, select a specific trail to be explored, but keep a backup in mind in the same area in case the favored trail is unreachable. Your next task is to assemble your equipment and become knowledgable about the area you will be hiking and about safety issues.

A GEOLOGIST'S EQUIPMENT

To make observations, record data, and collect samples, geologists use a variety of equipment, some of it simple and cheap, some expensive. The amateur geologist, however, needs much less for a satisfying and enjoyable experience. The following brief list is a good starting point.

Hand lens. Plenty of cheap lenses are available, but buying a decent one is worth it. Get the type known as a "Hastings triplet," with about 7x magnification. Bausch and Lomb makes good ones. A lens is used to magnify small grains, minerals, or fossils in a rock. You can find plenty of other uses for it as well, like searching for a splinter in your finger.

To use a hand lens properly, put it right next to your eye, then bring the rock close to the lens until it is in focus. You need plenty of light to make out details in the rock, so turn both the rock and yourself until sunlight strikes the area you are looking at. It is important to examine a fresh rock surface, not a weathered one. If you cannot find a fresh surface, a rock can be broken by striking it against another one or you can look for water-worn rock in a wash.

Notebook. If you go to the trouble of making observations, collecting samples, or photographing interesting features, a notebook is a good investment for recording the information. You can start with a small spiral-bound one, but eventually you may want to progress to a professional, surveyor-type notebook. K & E is one brand. You also need something to write with.

Camera. One of the pleasures of a geologist is taking photos of interesting features, not to mention the fine landscapes. Print film has the advantage that prints can be collected in an album, together with appropriate captions. Sketches accompanying the photo can also be useful: the camera does not see things nearly as well as the eye, which can select features of interest and ignore others. Most people nowadays use small automatic cameras, which have the advantage of being light, cheap, and simple to use. If you can handle the extra weight and cost, there is nothing like a good single-lens reflex camera with a zoom lens and a few filters. It allows so much more control and flexibility.

Binoculars. These are an important piece of equipment and not just for geology—who knows what interesting animals and birds you might encounter? A lightweight version works well, and the 8 x 20 size is quite adequate. For nearly thirty years, I have never been on a hike without my tiny Zeiss binoculars.

Maps and Reference Books. Maps are indispensable items, not only to find the way but also to learn about the geology of the area. The most useful topographic maps are USGS 7.5-minute quadrangles at 1:24,000 scale. USGS 1-degree quadrangles at 1:100,000 scale can be used in a pinch and are also useful for driving to the trailhead. Geologic maps show what geologic features are to be seen and give brief descriptions of the geologic units of the area and their mutual relationships. Some also give an account of the geologic history. If you are lucky, you may find a geologic map designed especially for the amateur geologist.

Maps can be found in book stores and outdoor equipment stores. They can also be obtained from the Arizona Geologic Survey, the USGS, and visitor centers at national parks and monuments. Another source is the USGS Survey Map Distribution Center, from which maps can be ordered by mail. Check out their website at *www.mapping.usgs.gov.* Convenient sources for topographic maps are the websites *www.topozone.com* and *www.mapquest.com.* When using maps on the trail, keep them clean and dry by placing them in large zip-lock baggies.

THE TEN ESSENTIALS AND OTHER GEAR

The Mountaineers have distilled what you should bring on a hike in wild country into the following list of Ten Essentials:

1. Flashlight/headlamp—with extra bulbs and batteries
2. Maps—take the right ones for the trip and know how to use them
3. Compass—know how to use it
4. Extra food—so that something is left over at the end of a trip
5. Extra clothing—more than is needed in good weather
6. Sunglasses—especially important for desert sun and snowy alpine destinations
7. First-aid supplies—hiker should also be versed in basic first aid, with cardiopulmonary resuscitation (CPR) skills a plus
8. Pocket knife—for first aid and emergency fire building
9. Matches—in a waterproof container
10. Fire starter—a candle or chemical fuel for starting a fire with wet wood

In addition to the Ten Essentials, other miscellaneous gear is helpful. A decent, comfortable pack is essential because you will be carrying not only items normally carried on hikes, but also geologic paraphernalia and perhaps rock samples. Always wear good footgear and clothing suitable for the place and season, not forgetting rain gear. Bring along several water containers (one-liter plastic beverage bottles are great for this). A wide-brimmed hat, suntan lotion, lip balm, and bug juice are important in the summer. Extra warm clothing is essential in winter. If you are traveling with other people, it's worthwile for each person to bring a whistle for keeping in touch with the other hikers. Some toilet paper is always a good idea. Finally, extra fruit and energy bars are a great additional nutrition source.

SAFETY

A geologic hike is no different from other hikes when it comes to staying safe, being well prepared, and knowing how to deal with emergencies. The first thing to consider is where to go. In a state like Arizona, which has both topographic and climate extremes, favor the cool mountains during the heat of summer and the warm deserts in winter. The summer thunderstorm season brings with it much danger of lightning, so avoid high exposed places in July and August. In these months, start hikes early enough to get back down to lower country by noon. Avoid hiking in snowy or icy conditions in the winter, especially on steep trails.

Many trailheads are reached by dirt roads. These can get pretty messy in wet weather, especially when snow melts in the spring. Be prepared for this, and do not hesitate to give up on the hike if the going gets tough. Digging vehicles out of the mud is no fun. For the same reason, keep an eye on the weather during the hike—the road that was fine going in may become impassable when it is time to return.

Many feel that a cell phone is a good thing to have on a hike in case of an emergency. Maybe yes, maybe no. True, you may be able to call out for help, but you may also find out the darn thing does not work in remote country. Then, if you had relied on the phone and neglected to bring self-help gear, you would be in real trouble.

Whenever you hike, recognize your personal capabilities and limitations and those of your party. Be alert to trail hazards such as frosty footbridges, slick rocks in streams, downfalls, eroded or collapsed trails, exposed sections, reroutes, obscure trails, and cliffs. Be alert to location hazards such as poison ivy, uneven or unstable terrain, rattlesnakes, bees, ticks, and other safety threats.

Respect the land you walk through: leave no litter, make no mark, throw away no cigarette, lit or unlit. Make no unnecessary fires, leave no fire unattended, and never leave a fire without first putting it out completely. In other words, walk so no one can tell you walked.

These warnings and recommendations should not discourage anyone from enjoying the pleasures of hiking. The vast majority of hikes are on well-marked trails, the weather is good most of the time, and everything is more likely than not to go smoothly. But it is wise to be prepared for the unexpected, because it is the unexpected that can bring you grief.

Rocks exposed in the walls of the Grand Canyon near the Tanner Trail

Part 1
COLORADO PLATEAU

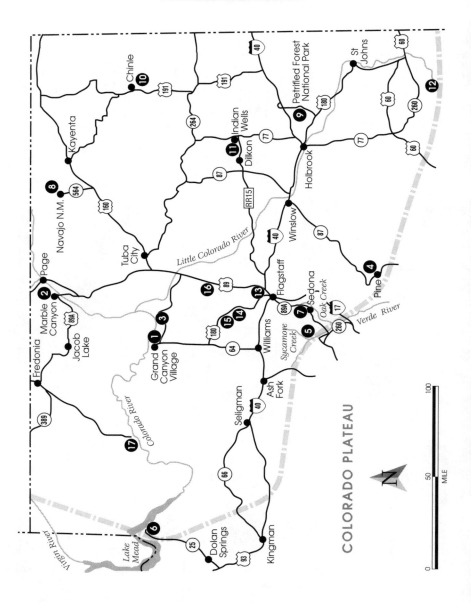

The Colorado Plateau occupies approximately the northeastern one-third of Arizona and extends into Colorado, New Mexico, and Utah. At a typical elevation of 5000 feet, it is considerably higher than most of its surroundings.

The distinctive geologic character of the plateau is given by its general lack of deformation and the Mesozoic strata that cover much of the surface. The plateau has escaped serious deformation for a remarkably long time—the nearly

600 million years since the beginning of Paleozoic time. Because of this, the strata are nearly horizontal, with an imperceptible dip to the northeast. At the southern margin, the dip steepens to a few degrees. This increase telegraphs the proximity of the Central Arizona Highlands, a mountainous belt formed during the Laramide orogeny, about 60 million years ago, but since foundered. Taken together, the dips give strata of the plateau a saucer-like shape.

In addition to the dips, the Laramide orogeny produced broad folds that disturb the flatness of the strata here and there. Most are of two kinds: anticlinal domes and monoclines, the characteristic folds of the plateau.

The Mesozoic strata differ from the underlying Paleozoic section in being composed primarily of sandstone, siltstone, and shale, so are much softer. These rocks are easily eroded and give the Colorado Plateau its open aspect. Harder layers above softer ones produce the characteristic step-like topography of scarps and mesas called the *tablelands*. As the rocks are worn away by erosion, the harder caprock layers protect the softer material underneath. This process

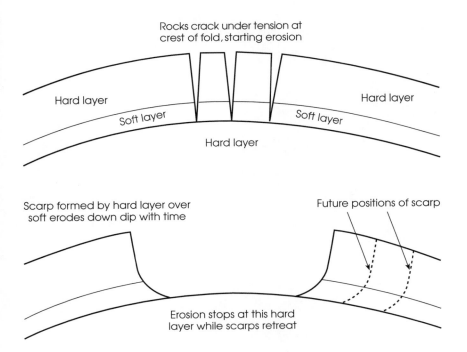

Figure 8. Scarps on the Colorado Plateau are formed by a hard layer over a soft one. The layers crack under tension at the crest of anticlines and monoclines. This allows erosion to start, forming a scarp. The face of the scarp then gets eroded back, retreating down dip over time.

forms mesas where the dip of the strata is very low, and cliffs where it is steeper because of a fold. Black Mesa and Vermilion Cliffs are examples of the former, Echo Cliffs of the latter. The hard caprock forms the top of the mesas and scarps. Many scarps were originally formed near the top of a nearby fold, but have retreated down dip with time because erosion is constantly undermining and wearing away the cliff faces (see figure 8).

Carved into the open landscape of the plateau are the *canyons,* which have made this region famous worldwide. The undisputed king of these is the Grand Canyon, carved by the Colorado River, the master stream of the region.

In central and western Arizona, the Colorado Plateau ends at impressive *rims*—the Mogollon Rim and the Grand Wash Cliffs. These are bold escarpments that are a dominant feature of the landscape and can be seen from many miles away. Many geologists think that the southern edge of the plateau is being eaten away by extensional faulting, so that unfaulted plateau becomes faulted Arizona Transition Zone with time. One line of evidence for this is the *volcanic fields* that are clustered near the southern margin of the plateau. This is because volcanism usually signals heating of the crust and the onset of some kind of tectonic event, most commonly extension. In other words, first you get volcanoes, then faults and rifting.

CANYONS

One of the most remarkable aspects of the Colorado Plateau is surprise. The visitor has been traveling through a flat, perhaps even boring, landscape. Suddenly, the path is interrupted by a totally unexpected and otherwise invisible chasm, one of the many canyons that slice through this stony region. People visiting the South Rim of the Grand Canyon often comment on this: nothing can be seen until you are a few feet from the rim. There, the land drops away from you, suddenly, for thousands of feet, and the view is now filled with a surreal, unexpected landscape.

This was even more true and troubling for Captain García López de Cárdenas, a member of Coronado's great expedition of 1540, and the first white person to see the Grand Canyon. His Native American guides had been alluding to a major impediment, but this was hard to believe after riding through so much flat country. And then, there it was, this awesome hole, squarely astride the intended route. But the Spaniards were not easily dissuaded, and they attempted to cross the obstacle. The silver river glimpsed at the bottom seemed no more than a few tens of feet wide, they thought; the canyon could not be all that big. But nothing in their experience had schooled them to gauge the size of a chasm like this one. The river sliding down there was the Colorado River of the West, and the canyon was very, very big. Cárdenas and his men turned back.

The Colorado is the master stream of the arid West. Like a giant knife, it has cut a 1-mile-deep and 8- to 10-mile-wide gash in the Earth's crust, exposing rocks that record one-third of the Earth's history, back to 1.8 billion years ago. For all practical purposes, the gash records the history of life on the planet.

No one who has seen the Grand Canyon is likely to soon forget it—the cliffs and slopes of the horizontal Paleozoic strata, stepping downward from the Kaibab limestone rimrock to the distant Tapeats sandstone at the base, about 600 million years old. Below in the sinister Inner Gorge, insignificant seeming but 1000 feet deep, the rock is all dark Proterozoic schist and gneiss, black laced with pink granite veins. Its youngest rocks are 1400 million years old and the oldest about 1800 million. In its own beautiful way, this looks like the portal of Hell. No wonder explorer John Wesley Powell was apprehensive when he entered this slit with his boats.

In most places, these rocks are deep below the surface, certainly on the Colorado Plateau, whose surface is mantled by rocks one tenth as old. Only because of the Colorado River's toil can we see what lies below the region. We are even more fortunate in this, because the Colorado, a stern taskmaster, forces all its tributaries to cut down whenever it does. So, they too have cut down deeply, fretting the land and exposing what is below the surface.

A geologist gazing at the precipitous Grand Canyon is sure to mutter the words "youthful landscape." Indeed, this is a young, angular, abrupt, energetic landscape that has not had the time to smooth out its sharp corners. The rivers have cut down at breakneck speed, leaving no time to erode the sides of the canyons back and away from the rivers, to open up the valleys and make them more subdued. Seen in a satellite image, these canyons look like giant fingers reaching into an older, subdued landscape.

Geologic observations of many kinds lead to the proposition that the Colorado River is younger than about 5 million years. The newly established river was greatly aided in its downcutting by uplift during this same time interval. The result was very rapid cutting down, in good agreement with the youthful topography so typical of the canyons. It also appears that Glen Canyon, and probably all the canyons of that area, came into being more recently than about 500,000 years ago, only yesterday in geologic terms.

The canyons are extending themselves into the much older subdued landscape that dominated the Colorado Plateau before its recent uplift and before the new river system came into being. With time, this old landscape will all be gone.

Hike 1

KAIBAB TRAIL

See Grand Canyon's colorful and spectacular layers, representing nearly 2 billion years of Earth's history.

LOCATION ■ Grand Canyon National Park

DISTANCE ■ About 3 miles one way

ELEVATION ■ 7200 to 5160 feet

DIFFICULTY ■ Moderate

TOPOGRAPHIC MAPS ■ Phantom Ranch, AZ, 1:24,000; Grand Canyon, AZ, 1:100,000; USGS Bright Angel, AZ, 1:62,500 shaded-relief map with descriptive text.

GEOLOGIC MAPS ■ 1

PRECAUTIONS ■ This hike is hot in the summer, so you must carry plenty of water. Hiking in the cool season is best. Watch out for ice in the winter.

INFORMATION ■ Grand Canyon National Park

Landscape and Geology: The Paleozoic rocks in the Grand Canyon actually underlie much of the Colorado Plateau, but are magnificently exposed here as horizontal bands (see figure 9). They are composed mostly of limestone, sandstone, and shale. To help you get oriented, note that the conspicuous cliff bands are, from the top, the Permian Kaibab limestone forming the rimrock, the Permian Coconino sandstone, the Mississippian Redwall limestone, and the Cambrian Tapeats sandstone at the base. Each of these layers is called a *formation* because it is made up of the same rock and was deposited under relatively uniform conditions. Taken together, the Paleozoic rocks represent about 350 million years of geologic time.

At the end of the hike, you can see even older rocks that are tilted and faulted. These Proterozoic sedimentary rocks have been assembled into a geologic unit called the Grand Canyon Supergroup, which is made up of smaller geologic units called *groups,* in this case the Unkar and the overlying Chuar Groups. Groups are made up of formations, which are even smaller units.

Only the lower part of the Unkar Group is visible here. Primitive forms of life, mostly algae, already existed when these ancient rocks were deposited between 1200 and 850 million years ago. The oldest rocks of all are the dark-colored metamorphic and igneous rocks of the Inner Gorge.

The geologic story told by these rocks is awe inspiring. In the dim antiquity of perhaps 1800 million years ago, sediments were deposited at the margin of the continent, which by that time had grown outward to this area from its ancient core in Canada and Greenland. This growth had taken as long as the entire interval between the present and the time when these continent-margin sediments were laid down.

Then, between 1700 and 1800 million years ago, the sediments were squeezed and heated by forces unleashed when plates collided to the west. Later, about 1400 million years ago, the rocks were invaded by granite, and both were later subjected to a long period of erosion that produced a remarkably even surface of huge extent.

About 1200 million years ago, an ancient sea advanced upon this surface, depositing a thickness of nearly 3 miles of the Grand Canyon Supergroup, whose middle is marked by basalt flows dated at 1090 million years old. The sea remained shallow while this remarkable thickness of rocks was laid down. Algae flourished late in this interval. The red color of many of these rocks points to oxidation, indicating that oxygen existed in the atmosphere by this time.

Deposition ended perhaps around 850 million years ago when the Proterozoic rocks were faulted into tilted blocks. Erosion then held sway once again for 250 million years, beveling tilted strata and old metamorphic rocks alike. At this time, the region became part of the *continental shelf,* an area covered by shallow sea water at the margin of continents.

63

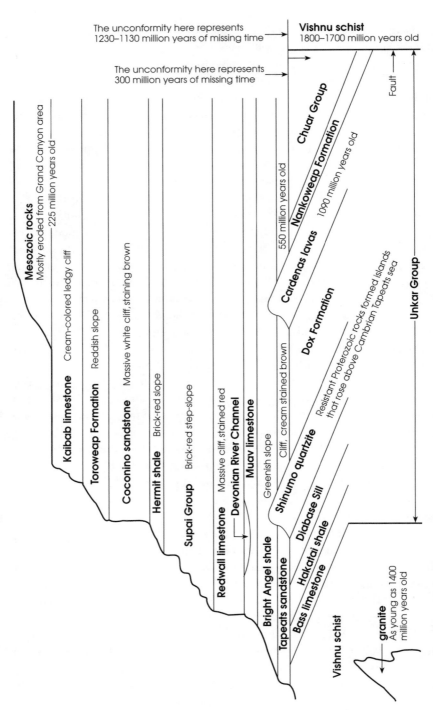

Figure 9. Geologic section of the Grand Canyon showing its stratigraphy

About 590 million years ago, the first of several Paleozoic marine incursions and retreats began, probably caused by changes in sea level. During this time, life exploded, first in the sea, then on land as well.

About 250 million years ago, Paleozoic time ended with a great crisis in which many organisms became extinct.

Trail Guide: As of 2001, visitors are not allowed to drive private cars to the trailhead. Once in the South Rim area of Grand Canyon National Park, take a shuttle bus from Yavapai Lodge or the Maswik Transportation Center at the Village to Yaki Point. The road to Kaibab Trail is a spur off the Yaki Point road. Bus schedules and other information are handed out at the park gate. Outhouses, drinking water, and a public phone are at the trailhead.

The hike described here goes about halfway down the south canyon wall. It can be done easily in one day without the need to obtain a backcountry permit or lodging at the bottom of the canyon. It is possible to hike down into and out of the canyon in one long day, but this is inadvisable for most people and pointless if you are interested in experiencing the place and learning something.

At first, the trail switchbacks impressively down through the Kaibab limestone, which contains abundant *chert* (very finely crystalline silica) and *brachiopod* (lampshell) fossils. The straight stretch that follows is in a bench at the foot of the Kaibab cliff. The bench is formed by the poorly resistant Toroweap Formation, whose reddish contorted mudstone, reddish cross-bedded sandstone, and gray limestone are all exposed along the trail. These sedimentary rocks were deposited near the shoreline of a shallow fluctuating sea.

After about one-half mile, the trail switchbacks down through a cream-colored cross-bedded sandstone made up of grains that are fine, well sorted, well rounded, and "frosted" (they look like frosted glass). This is the Coconino sandstone, the product of an ancient "sea" of pure sand. The cross beds represent slip faces of ancient sand dunes. The Coconino forms the sheer 500-foot cliff below the Kaibab limestone. This cliff is conspicuous throughout the Grand Canyon and helps you work out the sequence of strata even at a distance.

Views across the canyon to the west show how the various upper Paleozoic formations tend to erode or *weather*. This characteristic weathering profile is useful for identifying formations at a distance: the Kaibab cliff at the rim, the Toroweap slope below it, then the white to tan Coconino cliff, followed by the red Hermit slope, the red cliff and slope of the Supai, and finally the second conspicuous cliff band of the Grand Canyon, the 500-foot Redwall limestone.

The switchbacks end at Cedar Ridge, 1.5 miles from the trailhead. This is an overused place that is the destination for most day hikers. There are toilets but no drinking water. Continue down the trail, which has many fine exposures of red cross-bedded sandstone of the Supai Group of late Paleozoic age. The Supai was deposited on a coastal plain, much of it as sand dunes.

Figure 10. View to the northwest from the top of the Redwall limestone along the Kaibab Trail. The sketch identifies the geologic units visible from here.

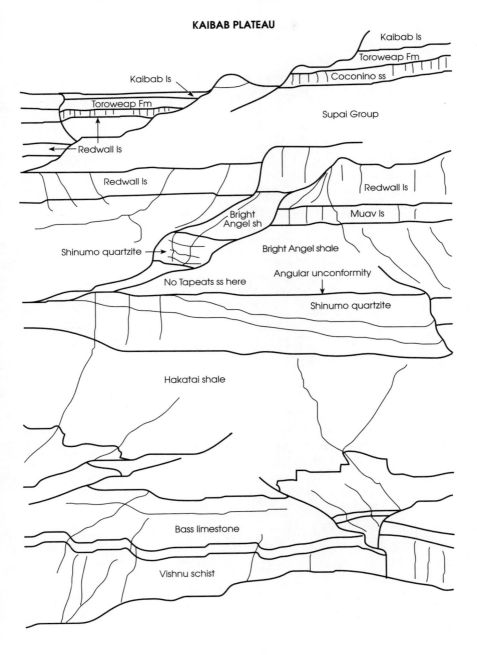

KAIBAB PLATEAU

Kaibab ls

Toroweap Fm

Coconino ss

Kaibab ls

Toroweap Fm

Redwall ls

Redwall ls

Supai Group

Redwall ls

Muav ls

Bright Angel sh

Shinumo quartzite

Bright Angel shale

No Tapeats ss here

Angular unconformity

Shinumo quartzite

Hakatai shale

Bass limestone

Vishnu schist

After rounding prominent O'Neill Butte, the trail enters a flat area on top of the Redwall limestone. Where the trail starts dropping off the Redwall at about 3 miles, go left instead for a few hundred feet to the edge of the Redwall cliff. This viewpoint offers good places to sit, remarkable views to the west and north, and an opportunity to examine the Redwall close up.

The Redwall is a light gray to white sugary limestone with chert layers and much fossil material. It appears red in color because it is stained by the Supai from above. This formation was deposited in a shallow sea, teeming with marine life, on the continental platform.

The next ridge west of the viewpoint shows the lower part of the Paleozoic strata. At the base of the cliff formed mostly of the Redwall, you can see the thin-bedded Muav limestone. This unit is Cambrian in age, whereas the Redwall above it is Mississippian, so about 150 million years are missing at the contact between the two formations, either because rocks of this age were never deposited or because they were eroded away. This gap in the rocks is called an *unconformity*.

Below the Muav, you can see a greenish slope cut into the Bright Angel shale and ending on a prominent bench. This bench is called the Tonto platform and is developed on top of the resistant Tapeats sandstone, which forms the brown cliff that rims the Inner Gorge. All three units are Cambrian in age and represent the advance of the Cambrian sea: the Tapeats is the ancient beach sand, the Bright Angel represents mud deposited in shallow water near the shore, and the Muav is from deposition in clearer water farther offshore.

The normal sequence of Grand Canyon rocks is absent between the mouth of Bright Angel Creek and Cheops Pyramid to the northwest (see figure 10). Here, a brownish cliff that looks like the Tapeats is underlain by an orange slope below which are brown ledges. These are, respectively, the Shinumo quartzite, the Hakatai shale, and the Bass limestone, all at the base of the tilted Grand Canyon Supergroup of Proterozoic age. The orange Hakatai is especially easy to spot. The Shinumo is the beach sand of an ancient sea, which explains why it is similar to the Tapeats. The Tapeats itself is not present here.

These tilted Proterozoic strata are overlain by the horizontal Paleozoic ones. The contact between the two is another example of an unconformity. This one, however, is called an *angular unconformity* to reflect the fact that the strata above and below the unconformity have different dips, and so make an angle with each other.

Within the Inner Gorge, the dark rocks are the Vishnu schist, and the lighter-colored, pinkish rocks are granitic intrusive masses. These are the oldest rocks in the area.

SPENCER TRAIL

See colorful Mesozoic rocks and learn a history lesson on this adventurous and scenic trail.

LOCATION ■ Lake Powell National Recreation Area

DISTANCE ■ About 4 miles round trip

ELEVATION ■ 3200 to 4440 feet

DIFFICULTY ■ Moderately strenuous

TOPOGRAPHIC MAPS ■ Lees Ferry, AZ, 1:24,000; Glen Canyon Dam, AZ, 1:100,000

GEOLOGIC MAPS ■ 2 and 3

PRECAUTIONS ■ This rough and unmaintained trail requires scrambling in a few spots; a walking stick is a good idea. Carry plenty of water or avoid hiking in the summer.

INFORMATION ■ Glen Canyon National Recreation Area

Landscape, Geology, and History: Lees Ferry, the launching point for river trips down the Grand Canyon, is at the intersection of the Paria River valley and the Colorado River where the latter emerges from Glen Canyon. Paria is a *strike valley* carved into a belt of the weak Chinle Formation of Triassic age (see figure 11) that extends along the *strike*, or horizontal extent, of this formation.

Much of the Chinle here consists of the Petrified Forest Member (a *member* is a smaller part of a formation), made up of colorful green and purple shale that is prominent at the foot of the cliffs in this area. It was deposited in swampy and forested plains, similar to those of today's Amazon basin. Abundant volcanic eruptions contributed ash, which eventually weathered into colorful clay. The Petrified Forest Member is famous for its petrified trunks of large trees, especially in Petrified Forest National Park (see Hike 9). One such tree, about 220 million years old, is exposed a short distance up the wash behind the restrooms at the launching ramp. Look, but don't touch.

Older formations below the Petrified Forest Member can be seen downriver from here. The lowest member of the Chinle is the Shinarump Conglomerate, a whitish to tan coarse-grained pebbly sandstone layer that caps the *hogback* (ridge made up of tilted strata) just west of the parking lot at the ramp and across the river near the gauging station (marked by a cable). This unit was deposited by ancient streams.

Below the Shinarump is the brown-red Moenkopi Formation, also of Triassic age, which forms the bluffs on both sides of the river downstream from the ferry site. This unit was deposited on a coastal plain.

The hard, gray rock below the Moenkopi is the Kaibab limestone, the top of the Paleozoic rocks that form the Grand Canyon. This formation is well exposed downstream of the ferry area, where the Colorado River enters a gorge. This is the beginning of Marble Canyon, which many consider part of the Grand Canyon.

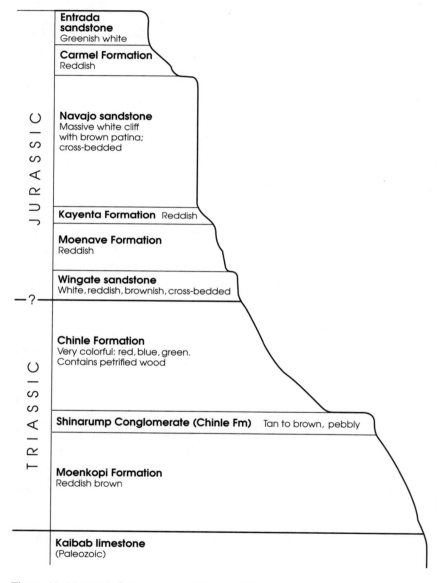

Figure 11. Mesozoic formations visible from hikes on the Colorado Plateau. The upper Mesozoic section is not present along the hikes and is thus not shown on the drawing.

Rocks above the Petrified Forest Member can be seen upstream from the boat ramp. Above the colorful Chinle are formations that collectively form the Glen Canyon Group. These rocks are more resistant to erosion than the Chinle, so they form prominent cliffs such as the Vermilion and Echo Cliffs, and the cliff climbed by Spencer Trail east of Lees Ferry.

The mostly Triassic Moenave and Kayenta Formations are not easy to distinguish from a distance and form the purplish and orange-red sandstone beds in the lower part of the cliff. The upper part is composed of the Jurassic-age buff-colored and cross-bedded Navajo sandstone. The lower rocks were deposited by rivers on nearly flat plains, on which large and small reptiles were common, including dinosaurs. By the beginning of Jurassic time, this landscape was replaced by a sandy desert comparable in extent to the modern Sahara, complete with large and shifting dunes. This was the world of the Navajo sandstone.

The tilt of the strata around the Lees Ferry area is an expression of the Echo Cliffs *monocline*, a large fold or bend in the rocks.

Lees Ferry stands at the boundary between the Mesozoic world of the Colorado Plateau and the Paleozoic and Precambrian world of the Grand Canyon. The Paleozoic rocks are tough and hard to erode, and form canyons. Some of the Mesozoic rocks are less resistant and tend to form a more open and subdued landscape. This is especially true of the Chinle and Moenkopi Formations. The presence of these rock units has funneled human activity into the Lees Ferry area from prehistoric times until today because they produce a

The Lees Ferry area and the beginning of Marble Canyon

landscape that is easy to travel through and create the only place in northern Arizona where the river is not in a canyon and is thus easily reached and forded. For this reason, Lees Ferry has been used from time immemorial by prehistoric people and then by Europeans, starting with the journeys of Spaniards based in Mexico.

John Wesley Powell, the first person to float through the canyons, interrupted his 1871 Colorado River trip here and cached his boats for the winter. However, an established ferry awaited the arrival of John D. Lee in that same year. Lee, a fugitive from the law, was eventually brought to justice, and his place was taken by the Johnson family and others, who took over Lonely Dell Ranch and operation of the ferry.

The ferry served a wagon road much used by Arizona's Mormon settlers for their travels to Utah. This trip was customary when distant settlers got married, so the road acquired the name "Honeymoon Trail." You can still see the old road south of the river and downstream from the gauge, where it is carved precariously into the reddish cliff of the Moenkopi Formation.

The ferry remained in operation through 1928, when Navajo Bridge was completed near the present settlement of Marble Canyon. For decades, this bridge afforded the only car crossing of the Colorado River in Arizona upstream from Hoover Dam, hundreds of miles to the west.

Today, Lees Ferry is the launching point for river trips down the Grand Canyon. It has also become a world-class fishery renowned for its large trout, which flourish in the clear, cold water that has been brought about by the construction of Glen Canyon Dam in 1962.

Spencer Trail was built in 1910 by Charlie Spencer in an attempt to bring coal by mule train from Warm Creek to the north. The coal was needed for the boilers used to run pumps and sluices that were part of his gold-dredging operation. This method soon proved inadequate, causing Spencer to resort to a steamboat. This, too, failed when he discovered that the boat used more coal to steam upriver than it could bring back down. The amount of gold was found to be minimal anyway, and the operation soon ceased.

Trail Guide: Lees Ferry is reached by a paved and signed spur road that branches off US 89A just east of the Marble Canyon settlement and north of the bridge across the Colorado. The trailhead is reached by driving to the boat-launching ramp at the end of the road, where you will find sanitary facilities and (sometimes) drinking water.

Start on the trail that goes east (upriver) from the dirt lot, past several old stone buildings. At the last of these, watch for a sign indicating the Spencer Trail. Go left and follow the trail for about 200 yards to a gentle rise, beyond which the trail approaches the river again. On the rise, watch for rock cairns on the left (north) side of the trail or scout around until you find Spencer Trail itself. It is indistinct at this point but soon becomes better defined. The well-beaten trail continuing along the river is used mostly by fishermen.

As Spencer Trail gets steeper, you can catch your breath and save face by looking at the geology. The extensive irregular terrain developed on chaotic red-brown material across the river is a landslide composed of Kayenta, Moenave, and Upper Chinle rocks that slid over the Petrified Forest Member. This member contains clays that swell and become soupy when wet. Slides like this one are common at the foot of the cliffs composed of rocks of the Glen Canyon Group. Most moved during the last glacial period, when the climate here was wetter than now.

On the south side but high above the river is an area of yellowish material. This is a *falling dune,* formed when sand carried by the prevailing southwesterly winds goes over the ridge and is trapped in the still area on the lee side of the Echo Cliffs.

Outcrops, or exposures of bedrock, become abundant about halfway up the cliff. The rock is buff, pink, and light gray and has conspicuous cross bedding (see figure 12). Using your hand lens, you can see fine, well-sorted, well-rounded, frosted grains of quartz, all characteristic of windblown sand. Between the quartz grains is whitish calcite cement that holds the rock together. This is the Navajo sandstone.

On top of the ridge at about 2 miles, go a few hundred feet down the other side to a spectacular view toward the east. This is the terminus of the hike. Straight up canyon is the Navajo Generating Station. The extensive topographic bench (flat area) below you is on the top of the Navajo sandstone. The bench is there because soft rocks above the Navajo have been stripped away by erosion. To the left of the generating station is Navajo Mountain, a dome of strata bowed up by an igneous intrusion and sacred to the Native Americans of the region. Still farther left is the town of Page, built during construction of Glen Canyon Dam.

The top of the Navajo sandstone on the ridge here is several hundred feet higher than it is to the east across the river. This is because the Navajo is folded down along the Echo Cliffs *monocline,* with the lower part of this fold below you. The fold is marked by a belt of shattered Navajo rock along the river, which contrasts markedly to pristine rock farther upstream. The shattering happens when a rigid and thick rock layer like the Navajo is folded sharply.

The view ahead of you contains an important clue on how ancient dunes can be turned into stone instead of simply blowing away. The answer is groundwater. In many dune areas of the world, the *water table* is near the surface. The water table is the highest level underground at which rocks are saturated with water, like a sponge. Since wet sand does not blow but dry sand does, the dry sand above the water table forms dunes while the wet sand below it stays in place. If the water table gradually rises, more and more of the dunes are preserved. People studying the desert areas of the world have noted that hollows between dunes are sometimes occupied by shallow pools of water, indicating that the water table is right at the base of the dunes.

On the opposite bank of the river just south (right) of the bend, you can see a dark band that pinches out in both directions along the canyon wall. Dark bands like this are common in the Navajo and typically consist of limestone. These limestones originated in pools of water occupying low areas between dunes.

EOLIAN CROSS BEDDING

Cross beds are steep and parallel.
Sand grains are fine, well rounded, frosted, well sorted.

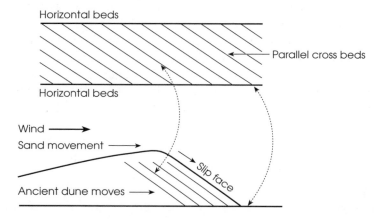

FLUVIAL CROSS BEDDING

Cross beds are low-angle and trough- or festoon-shaped.
Sand grains are fine to coarse, well-to-poorly sorted.

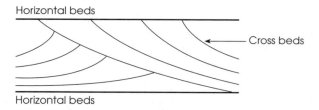

Figure 12. Characteristics of cross bedding produced by wind (eolian) and by rivers (fluvial). These features can be used to identify the origin of cross bedding in the field.

The gorge below you is the downstream end of Glen Canyon. As you can see, it is narrow and steep-walled, although the rock that forms the walls—the Navajo sandstone—is soft and erodes easily. The conclusion is that the canyon is geologically young, otherwise the walls would have eroded back, forming an open valley.

The canyon near Lees Ferry is also young, as you can see by looking west from the ridge. River gravel on Johnson Point (the mesa just north of the water tower) is about 500,000 years old. At that time, the river was flowing at the level of the top of Johnson Point. The flat-topped gray patch of land with the trees and park service housing is a river terrace about 100,000 years old. At that time, the river floodplain was at this level. Still looking west, the tree-rich area up the Paria River about one-third mile north of the paved road is Lonely Dell Ranch, original home of the Lee family. In the great flood of 1883, water of the Colorado River reached the orchard, enabling hydrologists to estimate a huge discharge of 300,000 cubic feet per second, about ten times the peak annual discharge since the dam was built. About 2 miles downstream from Lees Ferry, the river enters a narrow slot cut into a gray surface. The slot is the beginning of Marble Canyon, which, together with the Grand Canyon proper, extends more than 270 miles downstream from here.

Retrace your steps back down the trail to your car.

Looking south from the top of Spencer Trail, you can see the Echo Cliffs monocline and falling dunes.

TANNER TRAIL

Hike 3

This outstanding geologic and scenic hike in the Grand Canyon shows the entire Paleozoic sequence and ends at a breathtaking viewpoint. One of my favorites.

LOCATION ■ Grand Canyon National Park

DISTANCE ■ About 4.2 miles one way

ELEVATION ■ 7400 to 5560 feet

DIFFICULTY ■ Moderately strenuous. This is a rough backcountry trail. Parts are steep.

TOPOGRAPHIC MAPS ■ Desert View, AZ, 1:24,000; Tuba City, AZ, 1:100,000

GEOLOGIC MAPS ■ 1

PRECAUTIONS ■ Spring and fall are the best times to hike this trail due to snow and ice in the winter and heat and lightning in the summer. Carry plenty of water.

INFORMATION ■ Grand Canyon National Park

Landscape and Geology: In addition to being a scenic wonder, the Grand Canyon is one of the world's premier sites for geology. From Tanner Trail, rocks representing nearly 2 billion years of Earth's history are visible (see figure 9). These include the ancient (1800 to 1400 million years old) metamorphic and igneous rocks of the Inner Gorge; the younger but still very old (1200 to 850 million years old) Proterozoic rocks exposed in a tilted block across the river north of the trail; the colorful horizontal Paleozoic strata that give the Grand Canyon its distinctive cliff and slope appearance; and the geologically young sediments deposited by the Colorado River.

In spite of the impressive thickness of these rocks, it is remarkable that more time is missing from the rock record in the Grand Canyon than is represented by the rocks that we see. The missing time is marked by *unconformities*—erosional surfaces formed when rocks either were never deposited (probably because the land was above sea level) or were deposited but then eroded.

The horizontally bedded Paleozoic rocks before you in the Grand Canyon are much less deformed than similar rocks in the Basin and Range Province. Still, you can see evidence for three periods of deformation from Tanner Trail.

The first and oldest happened between 1700 and 1800 million years ago, when ancient sediments and lava flows were metamorphosed, probably by an event related to plate collision. The result is the early Proterozoic Vishnu gneiss and schist in the Inner Gorge.

The second event probably happened about 850 million years ago and resulted in the northeast tilting of great blocks of crust. This event can be seen only where the middle Proterozoic sedimentary rocks are exposed, as they are here.

The third event took place about 65 million years ago, at the end of Cretaceous time. It is called the *Laramide orogeny*, a mountain-building event that happened because the Pacific plate to the west got shoved against the North American continent. This collision of plates squeezed and buckled the crust, forming many mountains. The Colorado Plateau escaped the worst of it, so all we see here are *monoclines* such as the Echo Cliffs and *domes* such as the Kaibab Plateau. Canyons have cut through some of these folds, enabling us to see that the folds are the draping of strata over faults at depth (see figure 5).

Trail Guide: Once in the South Rim area of Grand Canyon National Park, take the East Rim Drive toward Desert View and turn off to Lipan Point between mileposts 261 and 262, near the east entrance. Since transportation arrangements in the park are changing, check at the park entrance to learn the latest rules about driving versus public transportation. You may have to take a bus to Lipan Point.

At Lipan Point parking lot, take a few minutes to enjoy the fine view, then walk back down the road about 150 feet to the trailhead and information sign to the left (east) of the road. Views to the north show the great wall of the Palisades in the near distance, the Echo Cliffs in the far distance, and the dark hump of Navajo Mountain, sacred to the Hopi and Navajo, near Lake Powell.

View north from the top of the Redwall on the Grand Canyon's Tanner Trail

The trail plunges off the steep north slope at an area of faulting. When rocks are shattered by faults, they erode more easily, forming slopes instead of the usual cliffs. Most trails in the Grand Canyon use such faulted areas to get across the more formidable cliff bands. Many were Native American trails originally and are probably thousands of years old. Later, they were used by miners.

At first, the trail goes through the Permian Kaibab Formation, visible in the cliffs to the west and in cream-colored outcrops along the trail. Here the trail is rough, with rubble composed of angular fragments of hard *chert* (finely crystalline silica) that has eroded out of the limestone. The limestone contains many fossils, and you may see *brachiopods* (lampshells). The Kaibab was deposited in a shallow sea about 250 million years ago.

Partway down the switchbacks, you get a good view of the Paleozoic layers on the east wall of Tanner Canyon ahead of you—the ledgy cliff at the top is the Kaibab, the slope below it is the Toroweap Formation made up of gypsum and shale, and then comes the great cliff of white to brown cross-bedded Coconino sandstone. The small slope below the Coconino is in the Hermit shale, below which are the reddish ledges of the Supai Group. These rocks are Pennsylvanian to Permian in age, but the gray to reddish cliff beneath the Supai is the Mississippian-age Redwall limestone. These units are recognizable everywhere in this area, providing many opportunities for practicing identification.

The Supai forms the long red ridge to the north along which Tanner Trail winds its course. The first prominence on the ridge is Escalante Butte, named in honor of the eighteenth-century Franciscan friar who traveled widely in this country. The second is Cardenas Butte, named for Captain Cárdenas who, as part of Coronado's great expedition of 1540, was the first white person to see the Grand Canyon, some 265 years before Lewis and Clark's expedition to the West. The trail aims for the saddle south of Escalante Butte.   ·

At about one-fourth mile, the trail becomes sandy and easier to walk on. You are in the Coconino, a conspicuously cross-bedded sandstone (see figure 12) composed of very small well-rounded quartz grains that are *frosted*, looking like frosted glass. This tells us that this formation is made up of *eolian* (wind-blown) sand, once part of a Sahara-like desert of sand dunes. The cross beds represent the surfaces of ancient dunes that swept through this region some 170 million years ago.

If you keep your eyes peeled, you can see *outcrops*, or exposures of rocks, that tell you what formations you are walking through. The trail becomes reddish, and small outcrops of red parallel-bedded *shale* (a fine-grained sedimentary rock made of clay) point to the Hermit shale. Farther down, outcrops become more abundant and consist of parallel- and cross-bedded sandstone, also red. This is the Supai Group, on which you will be walking from here on.

The trail touches the bottom of the canyon occasionally, but basically stays on its west flank. At 1.5 miles, it leaves the canyon for good and heads for the prominent saddle at the head of 75-Mile Canyon. This is a good place to rest and view a new part of the geologic section.

Escalante Butte is capped by a remnant of light-colored Coconino, but in the canyon below you see new rocks—the great reddish-to-gray cliff of the Redwall limestone, then a greenish slope with minor ledges formed by the Bright Angel shale of Cambrian age. Still farther down and farther away is the brown cliff of the Cambrian Tapeats sandstone, the lowest unit of the Paleozoic section, nearly 600 million years old. Below the Tapeats are the dark metamorphic rocks of the Vishnu schist, 1700 to 1800 million years old. Where the Tapeats directly overlies the Vishnu, the unconformity between them represents 800 million years of time that has vanished from the rock record, more than the time from when the first complex organisms began to swim in the Paleozoic sea to the present day.

Deeper and steeper than Tanner Canyon to the east, 75-Mile Canyon will erode down faster. It will also erode headward, eventually destroying the saddle and capturing the upper reaches of Tanner Creek, which will be diverted into 75-Mile Canyon. This is the process of *piracy* and *capture*, swashbuckling but official geologic terms.

After the precipitous descent to this point, you may be tempted to turn back. But keep in mind that the end of the hike is at the same elevation as the saddle, so you have already coped with all the elevation difference by getting here.

Beyond the saddle, the trail meanders along the ridge in pretty country carved into the Supai Group. You may see a whitish mineral with radial, rosette-like arrangement of crystals in veins along the trail at about 2.8 miles. This is *barite* (barium sulfate).

About 1.4 miles beyond this point, the trail descends to a bench on top of the Redwall limestone, then plunges to the right along the usual broken-down faulted zone. At this point, go straight ahead along the top of the cliff for a few hundred feet to one of the most remarkable geologic and scenic viewpoints anywhere (see figure 13). This is the terminus of the hike.

To the east is the great rampart of the Palisades, displaying the familiar Paleozoic section. To the northwest is the Walhalla Plateau, an extremity of the Kaibab Plateau. Note the Coconino cliff high up, the Redwall cliff lower down, and the Tapeats cliff at the base. Under the Tapeats is something new— a section of black and brick-red beds tilted gently to the northeast. This is the Unkar Group of middle Proterozoic age. The black rocks are the Cardenas lavas, at the top of the Unkar and 1090 million years old. The red layers below are the Dox Formation, forming a good part of the Unkar.

If you look at the base of the Tapeats closely, you can see that this formation cuts across the Proterozoic strata, forming a splendid example of an

View of the Kaibab Plateau from Tanner Trail, looking north-northeast across the Grand Canyon

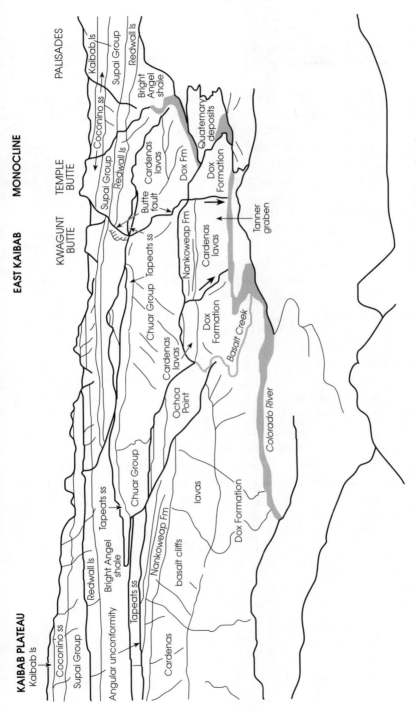

Figure 13. View to the north from the top of the Redwall limestone along Tanner Trail. The sketch identifies the geologic units visible from here.

81

angular unconformity. Following this contact from left to right, you can see that the Tapeats cuts higher and higher rocks of the Proterozoic "layer cake," that is, younger and younger units. This is an effect of erosion beveling a tilted block of strata.

At Ochoa Point, directly across the river, the black lava is overlain by purplish beds forming ledges and slopes. Farther right, north of an S-bend in the river, the purple beds are overlain by tan and gray slope-forming strata with a ledge near the top. This is the lower part of the Chuar Group, also Proterozoic in age and thought to be about 820 million years at the top. Together, these rocks form the Grand Canyon Supergroup, a section of ancient sediments that are rare in that they have never been metamorphosed and thus retain their original sedimentary characteristics. Here they are more than 2.5 miles thick, having been deposited over a span of nearly 400 million years. These rocks contain fossils, especially algae, that represent early forms of life on Earth.

The Proterozoic rocks were broken by faults and tilted into blocks about 850 million years ago. Later, the top of the tilted blocks was planed off by erosion and the Tapeats was deposited on this planed-off surface, which is an *angular unconformity*. Here, the well-displayed unconformity under the Tapeats sandstone represents erosion for more than 200 million years, almost the time from the end of the Paleozoic to today. Two of the faults responsible for the tilting are visible north of the river, just upstream from the S-bend, where the dark lavas are dropped down between red Dox rocks that are normally below the lavas. This structure is a *graben*, a down-dropped block bounded by faults on both sides. The easternmost fault is known as the Temple Butte fault, one of the major faults in the Grand Canyon.

The gently tilted reddish Supai and the Redwall beneath it can be traced eastward across the river. They can also be traced westward as they arch to near the top of the Walhalla Plateau, where they are much higher than near the river. This is the East Kaibab monocline, produced by renewed movement of the Temple Butte fault during the Laramide orogeny about 65 million years ago and some 750 million years after the initial movement. However, the later movement was in the opposite sense from the earlier one. Evidently, the old fault was a plane of weakness in Laramide time.

RIMS

The high country of the Colorado Plateau comes to an abrupt end in western Arizona at the Grand Wash Cliffs and in central Arizona at the Mogollon Rim.

The Grand Wash fault, a great normal fault, strikes north-south. West of this fault is the Basin and Range Province, produced by Tertiary and Quaternary pull-apart faulting, or *rifting*.

The Mogollon Rim is mostly an erosional scarp that started life retreating northward off the Mogollon Highlands, a Laramide-age mountain belt that once existed along the southern margin of the Colorado Plateau. The mountains foundered because of rifting in Tertiary time, forming the Arizona Transition Zone. This zone remains high today both topographically and structurally in spite of the foundering, attesting to its former loftiness.

DONOHUE TRAIL

Hike 4

Explore the Mogollon Rim and learn about its surprising geologic history. This is a pleasant walk, partly through forest, with fine views.

LOCATION ■ Mogollon Rim

DISTANCE ■ About 2 miles one way

ELEVATION ■ 5600 to 6700 feet

DIFFICULTY ■ Moderate (short but rocky)

TOPOGRAPHIC MAPS ■ Pine, AZ, 1:24,000; Payson, AZ, 1:100,000

GEOLOGIC MAPS ■ 4

PRECAUTIONS ■ Start early to get the climb done in the cool part of the day. Carry plenty of water. Walking sticks are a good idea for this rocky trail.

INFORMATION ■ Tonto National Forest

Landscape and Geology: Donohue Trail climbs up to a viewpoint on Milk Ranch Point at the spectacular escarpment of the Mogollon Rim, the boundary between the Colorado Plateau and the Arizona Transition Zone. North of the scarp is the relatively simple topographic and geologic terrain of the Colorado Plateau, with flat sedimentary layers and few faults. To the south are the intricate ranges, valleys, and basins of the Arizona Transition Zone.

In most places, the Mogollon Rim is distinguished by a great white cliff of

Coconino sandstone of Permian age. However, this formation has been eroded away where the trail climbs onto the rim, making the route passable here. Reconstructing the events that led to this erosion is important for understanding the age and development of the Mogollon Rim.

The geologic map shows that the lavas capping Milk Ranch Point are about 14 million years old, or middle Miocene in age. The *contact* (surface where the rocks meet) between the lavas and underlying formations was the surface of the Earth when the lavas flowed over the land. Geologists have discovered that an ancestral Mogollon Rim existed then near the south end of Milk Ranch Point. This rim was lower and had gentler slopes than the present one and was about 1 mile southwest of its present position.

Milk Ranch Point preserves the ancient scarp beneath the lavas, which are tough and do not erode easily. The location of the lava vents is not known for sure; several were to the north on the Mogollon Rim and two may have been on Milk Ranch Point itself. The lavas flowed south along a gentle valley, then over the ramp that marked the ancient rim, finally pooling at the foot of the ramp. The southern third of Milk Ranch Point, where the lava is thickest and exposed over a wide area, marks the foot of the ancient ramp. The point itself juts out from the general alignment of the present Mogollon Rim because it has been protected by its lava cap.

The separation between the ancient and the present rims indicates that the Mogollon Rim has been eroded back about 5300 feet in 14 million years, giving a rate of retreat of about 5 feet per 10,000 years.

The geology at Milk Ranch Point shows that the slope of the land's surface 14 million years ago was from high ground on the Colorado Plateau north of the rim to lower ground south of it. This is a reversal from the older Tertiary drainage direction, which was to the north from the Mogollon Highlands onto the Colorado Plateau. This ancient drainage direction is inferred from the Rim gravels, which were derived from the south and are common on top of the Mogollon Rim.

The drainage reversal documented at Milk Ranch Point helps us shed light on when and how the Mogollon Rim was formed, an issue that is still being debated among geologists. Several possibilities exist.

The first case to consider is that the Mogollon Rim is younger than or the same age as the foundering or collapse of the Mogollon Highlands and the formation of the Arizona Transition Zone. Thus, the rim may have been formed by faults that are parallel to the rim and moved down to the south. Such faults would probably be part of the foundering, and the Mogollon Rim would thus be a modified fault scarp. To test this, you would expect to find faults that run parallel to the rim all along it. Since this is not the case, this does not seem to be a good explanation.

Another possibility is that the rim formed after establishment of a south-

The Mogollon Rim near Milk Ranch Point. Cross-bedded Permian Coconino sandstone is in the foreground, forming most of the scarp, and the Arizona Transition Zone can be seen beyond. The Mazatzal Mountains form the skyline.

ward drainage system resembling the present one. In this case, the rim would be on the north side of an erosional valley with a course parallel to the rim. This by itself is not an adequate explanation because there are many streams at the foot of the rim, not just one. It is unlikely that many independent streams would just happen to produce a continuous and reasonably straight scarp like the Mogollon Rim.

Finally, it is possible that the rim predates foundering and was formed as an erosional scarp retreating northward off the flank of the Mogollon Highlands. In this case, regional stream flow would have been north onto the Colorado Plateau, but the scarp itself would have forced streams to flow parallel to its base in places before joining the general northward trend. Streams on top of the plateau but near the rim would probably have flowed southward into the low ground at the foot of the scarp.

Not enough information is available to solve this problem. Perhaps the best explanation is a combination of mechanisms: that the Mogollon Rim started as an erosional scarp on the flank of the highlands, then was modified after collapse of the highlands and development of southward drainage

Trail Guide: Drive southeast from Pine toward Payson on State Highway 87. About one-half mile beyond Pine, turn north off the highway at the brown sign for the Pine Trailhead. A large parking lot with some shade and a toilet is about one-fourth mile from the highway.

Take Trail #31, which goes past the outhouse and an informative sign. The sandy soil here is derived from the Coconino sandstone up slope. Beyond the gate, Trail #26 branches off to the left. Stay right on Highline Trail #31.

The Highline Trail was built in the 1880s to reach various ranches at the foot of the Mogollon Rim. It is well worn, showing its age. The mottled, nodular grayish cherty limestone along the trail near the beginning is the Pennsylvanian-age Naco Formation which is near the contact with the underlying Mississippian-age Redwall limestone. About 50 million years of erosion separate these two formations. During this time, the top of the Redwall eroded into an irregular *karst* topography, which was filled by the Naco deposits. Karst landforms and their characteristic sinkholes are formed by the subterranean solution of limestone. The boulders of *vesicular basalt* (lava rock pitted with gas bubbles) along the trail are derived from the basalt cap of the Mogollon Rim.

For the next one-half mile, the trail is flat and wanders through a pleasant forest of ponderosa pine, alligator juniper, and live oak. Box elders grow along a creek that has water during the wetter times of the year. The creek bed has large boulders of basalt brought in by floods. The trail follows the creek to a junction. Continue right across the creek on the Highline Trail, marked by the sign "Donohue Trail ½." The trail climbs onto a series of creek terraces, then onto a dry slope populated with juniper, chaparral, and agave. This slope is most likely a *pediment*, a surface cut on bedrock mantled by a thin veneer of gravel and sloping away from the mountains. This surface is littered with moderate-sized pieces of basalt from Milk Ranch Point above.

Turn left onto Donohue Trail #27, on which the going gets rough because this old trail is heavily eroded. As you climb the slope, think about the types of observations and reasoning that geologists use to make sense of what they see.

The reddish color along the trail is derived from the poorly exposed Pennsylvanian and Permian redbeds that underlie the slope and are roughly equal in age to the Supai Group of the Grand Canyon. One exposure of these redbeds is in a narrow washed-out part of the trail about halfway up the slope. The overlying light-colored Coconino sandstone is visible on the next prominence to the west, but has been eroded away where the trail climbs up to Milk Ranch Point.

Along the trail, an occasional broken boulder of basalt shows a fresh surface that is gray in color instead of the tan of a *weathered* surface. If you look at a fresh surface with a hand lens, you can see many rust-colored crystals. Originally, these were the greenish mineral *olivine*, which is rich in iron. The iron has weathered into iron oxide, forming the mineral *iddingsite.* Also visible in places are dark crystals of *pyroxene* and whitish crystals of *plagioclase*.

At about 1.7 miles, exposures of basalt increase as you near the crest of the trail, but it is still hard to locate the base of the flows precisely. You can use a field geologist's trick and figure that you are in basalt bedrock when exposures are large and fractures in the rock have the same orientation throughout the outcrop. This is because fractures in a boulder deposit would have many random orientations.

Even if you can't locate the base of the basalt, you can be sure that the basalt here rests on the redbeds. This means that the overlying Coconino and Kaibab Formations were eroded before the basalt flowed over this area. Yet, most of the Mogollon Rim is formed by the white, cross-bedded, and cliff-forming Coconino sandstone, which you can see on the next prominence to the west. The conclusion is that what is now Milk Ranch Point was actually a valley during the time of the basalt flow.

When you crest the hill, you can get to a good viewpoint by bushwhacking southeastward along the rim through the chaparral. Starting at the last switchback, go south a few hundred feet through brush to a basalt ledge at the edge of the mesa. This is the end of the hike. Here you can rest and have a good view of the Arizona Transition Zone country to the south.

Much of the low area at the foot of the rim is in the drainage basin of the East Verde River. Directly south is the broad hump of the Sierra Ancha (Hikes 18, 21, 22, and 24), to the west of which is the Mazatzal Range, whose highest points are Four Peaks (Hike 23) and Mazatzal Peak (Hike 19). Farther west still is Verde Valley and the Black Hills, which form its southwest margin (Hike 20).

From here, return to Pine Trailhead the way you came.

Hike 5

PARSONS TRAIL

This charming year-round canyon hike along a perennial stream will show you limestone and basalt flows as well as springs and a deep pool for taking a refreshing dip.

LOCATION ■ Sycamore Canyon Wilderness, Coconino National Forest

DISTANCE ■ About 2.5 miles one way to the recommended stopping point; about 1 mile farther to Parsons Spring

ELEVATION ■ 3600 to 3760 feet

DIFFICULTY ■ Easy

TOPOGRAPHIC MAPS ■ Clarkdale, AZ, 1:24,000; Sycamore Basin, AZ, 1:24,000; Prescott, AZ, 1:100,000

GEOLOGIC MAPS ■ 5

PRECAUTIONS ■ Sycamore Creek may be high enough in the spring and after summer storms to make crossings difficult. Carry walking sticks and plenty of water.

INFORMATION ■ Coconino National Forest

Landscape and Geology: The trail starts near the confluence of Sycamore Creek with the Verde River, then follows the creek upstream through picturesque Sycamore Canyon, carved by the creek into the eroded edge of the Colorado Plateau, here the northwestern end of the Mogollon Rim. The hike starts in the Verde Valley, a structural depression that is part of the Arizona Transition Zone and was formed in Cenozoic time. The Verde River flows though the valley, which it helped create.

The cliff-forming Redwall limestone of Mississippian age forms most of the walls of Sycamore Canyon here. The limestone is riddled with caverns

Columnar basalt cliffs are reflected in Sycamore Creek along Parsons Trail.

produced by *groundwater* flowing through and dissolving the rock. The top of the Redwall is irregular, an example of *karst topography,* which was caused by solution and collapse of the limestone before the overlying Permian redbeds were laid down. The redbeds were long considered part of the Supai, well exposed in the Grand Canyon, but are now thought to be slightly younger. The Martin Formation of Devonian age crops out here and there beneath the Redwall.

Remnants of basalt flows that once coursed down the canyon are preserved along its walls, where they form ledges about 80 feet above the floor. These exposures show prominent *columnar jointing,* vertical joint patterns that resulted from shrinking when the lava was cooling. A remnant of higher and older basalt is near the trailhead. These basalts make it possible to determine the rate at which the canyon was cut.

Two big springs along the trail—Summers and Parsons Springs—produce most of the flow in the creek. The water of Summers Spring is probably forced to the surface by a down-to-the-east fault. The lower part of Sycamore Canyon is carved along this fault.

Trail Guide: Set the odometer to zero at the junction of Arizona Highways 89A and 260. Drive toward Cottonwood and Clarkdale, leaving Highway 89A at the next big junction. Once in the undeveloped area north of Cottonwood, turn right at mile 4.7 onto the paved road to Tuzigoot National Monument, marked by a brown sign. Immediately after crossing the Verde River, turn left onto paved Sycamore Canyon Road, marked by a green street sign. The road follows the Verde River and becomes a wide all-weather dirt road at mile 6.6. At mile 14.7, the road deteriorates and becomes steep and rutted; a nimble passenger car should be able to make it with care. There is plenty of parking but no overnight camping at the trailhead, mile 15.7. Dogs must be leashed when walking on the trail.

Stop at the trailhead for a fine view upstream into lower Sycamore Canyon. The large pool you see is in the *alluvium* of Sycamore Creek—the sediment deposits of this stream. This alluvium forms the flat floor of the canyon. On the right, you can see a cliff-forming formation that is rose- to gray-colored below, and reddish and pitted on top. This is the Redwall limestone of Mississippian age, well known from the Grand Canyon. The irregular upper part is due to irregular masses of *chert* (fine-grained silica) that weather, or erode, more slowly than the limestone and get left behind while the limestone is dissolved. The pocked and pitted top of the unit is due to karstic solution, or dissolving of the limestone by groundwater and surface water. Many fissures and caverns, all produced by solution, are evident in the Redwall limestone throughout the canyon.

The red, well-bedded Supai sandstone forms most of the skyline above the

Redwall. The Supai stains the Redwall, which is actually a thick-bedded light gray limestone. Look for the true gray color in the talus (or scree) along the trail, just after the gate, for example.

The dark gray ledge forming the skyline east of the trailhead is a basalt flow. A lower and younger flow is visible on both sides of the canyon upstream. This basalt is about 4.6 million years old and flowed down Sycamore Canyon when the canyon floor was about 80 feet above its present stand. This gives a downcutting rate of about 17 feet per million years for this part of the creek.

After starting on the hike, you can see the lower basalt well exposed near the trail in the area of the gate just beyond the trailhead, where it is overlain by well-rounded river gravel.

Upstream from the limestone-ledge pool, boulders of red Supai sandstone are scattered around a stream crossing.

After reaching the canyon floor, go right at the junction, following the trail marked Parsons Trail, #144. The delightful Summers Spring is about 1.25 miles from the trailhead. The spring is here for two reasons. One is that the rock below the Redwall limestone is more impermeable to water, preventing water from seeping through it. The other reason is a fault. The fault ground up rock, producing a clay-rich *fault gouge* that is also impermeable. These two features together provide a barrier that forces groundwater to the surface.

Beyond the spring, the trail crosses the creek twice at places marked by rock cairns, then continues around three prominent river meanders. The well-bedded and laminated Martin limestone of Devonian age crops out along the trail here. This formation consists of interbedded limestone, dolomite, siltstone, and sandstone.

Just before straightening out to a northerly trend at 2.3 miles, the trail crosses some conspicuous black *scree* (bouldery rubble) derived from basalt on the canyon wall above. The canyon is narrow here, and its precipitous limestone walls are riddled with caverns produced by groundwater flowing through the limestone and dissolving it.

A few hundred yards upstream from the scree slope at 2.5 miles, the trail follows a ledge in the Martin limestone that overlooks a beautiful pool, whose upper part is deep enough for swimming. This is a great place to end the hike.

If you decide to continue, the trail crosses the creek four more times and is relatively rough. Picturesque boulders of red Supai sandstone are scattered in the stream at the first of the four crossings, a few hundred yards upstream from the pool. Parsons Spring, about 3.5 miles from the trailhead, is a nondescript pool, upstream from which the creek bed is dry most of the time.

PIERCE FERRY VIEWPOINT– GRAPEVINE CANYON HIKE

Drive to one of the premier scenic and geologic viewpoints in Arizona, where you can see Lake Mead, the mouth of the Grand Canyon, and the spectacular escarpment of the Grand Wash Cliffs. Then walk through a nearby wild canyon with towering limestone walls.

LOCATION ■ Lake Mead National Recreation Area

DISTANCE ■ About 2.8 miles round trip for the hike

ELEVATION ■ 2680 to 2280 feet

DIFFICULTY ■ Getting to the viewpoint is an easy drive. The nearby hike is short and not steep, but the absence of a trail makes for some scrambling.

TOPOGRAPHIC MAPS ■ Meadview North, AZ-NV, 1:24,000; Lake Mead, NV-AZ, 1:100,000; Mount Trumbull, AZ, 1:100,000

GEOLOGIC MAPS ■ 6

PRECAUTIONS ■ The hike is in a canyon subject to flash flooding, so do not hike in summer if thunderstorms threaten.

INFORMATION ■ Lake Mead National Recreation Area. Also, ranger station at overlook a short distance north of turnoff to Meadview.

Landscape and Geology: Everyone who comes to the point at the north end of Grapevine Mesa near the airport is impressed by the outstanding view of Pierce Ferry and the surrounding region. Few places show as many geologic features so well.

From the viewpoint, you can look north across the valley of the Colorado River, now occupied by Lake Mead, into the Grand Wash. This is the first basin of the Basin and Range Province, which extends from here westward to the Sierra Nevada range of California.

To the east, you can see the imposing scarp of the Grand Wash Cliffs, here composed of Paleozoic limestone, dolomite, sandstone, and shale. This is the abrupt western edge of the Colorado Plateau, which extends eastward into New Mexico and northeastward into Colorado and Utah. If you look carefully, you can see the mouth of the Grand Canyon where Lake Mead comes up to the cliffs.

The Grand Wash Cliffs cut the *strata* (sedimentary layers) at an angle, so the strata rise toward the south until the entire cliff is made up of Precambrian granite and gneiss 1.8 to 1.4 billion years old. These are the rocks exposed in the Inner Gorge of the Grand Canyon.

North of the Canyon, the cliffs include an upper step. These are the Upper Grand Wash Cliffs which reach an altitude of 6700 feet at Snap Point, whose dark cap is a basalt about 9 million years old. Some of this basalt flowed down the face of the scarp, indicating that the Grand Wash Cliffs of 9 million years ago were much as they are today.

The Virgin Mountains, capped by Paleozoic sedimentary rocks, form the skyline far to the north. Just to the east of them, and about 40 miles away, the Grand Wash trough ends in mesas capped by late Cenozoic basalt. To the northwest are the rugged South Virgin Mountains, whose highest point, Gold Butte, is underlain by a distinctive light-colored granite with large crystals of potassium feldspar. This rock once played an important role in filling the Grand Wash trough with debris.

Wheeler Ridge, in the middle distance, is made up of steeply dipping sedimentary rocks. The reddish ones north of Lake Mead are the same as exposed in the face of the Upper Grand Wash Cliffs. Perhaps you can see that the arrangement on Wheeler Ridge resembles that of the Upper Grand Wash Cliffs: a scarp in upper Paleozoic rocks, but here faulted down and rotated to an eastward

The mouth of the Grand Canyon

dip. This shows that the land's surface on top of the Grand Wash Cliffs extended farther west before faulting.

The nearly horizontal layers that form most of the landscape in the Pierce Ferry area in front of you are Miocene basin beds. They filled the trough created by movement on the Grand Wash and other faults. The trough had no outlet so it was an interior basin like many in the basin and range country of Nevada. However, this basin was later cut through by the Colorado River, giving us a rare opportunity to see the three-dimensional arrangement of rocks within the basin.

This is what we have learned from it: The basin gradually filled with sand and gravel eroding from nearby highlands, mostly from the west. These coarse-grained sediments formed alluvial fans and pediments near the mountains. An *alluvial fan* is a thick cone of debris dumped into a basin by a mountain stream or wash; a *pediment* is a surface sloping away from the mountains and underlain by a thin veneer of gravel. The land surface sloped down toward a low point whose axis was roughly where the boat landing is now. This low point was occupied by *playas*, flat areas occasionally covered by ephemeral lakes, in which sand, silt, and clay accumulated. In the later stages, the low point was flooded by shallow lakes. If you have been to Death Valley, you have an idea of what the landscape looked like here until maybe 5 million years ago.

The somber-colored, poorly bedded, and intricately dissected material banked up against the east side of Wheeler Ridge on both sides of the lake is *fanglomerate*—angular gravel deposited by debris flows in fans at the foot of mountain slopes. A *debris flow* is a slurry of mud and rock created by heavy rains. Similar fanglomerate is present all along the west side of Grapevine Mesa. Pebbles, cobbles, and huge boulders of Gold Butte granite are a major component of the deposit. You drove past some of these boulders on the way in. Some are also found right next to the Grand Wash Cliffs, indicating that the basin was filled mostly from the west. Initially, the gravel was transported into the basin through gaps in Wheeler Ridge, which you can still see. Later, the ridge was buried.

The Grand Wash Cliffs contributed a minor amount of material from the east side of the basin. You can see some of this material in form of a fan emerging from Pierce Canyon—the first canyon north of the Grand Canyon; another similar fan is at the mouth of Pigeon Canyon, several miles to the north.

At the center of the basin, near Pierce Ferry, the material of the fans gradually changes to sandstone and then siltstone deposited in the playas. These are exposed near the boat landing, together with a conspicuous white *air-fall tuff*, a deposit of volcanic ash that settled out of the air after an eruption. As the basin gradually filled, the contribution of material from the highlands decreased, and the bottom of the trough was occupied by a lake in which the

Hualapai limestone that you are standing on was deposited. With time, the lake gradually expanded to occupy more and more of the basin, and the limestone *transgressed* over the fanglomerate, meaning that limestone was deposited where previously only the fanglomerate had been laid down. Eventually, most of the basin was occupied by playa and lake, and the limestone was deposited over a substantial part of the Pierce Ferry area. This can be seen by driving down to Pierce Ferry and looking back at the face of Grapevine Mesa, which is capped by this limestone. The original top of the basin fill coincides roughly with the top of Grapevine Mesa, where the viewpoint is.

The Grand Wash fault is a normal fault along which the rocks were dropped down to the west. It forms the west boundary of the Colorado Plateau in this region. At Pierce Ferry, displacement is probably 10,000 to 16,000 feet. Near Kingman, the fault displaces a volcanic tuff that is 18 million years old. Near Pierce Ferry, the fault is buried by the undisturbed Muddy Creek Formation, which continued to be deposited until 5 to 6 million years ago. Thus, we know that the fault moved after 18 and before 5 to 6 million years ago, which allows us to "date" the fault (see figure 14).

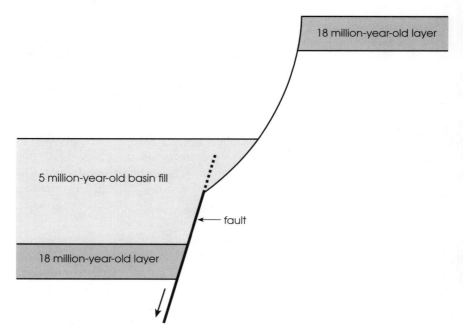

Figure 14. Method used by geologists to determine the age of a fault. The fault cuts the 18-million-year-old layer but does not cut the 5-million-year-old basin fill. Therefore, the fault moved after 18 million years ago and before 5 million years ago.

Wheeler Ridge is bounded on the west by Wheeler fault, another normal fault down to the west. This is the youngest fault in the area. It was active during deposition of the upper part of the Muddy Creek Formation and has continued to be active after deposition stopped because the fault offsets the Hualapai limestone by about 1000 feet. Movement thus started about 6 million years ago and continued to perhaps 2 million years ago. Wheeler fault has tilted the block to its west, much as Grand Wash fault has tilted Wheeler Ridge.

These and other faults in the region, and the sharply tilted blocks between them, define a remarkably sharp transition between the nearly flat strata of the Colorado Plateau and the tilted-block ranges of the Basin and Range Province.

The age of the western Grand Canyon has been the subject of much controversy. Geologists have used the basin beds in the Pierce Ferry area to establish a maximum age for the canyon. The beds were deposited in a closed basin with no outlet. Also, there is no evidence in the beds of material that would have been brought into the basin by the Colorado River had it existed at the time. The conclusion is that no Colorado River flowed through this area as recently as 5 million years ago, the age of the youngest basin beds. So the Grand Canyon and this part of the Colorado River are no more than about 5 million years old.

Trail Guide: At Dolan Springs, near milepost 42, turn off US 93 onto paved Mohave County Road 25 to Meadview and Pierce Ferry. Set your trip odometer to zero. At mile 40.4, you will see a paved road leading to the right towards Meadview, a nearby town with numerous facilities. Continue going straight. A short distance farther are a spectacular view from Grapevine Mesa westward and an inconspicuous ranger station east of the road.

To reach the view of Pierce Ferry, turn right through a cattle guard and fence onto a dirt road at 45.4 miles, just before dropping off the mesa. Follow the graded dirt road to the airport at 48.5 miles. Do not park right at the end of the gravel runway; this is an active landing strip. There are plenty of places to park nearby. From this point you can see all the geologic features described in the "Landscape and Geology" section.

To reach the start of the Grapevine Canyon hike, retrace your route from the airport to the paved road, but do stop for the spectacular view to the west along the way. Just before reaching the paved road, turn left (south) onto small dirt road 147, and reset the trip odometer. Although marked as "4-wheel drive recommended," the road is passable for normal vehicles when dry, unless there have been washouts. Be prepared to turn back if necessary, and do not drive off the track. This would be a nice mountain-bike excursion.

After 1.2 miles, cross a gate and stay on road 147. About 0.9 mile farther, the road crosses an obvious wash. This is one possible start for the hike, but one that requires climbing down several ledges and dry waterfalls. An easier

Looking north into the Great Wash trough

route is 0.4 mile farther along the road, where the first part of the hike is down an easy sandy wash that the road crosses. There is a sizable dry waterfall just beyond the confluence with the other fork of the wash. One can scramble down easily on the right side, looking downstream.

There is much to learn in this canyon. Catclaw, mesquite, willow, yucca, barrel cactus, and Mormon tea are the common plants. You may see a peregrine falcon if you are lucky. Here and there in the sand you can see concentrations of black sand composed of dark, heavy minerals such as magnetite and hematite which are rich in iron. These heavy minerals settle out of moving water first, as soon as the water velocity slackens. This concentrates them. Gold is also heavy and tends to settle out with the dark minerals. This property is used by placer gold miners.

You can see another effect of water velocity—that is, energy—below the waterfalls, where you often see a hollow at the foot of the falls. This is the plunge pool, produced because falling water has lots of energy with which to scour and pick up material. Just a little downstream from the plunge pool you can find a mound of sediment where the slackening water loses energy and drops its load.

The limestone on the lip of waterfalls is polished and scoured, witness to the floods that often run through these canyons. The polished limestone shows details of the bedding, as well as small cavities (called *vugs*) that are common in fresh-water limestone such as this. Reddish grains of silt and impressions that may be of plant stems are also common. Under your hand lens, a fresh

96

surface of the limestone looks sugary. This means that it is composed of small crystals of calcite, making the limestone *crystalline.*

After a few hundred yards, the wash enters some picturesque narrows that are not easily passable. Walk along the lip of the narrows, whose walls display fine bedding in the limestone. The many potholes along the bottom attest to vigorous running water. Potholes are formed when a rock is spun inside the hole by flowing water. Near the end of the narrows, the cliff exposure on the right (east) wall of the canyon displays a prominent down-canyon dip of the strata. If you look carefully, you can see that the dip decreases upward in the section. Since the lowest beds were deformed but the upper ones were not, this shows that the limestone was deforming as beds were being deposited: the oldest beds are deformed the most and the youngest ones the least.

The hike ends suddenly and impressively at a huge dry waterfall. Don't get too close to the lip. This is a lonely and eerie place. The immense wall across the waterfall is another place where you can see clearly the effects of deformation that occurred while the sediments were accumulating. Here, however, the lower strata are bent into a trough, and individual beds pinch out in both directions away from the low point. The bending and pinching out decrease upward, and the upper layers are horizontal and continuous. No deformation took place during or after deposition of these upper beds.

Hike
7

WILSON MOUNTAIN TRAIL

This fine but moderately strenuous trail rewards those who hike it with splendid views of the famed red rock country of Sedona, providing clues to the formation of the Colorado Plateau.

LOCATION ■ Red Rock/Secret Mountain Wilderness, Coconino National Forest

DISTANCE ■ About 6 miles round trip

ELEVATION ■ 4520 to about 7000 feet

DIFFICULTY ■ The distance is moderate, but the climb substantial. The chief part of the climb is along a hot south-facing slope. In places, the trail is rocky. For the most part, the trail is not steep.

TOPOGRAPHIC MAPS ■ Munds Park, AZ, 1:24,000; Wilson Mountain, AZ, 1:24,000; Sedona, AZ, 1:100,000

GEOLOGIC MAPS ■ 7

PRECAUTIONS ■ Best hiked in spring and fall due to snow in winter and heat in summer.

INFORMATION ■ Coconino National Forest

Landscape and Geology: The Wilson Mountain Trail climbs up the west side of Oak Creek Canyon, a rugged north-trending valley carved into the southern edge of the Colorado Plateau, known as the Mogollon Rim. The trail ends on top of Wilson Mountain, a basalt-capped outlier of the plateau. Wilson Mountain is surrounded on all sides by spectacular cliffs that are part of the famed red-rock country of the Sedona area.

The red rocks are composed mostly of the Schnebly Hill Formation of Permian age. This formation consists of parallel-bedded sandstone and mudstone, with thin interbeds of limestone and dolomite. The reddish-brown to orange color is due to iron oxide. The rocks were deposited on a low-lying coastal plain; the limestone beds represent temporary incursions of a shallow sea.

The prominent whitish cliff above the redbeds is the Coconino sandstone, also of Permian age. You can see large cross beds, which appear as slanted bedding surfaces. This rock is made of fine well-rounded grains of quartz weakly held together (or *cemented*) by the mineral calcite. This is characteristic of windblown sand; these are "fossil" dunes. The Coconino was once a huge "sea" of sand; the cross beds represent the downwind faces of ancient sand dunes (see figure 12). This unit is not well exposed along the trail.

The main branch of Oak Creek fault separates Wilson Mountain itself from "First Bench," a conspicuous bench, or flat area, crossed by the trail. Both are capped by dark-colored basalt flows. These lavas probably came from vents to the north or northeast. Similar lavas rim the east wall of the canyon. All are about 8 to 6 million years old (Miocene age).

In places along Oak Creek Canyon (but not along the trail), lavas cover gravel

Looking south into the Sedona red-rock country

that fills an ancient valley cut into the Permian rocks. The composition of the gravel shows that the stream that deposited it was flowing south. The valley is younger than 10 million years and probably is an ancestral version of Oak Creek Canyon.

Oak Creek fault is a high-angle, down-to-the-east normal fault that strikes north and is exposed for about 30 miles. In places, the fault splits into two strands. Along the trail, the main strand is west of First Bench and the smaller strand is east of it. The combined offset along the fault is visible from the higher parts of the trail, where you can see that the lava plateau east of Oak Creek is substantially lower than the same lava on Wilson Mountain.

The relationships between Oak Creek fault, the lavas, and the gravel in the valley have fueled much debate on the age of the Mogollon Rim and the time when drainage reversed direction along the rim.

To review briefly, the area south of the Colorado Plateau was once a belt of mountains called the Mogollon Highlands, formed during the Laramide orogeny at the end of Mesozoic time. Streams flowed from these mountains northward onto the Colorado Plateau, depositing the "rim gravels." At some time in the Tertiary Period, the mountain chain foundered (broke apart) because of tectonic rifting. The plateau was then bounded on the south by a great south-facing scarp, the Mogollon Rim. Drainage was reversed to a southward direction.

This is what geologists think has happened in Oak Creek Canyon:

1. Oak Creek fault began to move during the Laramide orogeny 65 million years ago, but with up-to-the-east movement, the opposite of what we see today. Rim gravels were deposited across the fault. Streams flowed north.
2. The Mogollon Highlands foundered. Streams in the Oak Creek area started flowing southward and carved the ancestral Oak Creek Canyon. This happened about 15 million years ago.
3. About 10 million years ago, the south-flowing streams deposited gravel in the ancestral canyon, which was then filled by lavas from the north.
4. Oak Creek fault was reactivated 6 million years ago or less, but this time with down-to-the-east movement. The modern Oak Creek Canyon was carved along the fault.

Trail Guide: The trailhead is reached by means of highway US 89A, which follows Oak Creek Canyon between Sedona and Flagstaff. Look for the metal Midgley Bridge, which crosses Wilson Canyon a little more than 1 mile north of Sedona, near milepost 376. (A bear hunter named Wilson was killed by a grizzly bear in this canyon in the mid-1880s.) There is a small and often-full parking area just north of the bridge. The trailhead is about 100 feet up Wilson

Canyon from the parking area. Look for a metal signpost where the trail climbs to the right up the side of Wilson Canyon. Do not continue straight up the canyon.

The trail switchbacks through a woodland of juniper, pinyon pine, and manzanita, with numerous outcrops of the reddish Schnebly Hill Formation, whose parallel bedding is well displayed. Soon, you are rewarded with fine views of the red cliffs of this formation and the overlying white Coconino sandstone on the east flank of Wilson Mountain, which is capped by dark-gray layers of basalt.

When you reach the wilderness sign in a small saddle at three-fourths mile, go straight ahead on the trail marked "Wilson Mountain." Just beyond the saddle, the trail enters an area of gray soil with no outcrops but abundant boulders of basalt. This is an eroded *pediment*, or apron of sedimentary debris, sloping from Wilson Mountain to Oak Creek. The weathering of basalt produces much clay, so this part of the trail can be quite sloppy when wet. Reddish bedrock is visible in many places.

The trail eventually crosses a prominent gully filled with water only in the wet times of the year. This gully roughly follows the west splay of Oak Creek fault, but the fault itself is covered with debris. Beyond the gully, the trail begins the serious and often hot climb to the First Bench in open chaparral country. Partway up, an attractive clump of Arizona cypress trees is a good place to rest and admire the red-rock country to the south. At roughly 1.7 miles, a switchback below a nose of First Bench passes through the base of an ancient flow of *olivine basalt*, which caps both First Mesa and Wilson Mountain. This documents a displacement of about 750 feet along the west splay of the fault, which passes through the saddle between First Bench and Wilson Mountain.

The top of First Bench, almost 2 miles from the trailhead, is littered with basalt boulders and can be muddy. The fine view of Wilson Mountain to the west shows that the mountain is capped by three distinct basalt flows, each delineated by a small topographic bench. The indistinct high terrain at the north end of the mountain is a *scoria cone*, a cinder cone surrounding a volcanic vent. The flow capping Wilson Mountain and First Bench came from this vent. The cone is cut by the west strand of the fault, and its down-dropped side is near the north end of First Bench.

The trail climbs westward from First Bench saddle through magnificent alligator junipers, distinguished by their checkered bark. A trail junction is marked by a large cairn at 2.3 miles. Continue going up and westward. The other trail here comes up from Encinoso picnic area in Oak Creek Canyon and provides the opportunity for a one-way hike if you leave cars at both trailheads.

You are rewarded with fine views of the San Francisco Peaks to the north as you enter a forest of pine and oak, where snow patches are common into early spring. At about 2.6 miles, the trail crests at a subdued saddle near a shed that houses fire-fighting tools. A level trail goes northwest for about 1 mile to a viewpoint at the north end of Wilson Mountain, from which you can see the San Francisco volcanic field in the distance and the eroded edge of the Colorado Plateau closer by. The other trail goes south, through a burn, rising gently to a viewpoint about 0.4 mile away.

The southern viewpoint is on the thick flow of *vesicular* (pitted) olivine basalt that also forms the top of First Bench. In the middle distance below you, erosional pinnacles of cross-bedded Coconino sandstone overlie the horizontally bedded and slope-forming Schnebly Hill Formation. Farther south is the town of Sedona, in the middle of which is a *mesa* with the town's airport. The many *buttes* surrounding Sedona are erosional remnants of Coconino and Schnebly Hill Formations. Some are capped by dark layers of lava.

Verde Valley, in the distance, is a linear trough aligned northwest. The valley is within the Arizona Transition Zone and was formed in part by down-to-the-northeast movement along the Verde fault on the other side of the valley. Beyond the fault is the scarp of the Black Hills (Hike 20), which are capped by dark layers of basalt 10 to 15 million years old.

The Bradshaw Mountains loom far to the south near Prescott. They are composed of Precambrian granite and gneiss. You can also make out the rugged Mazatzal Mountains far to the southeast and composed largely of Precambrian metamorphosed sedimentary rocks. Both are in the Arizona Transition Zone. In these ranges, Precambrian rocks are at a higher elevation than upper Paleozoic rocks of the Colorado Plateau rim, in spite of the foundering of the former Mogollon Highlands. Since Precambrian rocks originally are below Paleozoic ones, the still-high position of Precambrian rocks shows that the Mogollon Highlands must have towered above the plateau before the foundering took place.

Midgley Bridge and the trailhead are in plain view to the south, some 2300 feet below the viewpoint.

TABLELANDS

Tablelands are the characteristic landscape of the Colorado Plateau—far-ranging vistas across grassland to distant flat-topped mesas and small, sharply pointed buttes.

The tablelands owe their unique existence to three factors. First, they are cut into Mesozoic rocks, which are relatively soft and easily eroded. Second, this landscape is old—erosion has been in play for a long time, softening the contours of the land and bringing wide areas down to a common level. Third, the Mesozoic section is characterized by many alternations of relatively soft and hard strata. Certain hard-over-soft couplets tend to form scarps. These scarps rim mesas or form imposing cliff lines.

Hike 8

KEET SEEL RUIN TRAIL

This hike displays the Colorado Plateau's tableland and canyon country at its best and leads to untouched ruins of the prehistoric Puebloan people.

LOCATION ■ Navajo National Monument

DISTANCE ■ 8.5 miles one way

ELEVATION ■ 7270 feet (trailhead), down to 6310 feet (Laguna Creek), then up to 6840 feet (Keet Seel Ruin)

DIFFICULTY ■ Demanding

TOPOGRAPHIC MAPS ■ Betatakin Ruin, AZ, 1:24,000; Keet Seel Ruin, AZ, 1:24,000; Kayenta, AZ, 1:100,000

GEOLOGIC MAPS ■ 8

PRECAUTIONS ■ Permission must be obtained from the park service. Carry plenty of water on this summer-only trail.

INFORMATION ■ Navajo National Monument

Landscape and Geology: Keet Seel and Betatakin Ruins are in canyons that fret the tableland of Skeleton Mesa. This mesa, its neighbor Tyende Mesa, and Monument Valley to the northeast are all part of a broad and complex belt of structurally high terrain that is made evident by the presence of Paleozoic rocks at the surface in Monument Valley. Mesozoic rocks underlie the rest of this region.

Navajo National Monument and Skeleton Mesa are underlain by the Navajo sandstone of Jurassic age. This massive, cliff-forming sandstone consists of fossil sand dunes. The cross bedding so characteristic of the unit represents the slip faces of the ancient dunes (see figure 12). When eroded, the Navajo breaks down into its original sand grains, which are very fine grained, well rounded, and frosted, all characteristics of windblown sand. This means that the sand weathered from the Navajo is just right for being blown around by the wind. The result is that ancient dunes have given birth to modern ones. Since the Navajo and other *eolian* (windblown) sandstone units are common on the Colorado Plateau, modern sand dunes are abundant here.

The canyons near Navajo National Monument are floored by *alluvium*, material eroded from each drainage basin and carried down into the canyon by the wash within it. The alluvium here is tens of feet thick and represents a period when the washes were *aggrading*, that is, depositing material and building up their bed. This happens when streams are overloaded because more material is brought to them than they can carry away. This happened during the *Holocene Epoch*—the 10,000 years or so since the waning of the last ice age.

When the streams were aggrading, the bottoms of the canyons were flat floodplains, and the streams were at this level. There was no downcutting. This made the floodplains ideal for farming. The *Anasazi*, prehistoric Puebloan inhabitants of the region, made good use of these moist, fertile floodplains. Later, aggradation ceased and *incision,* or arroyo cutting, began. Streams cut their way down to well below the floodplain level, making irrigation of fields impossible. The water table sank as well, drying up springs.

This may have contributed to the departure of the Anasazi from their cliff dwellings about 1300 A.D. But this downcutting was then followed by renewed aggradation that lasted until very recently. Oral accounts by the Navajo who reside in the area hold that arroyo cutting began some 100 years ago, in keeping with historical records from elsewhere in the region. Before then, Laguna Creek was dotted with marshes and lagoons, which gave the creek its name.

Trail Guide: Navajo National Monument is reached by paved Highway 564, which branches off US 160 at Marsh Pass about 19 miles south of Kayenta, Arizona. The monument has a pleasant campground with drinking water and toilets and an informative visitor center.

The hike to Keet Seel is demanding because of the length, lack of water, and the heat during the Memorial Day through Labor Day season when the hike is allowed. Exceptionally fit people can do the 17-mile round trip in one day, carrying a day pack and all the water needed, both ways. The rest of us are wise to stay overnight at Keet Seel, which requires backpacking in.

In either case, reservations must be made by writing or calling no more than

Keet Seel: The Anasazi farmed fields on top of the alluvium.

60 days before your planned hiking date and must be confirmed no later than 7 days before. A permit tag must be carried, obtainable at the mandatory orientation meeting at 4:00 P.M. the day before the hike or at 8:15 A.M. the day of the hike. Camping at Keet Seel is permitted for one night only. All drinking water (one gallon per person per day) must be carried in, as well as a cooking stove—no wood fires are permitted. You are well advised to start walking at first light so you can do a good part of the hike in the shade. Full information and instructions are available on the website or by mail (see "Addresses and Contact Information" at the back of this book). The following guide assumes that hikers are using the park service's instruction sheet for finding the trail.

The hike begins along a dirt road on the Navajo sandstone, outcrops of which are visible once one drops off Tsegi Point, which also provides splendid views into the canyon of Laguna Creek, 1000 feet below. The Navajo sandstone displays prominent cross beds in large *sets*—bands of rock with uniform cross beds, separated from other sets above and below by horizontal planes (see figure 12 and Hike 2 for how these features are formed).

Once you have clambered down through the Navajo, you will be in another sandstone unit but this one has parallel bedding on a large scale, forms slopes instead of cliffs, and contains layers of mudstone and shale. This is the Kayenta Formation, which was deposited mostly by rivers. Along the trail down to Laguna Creek, much of this bedrock is mantled by modern sand dunes that make walking difficult. The sand is eroding from the Navajo and Kayenta.

Just before getting to the creek, the trail drops steeply off a flat-topped terrace that is prominent along Laguna and all other creeks in this region. The terrace is on the Holocene *alluvium* (river sediments) that once filled the canyon to this level. The rest of the hike is on the present floodplain.

Laguna Creek is a shallow *braided stream*, indicating that it is overloaded with sand. Overloaded streams do not erode, yet this stream has clearly cut down into the terrace on top of which it once flowed. There must be times when the stream is not overloaded, probably during floods.

Just beyond milepost 3.5, the stream flows on bedrock and the alluvium above the bedrock consists of coarse gravel. The valley had been carved to this depth when the aggradation began. The alluvium buried the debris that had littered the channel.

Much of the alluvium in the walls of the arroyo has a striped appearance. The dark bands are mud and clay layers deposited in slackwater when the energy of the stream was low. The tan-colored bands consist of cross-bedded sand and were the product of floods, when the water was flowing faster and had more energy. By looking carefully, you will see that many sand layers grade upward into mud layers. Sand and mud represent a single flood—the sand was deposited during the peak of the flood, and as the flood waned, it was gradually replaced by mud.

As you walk notice that the top 6 feet or so of the alluvium consist of irregularly bedded tan sand that fills channels cut into the underlying striped section. The contact between tan sand and the striped layers is an *unconformity* (a gap in the geologic record). The channels show that the overall aggradation was interrupted by a period of *incision*, or downcutting, that formed the channels. When aggradation resumed, the new channels were filled by the tan sandy alluvium. Could this incision be the arroyo cutting that occurred about 1300 A.D.?

The first of several waterfalls along the trail is at the junction of Keet Seel and Dowozhiebito Canyons, about 1 mile from the crossing of Laguna Creek. This waterfall is not caused by a ledge of more resistant bedrock, as is the usual case. Instead, Keet Seel Canyon is a *hanging valley*, meaning that it has been left "hanging." This may be because Dowozhiebito Canyon has a larger drainage basin than Keet Seel Canyon and thus more frequent and bigger floods, so it is able to cut down faster.

As you complete the distance to the ruins, you will find two more interesting waterfalls in Keet Seel Canyon. These were produced by landslides that filled the stream channel and dammed the stream. The stream then spilled over the lowest part of the landslides and cut new channels. Deposits of light-colored sand along the stream above the waterfalls represent deltas built by the stream into the landslide lakes.

Keet Seel Ruin is in a huge south-facing alcove carved out of a single cross-bed set in the Navajo sandstone. The location was carefully chosen by the Puebloans to provide sun in the winter when the sun is low and shade in the summer when the sun is high.

The alcove also provided a spring, now dried up. It is likely that the spring itself was partly responsible for creating the alcove by weakening and sapping the canyon wall.

The inhabitants of Keet Seel probably had their fields on the alluvial terrace below the ruin. At that time, the stream flowed just below the level of the terrace.

PETRIFIED FOREST NATIONAL PARK

Hike 9

In three short scenic hikes, you will see the remnants of a great 200-million-year-old forest now in the form of beautiful petrified logs.

LOCATION ■ Petrified Forest National Park

DISTANCE ■ Less than 1 mile for each of three hikes

ELEVATION ■ The park is at an elevation of 5500 to 6000 feet. The maximum elevation difference on the walks is 120 feet.

DIFFICULTY ■ Very easy (the paths are paved)

TOPOGRAPHIC MAPS ■ Adamana, AZ; Agate House, AZ; and Kachina Point, AZ, all 1:24,000; St. Johns, AZ, 1:100,000

GEOLOGIC MAPS ■ 9; also Geologic Map of Petrified Forest National Park (by G. W. Billingsley) can be purchased at the park museum.

PRECAUTIONS ■ You are strictly prohibited from removing any petrified wood from the park. Have plenty of water in your car if it is hot.

INFORMATION ■ Petrified Forest National Park

Landscape and Geology: Petrified Forest National Park is in country typical of much of the Colorado Plateau—wide expanses of grassland and shrub punctuated by buttes and mesas and traversed by shallow washes, all at an elevation between 5000 and 6000 feet.

The park displays an erosional landscape cut into the Chinle Formation of Triassic age, and specifically the Petrified Forest Member, which forms the lower half of the formation here. These rocks were deposited more than 200 million years ago in a swampy plain traversed by sluggish meandering streams that flowed generally north. The streams carried very fine material, especially clay, but during floods were also capable of carrying coarser grained sand and gravel. To the southwest, volcanoes created by subduction along the western edge of the continent produced clouds of volcanic ash that drifted northward and settled in the plain, where it weathered into clay.

Petrified log

Life was abundant on the plain. Flowering plants first made their appearance about this time. Large trees were common, especially the Norfolk Island pine and large horsetails and tree ferns. Occasional floods swept trees away and concentrated them in logjams, where they were eventually buried and preserved by river sand and clay.

Large and small reptiles patrolled the forests and swamps of this Triassic floodplain. All were archosaurs, a group that includes the well-known dinosaurs, which were just making their appearance. Today, archosaurs are represented only by crocodiles.

More sediments were laid on top of the Chinle in Mesozoic time, then the Cenozoic ushered in a time of erosion. This has been going on for 50 million years, but at a slow pace, largely because canyon cutting has not yet reached this area. What you see here is the old, mature landscape that once existed everywhere on the Colorado Plateau before canyon cutting began.

The slow and peaceful erosional lowering of this area has been interrupted several times by volcanic activity. Between 14 and 7 million years ago, volcanoes of the Hopi Buttes field emitted ash and basalt lava flows. The southernmost volcanoes of this field are just within the park. Volcanoes of the Springerville and White Mountains volcanic fields (about 50 miles to the southwest) started erupting about 9 million years ago and have been active until recently.

Trail Guide: Petrified Forest National Park is traversed by a 28-mile paved road. At its north end, this road connects with Interstate 40 at Exit 311, 25 miles east of Holbrook. The visitor center is here. At the south end, the road connects with US Highway 180, 19 miles east of Holbrook. The Rainbow Forest Museum is at this end. This guide is for a trip through the park from south to north.

The park is open from 7:30 A.M. to 5:00 P.M., longer in the summer. All roads in the park are paved. There is no lodging or camping in the park. Pets must always be leashed.

Pilfering of petrified wood from the park has long been a problem, and park staff are sensitive to it. The risk of getting caught is considerable, as are the fines. More important, even a small piece, when multiplied by a million visitors per year, adds up to a substantial loss of an irreplaceable resource. So, please take photographs, not wood. Petrified wood obtained from private quarries can readily be bought in and near the park.

After taking a look at the worthwhile Rainbow Forest Museum and strolling through the Giant Logs area behind it, drive less than 1 mile to the parking lot for the Long Logs and Agate House Trails.

Looking south from the parking lot, you can see a light-colored cross-bedded sandstone layer. This is the Sonsela Tongue of the Petrified Forest Member of the Chinle Formation. The name "tongue" comes from the fact that this bed pinches out in certain directions; in three dimensions, it would look like a thin tongue.

On your way to Agate House, ponder how this amazing collection of petrified wood came to be here. Most of the petrified logs in the park are in the sandstone of the Sonsela Tongue, which was probably deposited by rivers in flood stage. The flooding rivers also carried many tree trunks, which got caught in logjams. The remarkable concentrations of ancient tree trunks that you see along this trail probably represent such logjams.

After the floods subsided, finer sediments such as clay buried the logs, excluding oxygen and preventing decay of the wood. At the same time, volcanoes erupting far to the southwest repeatedly blanketed this area with volcanic ash. The ash gradually weathered into the colorful and picturesque clays that are so characteristic of the landscape here.

With time, the mineral silica (SiO_2) leached from the volcanic ash into the groundwater. The microcrystalline silica then came out of solution, or *precipitated*, into the woody fibers, eventually replacing them. The wood's internal structure was hardened and preserved. Impurities gave the silica vibrant colors so vividly displayed in the petrified trees.

Most logs now rest below their original positions because material is eroded from below them, allowing them to drop down. Many concentrations of logs effectively protect the underlying layers of rock from further erosion. Unprotected areas erode farther down, leaving concentrations of logs as ridges.

As you walk, note that the logs are broken into cylindrical segments. This happened long after burial when the wood had become petrified and brittle.

Agate House is a partially restored prehistoric pueblo with walls made up mostly of petrified wood pieces, giving you the opportunity to closely examine the intricate structures and colors of petrified wood. A hand lens is useful here. Maybe the ancient builders had a well-developed aesthetic sense and selected the wood for its pretty colors. More likely, they made use of whatever material was abundant and close at hand. They enjoyed a fine view of the Painted Desert and the volcanoes of the White Mountains and Springerville fields to the south and southeast.

Return to the main park road and drive about 6 miles north to the Crystal Forest turnout, east of the road. This 0.75-mile loop takes you through an area that is littered with spectacular petrified logs.

Some of the logs are highly *opalized* (filled with the microcrystalline silica opal), while others show the structure of the wood very well. The logs came from a light-colored layer of pebbly sandstone, then were dropped into their present positions on the clay beds by erosion. Notice the conspicuous hollows on many of the logs—these were caused by people removing the crystals of quartz and amethyst that gave the place its name. The national park was established here to stop the intensive collection of these crystals and the destruction of priceless and irreplaceable fossil trees.

As you walk through these remnants of ancient forests, you may be asking, "Why is petrified wood so common in the Chinle Formation?" Not only is this a logjam deposit, but another factor is at play here—preservation. The Chinle trees were preserved by becoming impregnated with silica, which was derived from volcanic ash. Support for this idea is provided by fossil trees in Yellowstone National Park, which were also preserved by ash falls from the Absaroka volcanoes of that region.

Upon returning to your car, drive north about 5 miles to the turnoff to Blue Mesa. This mesa gives you fine views of the countryside and is the start of a trail that illustrates the workings of erosion on soft strata like those of the Chinle.

The trail starts on a layer of light-colored, coarse-grained, cross-bedded sandstone that includes a layer of pebbles. These are well rounded and made of resistant rock types such as quartz and chert. The pebbles and coarse sand tell you that the stream that deposited them had enough velocity and energy to move material of this size. This may have happened during a flood.

Pebbles of hard rock types like these are nearly indestructible and keep

Microgullying in claystone along the
Blue Mesa Trail

getting recycled by being eroded in one place, then redeposited in another. In the process, they may concentrate on a surface, forming an armor plate that protects the surface from further erosion. Many examples of this are visible along the trail.

At about 0.1 mile, just beyond the narrow ridge, is an example of *badland* topography. These badlands are formed by rapid downcutting along closely spaced rills; the pinnacles are created where harder layers form a caprock that protects softer layers underneath.

The switchbacks of the trail are in a clay layer, which shows the characteristic mud cracks produced by repeated wetting and drying of the clay. This clay contains *bentonite*, a clay produced by the weathering of volcanic ash that swells when wet and contracts when drying, forming the cracks. Many of the cracks are sinks that collect rainwater during storms.

Erosion of the clay slopes is rapid here, reaching inches per year. Hard objects like the petrified wood, however, do not erode as fast, so are left protruding from the slopes.

On the return part of the loop, you can see a log perched on a pedestal of clay a few feet high. This illustrates how quickly the clay erodes compared to the petrified wood and also how the wood protects the underlying clay from further erosion.

Return to the main road and continue north. At 10 miles, the road crosses Interstate 40 (no access here), then provides a series of viewpoints that look north into Painted Desert country. The big wash is Lithodendron Wash, whose name comes from the Greek, meaning "stone tree." The dark hills are the southernmost volcanoes of the Hopi Buttes volcanic field. One of the volcanoes forms the northern end of the mesa on which the road is built.

Hike 10

WHITE HOUSE RUIN TRAIL

Within the picturesque sandstone walls of Canyon de Chelly is a well-preserved prehistoric cliff dwelling.

LOCATION ■ Canyon de Chelly National Monument

DISTANCE ■ 1.25 miles one way

ELEVATION ■ 6210 to 5680 feet

DIFFICULTY ■ Easy

TOPOGRAPHIC MAPS ■ Del Muerto, AZ, 1:24,000; Canyon de Chelly, AZ, 1:100,000

GEOLOGIC MAPS ■ None, but the booklet *The Rocks and Times of Canyon de Chelly National Monument* (by Donald L. Baars, 1998) can be purchased at the visitor center.

PRECAUTIONS ■ Snow and cold in winter; heat and flash floods in summer.

INFORMATION ■ Canyon de Chelly National Monument

Landscape and Geology: Canyon de Chelly is carved into the west flank of the Defiance Plateau, a belt of high ground that extends northward across the New Mexico–Arizona boundary and reaches altitudes of more than 8000 feet.

The plateau corresponds to a zone of geologic uplift that has been active on and off since the beginning of Paleozoic time. The result of the uplift is that many rock units found in the vicinity, for example on Black Mesa and in the Grand Canyon, are missing from the Defiance Plateau. This is because they were either never deposited on the high ground, or were deposited but then eroded. The consequence is that rocks that in Grand Canyon are near the top of the Paleozoic section here rest directly on the Precambrian basement of granite and gneiss.

The massive pinkish cliff that forms most of Canyon de Chelly near White House Ruin is made of the Permian De Chelly sandstone, composed of well-rounded fine grains of quartz. This characteristic, together with the conspicuous *cross bedding* so well exposed in the canyon walls, shows that this sandstone is of *eolian* origin, meaning that it consists of ancient sand dunes that have hardened into stone. The cross beds represent the lee, or slip, slope of the ancient dunes (see figure 12). This formation forms the main part of the famous buttes in Monument Valley.

The De Chelly sandstone is capped by a layer of dark brown sandstone and conglomerate. This layer, the Shinarump Conglomerate, forms the rim of the canyon, and is the surface layer over much of the national monument.

Trail Guide: From US Highway 191, drive 2.7 miles east on Navajo Nation Route 7 through the town of Chinle to reach the visitor center for Canyon de Chelly National Monument. From there, drive east on South Rim Drive for 6.4 miles to the White House Ruin overlook, where a sign points to the trail. You are admonished that hikers are only allowed to go directly to the ruin, not elsewhere in the bottom of the canyon. The canyon is the home to Navajo families, who wish to retain their privacy.

The trail starts on the slickrock near the rim, then drops down through a short tunnel. In the walls of the tunnel and along the trail just beyond it, you will see layers of pebbly sandstone in which the pebbles are rounded and composed of hard rocks such as quartz and quartzite. The roundness of the pebbles shows that the sandstone was deposited in a high-energy environment, maybe a stream, maybe a beach.

These even layers are parallel to one another. If you look carefully, you can also see irregular, low-angle cross beds that are fan-shaped, and made up of coarse sand that is moderately rounded—features visible in the sand of a modern streambed. This rock was deposited by an energetic stream 225 to 230 million years ago. It is called the Shinarump Conglomerate.

Beyond the tunnel, the route switchbacks about 500 vertical feet down to the canyon bottom. As you descend the switchbacks, you will at first be on a slope below the Shinarump cliff. The slope is littered with large boulders from the caprock, and is carved into a softer, shaly unit.

At the second switchback, look carefully down the trail. You will see a dark brown channel cutting into the reddish sandstone below it. The dark brown rock is the Shinarump Conglomerate, and the reddish sandstone is the De Chelly. These two layers do not usually come into contact with each other. Layers such as the Coconino sandstone, the Kaibab limestone, and the Moenkopi Formation—layers representing tens of millions of years—normally appear between the De Chelly sandstone and the Shinarump Conglomerate. Here those intermediate layers are missing due to erosion, a phenomenon known as an *erosional unconformity.*

The De Chelly sandstone is well exposed from here on down, forming photogenic slickrock into which the trail is cut. Take a good look at this rock. The quartz grains are fine and very well rounded. A lens will show you that many are *frosted,* which occurs from being sand blasted. The cross beds are steep and parallel. These features are quite different from those of the Shinarump, and indicate that this sandstone is composed of ancient sand dunes. The cross beds here are the slip faces on the downwind side of ancient dunes.

At the foot of the cliff, the trail goes through a second tunnel then emerges into the bottom of the canyon, a picturesque and pastoral home for the Navajo farmers who live here with their fields and flocks.

Until maybe twenty years ago, the canyon floor had little vegetation and was occupied by the shallow, braided Chinle Wash. Braided streams are overloaded with sediment, which here came from the easily eroded walls of the canyon. The stream was *aggrading,* or building up its bed. This is not a friendly environment for plant life, which keeps getting flooded and smothered with sediment.

Today, the floor of the canyon is very different. Much is occupied by thickets of Russian olive, salt cedar, cottonwood, and willow, and the valley bottom is cut by sharp arroyos as much as 13 feet deep.

One possible cause of the arroyo cutting was the recently arrived vegetation. Plant life can stabilize the soil and force a stream into a narrow channel. Confined within this channel, the stream flows faster and therefore has more energy. It then erodes sediment rather than depositing it.

Walk north along the streambed, toward the ruin. Near the footbridge, about 1 mile from the trailhead, look at the base of the west (left) wall. You will see a horizontal line marked by a change in color. This line shows the recent location of the valley floor. Obviously, there has been quite a lot of erosion in only a few years.

White House Ruin is built in a south-facing alcove cleverly selected by the prehistoric Puebloan farmers

The sandstone walls of Canyon de Chelly enclose the White House Ruin.

to provide sun in winter and shade in summer. This was their common practice—an early and very successful form of environmental engineering. The prehistoric Puebloan people lived here until about 700 years ago and farmed the valley floor, much as the Navajo do today.

VOLCANIC FIELDS

The Colorado Plateau is a land dominated by erosion. For tens of millions of years, the land has been worn down gradually and the resulting detritus has been carried to the sea. However, even in this landscape of general destruction, you can find a few features that are constructional, that is, built up. The most conspicuous are the volcanoes that pepper the southern rim of the plateau.

TYPES OF VOLCANOES AND VOLCANIC FEATURES

Volcanoes are built of *magma*, liquid igneous rock carried up from the depths and solidified into lava at the surface. There are several types of volcanoes and volcanic deposits. Most conspicuous are composite volcanoes, also known as *stratovolcanoes*. These are made up of lavas such as *andesite* and *dacite* that are intermediate in silica content between silica-poor *basalt* and silica-rich *rhyolite* (see figure 1). Mount Fuji in Japan is a classic stratovolcano.

Stratovolcanoes form large, steep mountains such as the San Francisco Peaks near Flagstaff, and are built up of many lava flows layered (or stratified) with ash and other air-fall volcanic deposits. They sometimes become truncated late in their history when the summit either collapses or explodes in the manner of Mount St. Helens. As a result, the former summit of the mountain is gone and its place is taken by a central cavity.

Shield volcanoes are broad with gently sloping sides and are formed by fluid lava such as basalt flowing away from a central vent. Hawaii's Mauna Loa is a classic example.

Cinder cones are the most common features in many volcanic fields. They form during gassy eruptions when magma is ejected into the air and solidifies in flight, producing (in order of decreasing size) *bombs, cinders, lapilli*, and *ash*. These particles fall around the vent from which they issued, forming a circular mound surrounding a central crater. The sides of a cinder cone typically have a slope of about 32 degrees, which is the steepest slope on which unconsolidated material can stay without sliding down. Cinder cones can be as high as 1000 feet. Basalt flows sometimes issue from the base of the cones. Sunset Crater near Flagstaff is a good example of a cinder cone.

Lava flows form the bulk of many volcanic fields. They are the result of magma flowing over the surface of the land, then cooling and hardening. The most fluid magma flows so well that it resembles a river of molten rock. The surface

114

appearance of a flow provides information on the composition and temperature of the magma before it solidified. Very hot, low-viscosity basalt flows far
and fast and produces smooth, ropy surfaces. This type of flow has the Hawaiian name *pahoehoe.* Cooler, less fluid basalt flows form irregular, jagged
surfaces littered with blocks, called *aa lava.*

Magmas such as dacite and rhyolite that have high silica contents are cooler
and more viscous than basalt, so they do not flow far and need steep slopes
to flow at all. The resulting shapes are lobes, pancakes, and domes. Domes
often plug up the vent from which they issued, sometimes creating catastrophic explosions. This is how Crater Lake in Oregon was formed.

Eroded volcanoes are interesting because they give us a glimpse of the
interior plumbing along which the magma rose to the surface.

At the end of an eruption, magma solidifies in the conduits along which it
had been rising. This rock is more resistant than the shattered rock forming
the walls, so these lava-filled conduits are often left behind when the rest of
the volcano has been eroded away. The filling of the central vertical vent is
circular in cross section and forms a spire called a *neck.* The filling of cracks
along which lava rose forms nearly vertical tabular bodies called *dikes.* Volcanic necks and dikes are well displayed in the Hopi Buttes volcanic field.

Sometimes, magma works its way along cracks that are nearly horizontal,
often along bedding planes of sedimentary rocks. The result is horizontal, table-
like bodies of lava called *sills.*

VOLCANOES OF THE COLORADO PLATEAU

The youngest volcanic fields of Arizona's Colorado Plateau are clustered along
its southern margin. From west to east, they are the Shivwits, Uinkaret, San
Francisco, and Springerville–White Mountains fields, which range in age from
Miocene to recent times. The oldest age is about 10 million years, and the
youngest, 1065 A.D., is that of Sunset Crater.

Interestingly, volcanic activity in Arizona becomes younger to the northeast, both regionally and within a field. Geologists view this as evidence that
basin and range extension is gradually encroaching northeastward into the
Colorado Plateau. Extension often is accompanied by heating of the crust, the
result of which is volcanism.

The Hopi Buttes volcanic field (Hike 11) is away from the plateau's rim and
slightly older than the other fields, so it is not part of this most recent volcanic cycle. The volcanoes of the Hopi Buttes are unusual: many are *diatremes,*
also known as *maars.* These are funnel-shaped craters drilled out explosively
by gas-charged magma as it rises. Most of the craters were later filled by lakes
or late-stage basalt flows issuing from the vent.

The Springerville–White Mountains volcanic complex includes one large and dissected shield volcano, Mt. Baldy (Hike 12), and many cinder cones of various sizes.

The San Francisco volcanic field (Hikes 13 through 16) consists of one imposing composite volcano, which is the highest mountain in the state, several large mountains that are clusters of domes, and hundreds of cinder cones. All rise above a platform of basalt flows that are 5 to 6 million years old. These flows rest on the light-colored Permian Kaibab limestone and the brick-red Triassic Moenkopi Formation.

The four domes are aligned and become younger in a northeastward direction: Bill Williams Mountains (5 to 3 million years old), Sitgreaves Mountain (2.5 million years), and Kendrick Mountain (2.7 to 1.4 million years). The San Francisco Peaks (1.8 to 0.4 million years) are the broken remnant of a once much higher composite volcano. At the far northeast end of this trend are the young rhyolite volcanoes of Sugarloaf Mountain and O'Leary Peak.

The youngest volcanoes of the San Francisco field are cinder cones near its north and northeast margins: Sunset Crater (1066 to 1067 A.D.), Strawberry and O'Neill Craters (50,000 years old), and SP Mountain (71,000 years). This part of the field is still active today.

Humphreys Peak (Hike 13) provides the best overall view of the volcanic field; Kendrick Mountain (Hike 14) is a good example of a dome complex. Sunset Crater (which the park service does not allow hiking on) and SP Mountain (Hike 16) are uneroded cinder cones with spectacular basalt flows issuing from their bases and extensive ash blankets. The ash blanket from Sunset Crater had a great effect on the lives of the prehistoric Puebloan people of the area.

The Uinkaret volcanic field (Hike 17) is one of the most remote and least-visited fields on the south edge of the Colorado Plateau. This is a pity because it contains a remarkable and scenic geologic feature—great cascades of frozen lava that pour into the Grand Canyon. It exists because of two normal faults, the Hurricane on the west and the Toroweap to the east. The pull-apart forces related to these faults provided an easy path for magma to rise to the surface. Many of the volcanic features in this field are geologically very young.

**Hike
11**

COLISEUM DIATREME

Erosion of this diatreme has created a strange place resembling an immense sports arena.

LOCATION ■ Hopi Buttes volcanic field, Navajo Reservation
DISTANCE ■ About 2 miles
ELEVATION ■ 5860 to 5980 feet
DIFFICULTY ■ Easy

TOPOGRAPHIC MAPS ■ Na Ah Tee Canyon, AZ, 1:24,000; Winslow, AZ, 1:100,000

GEOLOGIC MAPS ■ 10

PRECAUTIONS ■ This is on the Navajo Reservation, so please be respectful of private property and keep away from dwellings.

INFORMATION ■ None available

Landscape and Geology: The Coliseum Diatreme is within the Hopi Buttes volcanic field, which occupies a fair chunk of the Navajo Indian reservation north of Holbrook and Winslow. The name "Coliseum" comes from the Roman Colosseum, that enormous and famous sports arena which this feature resembles.

Most buttes in this area are capped by basaltic lava flows that fill the crater from which they issued. These craters are *diatremes*, a Greek word meaning "object that cuts across." These funnel-shaped cavities were drilled out by gas-charged magma escaping at great velocity in explosive eruptions. The gas is water vapor produced when the magma vaporizes groundwater.

The diatremes were drilled through the reddish siltstone, sandstone, and shale of the Bidahochi Formation, which then covered the area. This unit was deposited either in one large lake or in several shallow and ephemeral ones. You can see the Bidahochi as reddish outcrops on the flanks of many of the buttes. The lava caps of the buttes mark the top of the formation. The Bidahochi is poorly consolidated and prone to sliding, producing the landslide aprons that surround many of the buttes.

The lavas above the formation, together with layers of volcanic tuff within it, bracket the age of the Bidahochi between about 14 and 7 million years. Erosion since then has lowered the landscape several hundred feet to its present level.

The fast-moving froth of magma and gas produced funnel-shaped cavities near the surface, where the gases in magma expand greatly due to reduced pressure. The froth itself cooled rapidly and solidified at the surface, forming *tuff breccia*, a chaotic rock composed mostly of solidified froth. The breccia owes its name to the many fragments of rocks within it that came from the volcano's walls through which the magma rose. Some of this material may even come from the *mantle*—the zone deep beneath the Earth's crust. Some of the froth was ejected into the air and settled back on the ground or in the crater lakes, forming well-bedded air-fall tuff.

Fish and other organisms lived in the crater lakes of these volcanoes. Thin-bedded limestones were often deposited in the lakes. Over time, the limestone and tuff within the craters settled and slumped downward and inward toward the center of the craters.

Trail Guide: From AZ 77, turn west toward Dilkon on paved Reservation Road 15. Reset the trip odometer to zero at the junction.

This is a Navajo reservation, where it is generally necessary to have a hiking permit. Getting a permit is a laborious process, not practical for a short walk like this. Wisdom counsels being tactful and inconspicuous: do not drive near people's homes, stay on the roads, and leave no litter. If challenged, explain that you are making a brief visit to a well-known geologic feature, you have no official connection, and you are leaving shortly.

The buttes north and south of the road are diatremes, capped by basaltic flows. The orange-red material cropping out on the sides of the buttes is the Bidahochi Formation. The jumbled aprons surrounding many of the buttes are landslides.

Driving along, Coliseum Diatreme comes into view on the north side of the road at 4.2 miles. The stadium-like shape of this volcano is due to two factors. First, no capping lava flow buried the crater of the diatreme. Second, the Bidahochi Formation, into which the diatreme was drilled, erodes more easily than the tuff and limestone in its interior. Consequently, the rock once forming the outside wall of the diatreme has been eroded away, leaving behind the diatreme's fill. The walls of the ancient funnel-shaped vent were just outside the present Coliseum's wall. The process by which a formerly low area becomes high through differential erosion is called *topographic inversion*.

Still driving, leave the highway toward the north, cross a cattle guard, and go left on a track that follows a wash through a gap in the Coliseum wall. Do not go toward the Native American dwelling. Park the car in an inconspicuous spot within the Coliseum. Walk up the jeep track that climbs the southwest wall of the diatreme about 200–300 yards from the gap.

The track is on a steeply dipping slope of tan, silty limestone. The bedded tuff on the rim dips the same way. Both are part of the crater fill. The rim is a good place to get an overall view of the diatreme, which is about one-half mile in diameter. The land to the west is flat and even with the rim. This tells you that originally the walls of the diatreme did not rise above the level of the surrounding land, as they do today, but were the margins of a depression below this level.

Walk clockwise along the rim toward the dam built across the main wash. The Bidahochi Formation, and a well-bedded tuff with layers of basalt and chert pebbles, are both easy to spot near the dam. The fine-grained layers you see are claystone and siltstone, deposited in the still water of the lake between eruptions.

You can also see cross bedding, possibly the result of a *base surge*—a cloud of gas moving rapidly outward from the center of the eruption (such as in a nuclear explosion). Small folds and faults in the beds indicate movement of sediment toward the center of the diatreme when they were squeezed inward by the walls of the funnel while settling downward. See if you can visualize how the geometry of the folds and faults is consistent with such movement.

The inward-sloping wall of the crater funnel is well exposed near a west-draining wash about 1000 feet north of the dam, where the rocks of the diatreme are in contact with the Bidahochi Formation.

As you drive out of the diatreme, look carefully at the west wall of the stream-cut gorge through which you enter and exit the diatreme. Here, you can see more faults and folds that indicate inward movement of the rocks.

WEST BALDY TRAIL

This alpine trail takes you up to timberline on glacier-sculpted Mount Baldy, a large shield volcano along the southern rim of the Colorado Plateau.

LOCATION ■ Springerville–White Mountains volcanic field, Mount Baldy Wilderness, Apache–Sitgreaves National Forest

DISTANCE ■ About 6 miles one way

ELEVATION ■ 9280 to about 11,360 feet

DIFFICULTY ■ Strenuous day hike, moderate 2-day backpack

TOPOGRAPHIC MAPS ■ Mount Ord, AZ, 1:24,000; Nutrioso, 1:100,000

GEOLOGIC MAPS ■ 11

PRECAUTIONS ■ Snow makes this trail impassable from November to April; in summer, the danger of lightning is severe.

INFORMATION ■ Apache–Sitgreaves National Forest, Springerville Ranger District

Landscape and Geology: Mount Baldy is within the Springerville–White Mountains volcanic field, which straddles the Mogollon Rim and consists mainly of hundreds of basaltic cinder cones. The ages of lavas in this field range from about 8.5 to 2 million years. Mount Baldy itself is a *shield volcano*, which has the shape of a flattened dome that is wide relative to its height. It formed between 7 and 9 million years ago. Most lava flows that formed the volcano erupted from a central vent between Mount Baldy and Mount Ord and from fissures radial to the central vent.

Mount Baldy is the second-highest of the volcanoes that rim the southern edge of the Colorado Plateau in Arizona, after Humphreys Peak in the San Francisco volcanic field. Because of its loftiness, it was glaciated four times during the Ice Age. Topographic features and glacial sediments along the hike give evidence for the glaciations.

Trail Guide: Traveling east on AZ 260 from Pinetop to Springerville, turn south onto AZ 273, just east of MP 277. Set the odometer to zero here. Continue past the ski area. At mile 5.9, the road becomes dirt and is not plowed from November to May. At mile 10.1, Sheep Crossing, park in some good spot before crossing the creek. The unofficial trail goes south from here. There are no facilities at this trailhead.

Note that this is a strenuous one-day walk. A better plan is to backpack in, camping in the last glacial meadow before climbing to the summit the next day. The best time to hike this trail is in the fall.

A trachyte dike with vertical flow banding along the West Baldy Trail

The large boulders at Sheep Crossing are part of the *terminal moraine* of a glacier formed during the oldest and most extensive of the four glaciations that affected this mountain complex. The moraine is composed of boulders and gravel carried down by the ice to the end, or terminus, of the glacier, where they were dumped. This glacier moved down the West Fork of the Little Colorado River some 700,000 years ago and was more than 3 miles long. More evidence for the glacier's action is the smooth, straight-walled U-shaped valley, typical of glacial valleys, and the carved-out *cirques* on the north face of Mount Baldy.

Boulders of a second terminal moraine are found at the end of the continuous meadows, about 2.5 miles upstream from Sheep Crossing, at an altitude of about 9500 feet. This glaciation occurred about 70,000 to 90,000 years ago and was less extensive than the previous one.

In addition to terminal moraines, the glaciers left *recessional moraines*, boulders and deposits that accumulated at the snout of the glacier as it receded. They also left their mark in the many meadows, or *cienegas* (as they are called in this part of the world), which here are glacial lakes filled in with sediment and vegetation.

The trail goes up the glacial valley through meadows that give fine views of the river and Mount Baldy ahead. Handsome spruce and fir dot the valley bottom, and aspen on the hillsides are a blaze of color in the fall. Among the few rock outcrops along this part of the trail are dark-colored *mafic* lavas—those rich in heavy iron and magnesium minerals—interbedded with reddish and tilted material that may represent *pyroclastic* deposits, the volcanic debris that is ejected from cinder cones. These rocks are older than Mount Baldy and were buried by lavas from that mountain. At about 3.0 miles (one-half mile beyond the end of the meadows and the second terminal moraine), a lovely little cienega offers fine campsites. Large boulders here are of glacial origin.

After crossing the creek, the trails starts sidehilling up the slope, along exposures of brick-red fine-grained weathered cinders. The terminal moraine of a still younger and smaller glacier complex is present at about 10,000 feet, a little up valley from this point. This glacier was active about 12,000 to 20,000 years ago. As you climb up the trail, you start seeing the kind of rock that makes up most of the mountain. It is gray, sheeted, with large crystals of white to nearly clear minerals. This is the uncommon volcanic rock *trachyte*, rich in the element potassium. The crystals you can see are mostly potassium-bearing feldspar, plagioclase (calcium- and sodium-bearing) feldspar, and some quartz. As you approach the crest of a ridge at about 4.5 miles after switch-backing under cliffy outcrops, you pass by a prominent cliff of trachyte in which the flow banding is vertical. This is a *dike*, a vertical sheetlike conduit that fed the trachyte flows. You can even make out the dike in the contours of the topographic map. A little farther up the ridge, the flow banding and sheeting are again horizontal—you are back in flows. The forest here is Engelmann spruce, which become smaller and more stunted toward timberline at the top.

From near the summit of Mount Baldy, the cinder cones of the Springerville–White Mountains volcanic field can be seen to the north.

Near the top of Mount Baldy, signs indicate the out-of-bounds area in the Apache Reservation, which includes the actual summit. However, a little effort gives views in most directions. To the north is the Colorado Plateau and the many cinder cones of the Springerville–White Mountains volcanic field; to the east, the large hump of Escudilla Mountain; to the southeast, the Gila Mountains in New Mexico; to the south, the dark hump of the Pinaleno Mountains; to the southwest, the Pinals; and to the west, the Sierra Ancha and Mazatzal ranges. Some of these features are more than 100 miles away.

Hike 13 HUMPHREYS PEAK TRAIL

Humphreys Peak is the highest point in Arizona, but is only the lower part of an ancient composite volcano whose top was removed by a cataclysm.

LOCATION ■ Kachina Peak Wilderness, Coconino National Forest

DISTANCE ■ 9 to 10 miles round trip

ELEVATION ■ 9300 to 12,633 feet

DIFFICULTY ■ Strenuous

TOPOGRAPHIC MAPS ■ Humphreys Peak, AZ, 1:24,000; Flagstaff, AZ, 1:100,000

GEOLOGIC MAPS ■ 12 and 13

PRECAUTIONS ■ Weather conditions are extreme. Windchill temperatures at the summit can dip below –100° F in winter. Watch for fierce thunderstorms in July and August and high winds any time.

INFORMATION ■ Peaks Ranger Station, Coconino National Forest

Landscape and Geology: Humphreys Peak is part of the San Francisco Mountain complex. This is the broken remnant of an extinct composite volcano—the only one of this type in the volcanic field. The volcano was formed between about 1.8 million and 400,000 years ago, then either blew its top or collapsed. Before this happened, San Francisco Mountain probably was 15,000 to 16,000 feet high, surpassing the present Mt. Rainier. It would have been quite a sight from Flagstaff.

San Francisco Mountain is a *stratovolcano*, also known as a *composite volcano*. It was built up partly by the eruption of lavas, partly by explosive activity. The lavas range in composition from basalt (silica-poor) to rhyolite (silica-rich). The most common rock types are andesite and dacite, which have intermediate silica contents. Of the two, dacite has the most silica and tends to have more abundant large feldspar crystals, a lighter gray color, and more rounded weathering forms. The top of Humphreys Peak is composed largely of andesite.

Many geologists now think that the cavity at the core of the San Francisco Mountains was formed when the volcano blew up in a manner resembling the eruption of Mount St. Helens. Other geologists prefer the older interpretation that the mountain collapsed into the cavity left when the magma was emptied from beneath the volcano. In either case, the internal structure of the volcano is now exposed: on its walls you can see the cross section of lava flows originating from vents in the now-vanished center of the mountain.

In spite of the cataclysm, Humphreys and its fellow peaks on the rim of the broken volcano remain high enough to be seen for hundreds of miles, and to be a sacred mountain for both the Hopi and Navajo people. The Hopi have a particularly fine view of the mountain from their distant mesa-top villages, and consider it the home of Kachinas, beings intermediary between humans and gods.

Trail Guide: The trail starts near the Arizona Snow Bowl ski area, in meadows with great views of the San Francisco volcanic field. Most of the ascent is on a ridge, first through dense stands of aspen, spruce, and fir, then through more open forest to timberline near a saddle on the rim of the broken volcano. Here bristlecone pines, contorted by the fierce winds, thrive where little else can grow. Among and above the bristlecones is the domain of tundra vegetation, the only such in Arizona, and above this is a desert of jumbled rocks, the home of thin air, wind, snow, and lightning—not to mention the Kachinas.

Reach the trailhead by driving north from Flagstaff on US 180. Continue 8.6 miles beyond the traffic light at the intersection of Humphreys and Columbus Streets. Just before milepost 223, turn right onto the paved road to the Arizona Snow Bowl. The gate to the ski area is 6.4 steep miles from the turnoff. Just before the gate, turn left into the dirt parking loop. At the far end of the parking loop is the marked trailhead (see figure 15).

From here, the official trail crosses the meadow, then switchbacks in the dense timber on the other side. (It is shorter and more scenic to follow a trail under the chairlift on the right side of the meadow, making a steep climb of about 300 feet to a junction with an upper trail. Beyond the junction, the trail crosses the meadow and connects with the official trail at the Kachina Peaks Wilderness sign and trail register.)

Follow the Humphreys Peak Trail as it switchbacks up through the forest. Count the switchbacks as you go, starting with the first switchback after the register. These switchbacks will be important milestones along this geologic hike.

You will see no outcrops, but many boulders, especially notable at a prominent gully that the trail crosses four times. The boulders are composed of dark- to medium-gray andesite, some with 1- to 3-mm crystals of glassy plagioclase. They are part of a *colluvial apron*, that is, boulders and other rubble weathered from outcrops and moved downslope by the influence of gravity.

At switchbacks one and three, you will have a fine view of a *boulder stream*. These typically form in or near glacial environments, where ground ice and

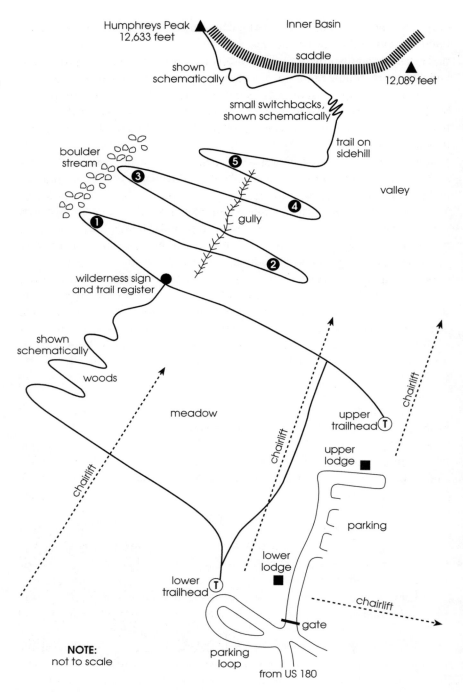

Figure 15. Sketch map of the Humphreys Peak Trail area (Hike 13)

freeze-thaw allow easy movement of boulders downslope. The forest is encroaching into parts of the now-stable stream.

At the third gully crossing, an outcrop of andesite can be seen just up the gully from the trail. At the fourth switchback, you will see several flat areas big enough for a tent, just downslope from the trail. Many people camp here; by doing the hike in two days, you can be on the summit early in the morning or late in the afternoon, when the light is best. There is competition for the sites on weekends.

Above switchback six, the trail sidehills in open timber, providing many views of the ski area and the forested country of northern Arizona. After grunting up several short and steep switchbacks, you reach the saddle on the rim, at 11,800 feet. This is a good place to rest and look around.

You are now on the jagged rim of the broken volcano. To the east, you look down into the central cavity, the Inner Basin, formed when the volcano blew up or collapsed. High on its left wall, below Humphreys Peak, you can make out lens-shaped cross sections of andesite and dacite lava flows that issued from vents in the now-vanished part of the volcano. Lower down and farther away on the left side of the Inner Basin, you will see features that look like vertical walls. These are *dikes*, consisting of lava that solidified within the conduits that once fed the vents. On the rim to the right of you is a conspicuous reddish

The view along the crest ridge shows a glacial cirque with glacial ridges, as well as the jagged rim. This is the remnant of a once-mighty volcano that collapsed and/or exploded.

zone composed of cinders and scoria, produced by a *parasitic cone* that once was active on the flank of the main volcano.

You may note subdued, gently curved ridges in the floor of the Inner Basin directly below you. These are glacial features, either moraines from tiny glaciers (or permanent snowfields) that occupied the hollows (*cirques*) in the wall to your right during the Ice Age, or boulder streams moving downslope. Opinions differ among geologists concerning the origin of these features.

North of the saddle, the rough trail continues up for another mile through outcrops of andesite and zones of cinders and scoria near ancient vents. Some of the flows are *sheeted*, that is, broken by closely spaced *joints* (parallel fractures), which cause the rock to weather into slabs.

On the summit, look closely at the rocks piled up to form the shelter, especially those near the entrance. You will be rewarded by a surprise: what look like splotches of gray-to-greenish glass on the surface of the rocks are *fulgurites*, the result of lightning strikes that melt the rock. Once you have learned to recognize them, you will see fulgurites everywhere here, which gives you some idea of how many lightning strikes hit this mountain.

The isolated summit of Humphreys Peak is ideal for viewing the geology of a large region at the south margin of the Colorado Plateau.

The basin formed by the collapse of San Francisco Mountain is to the right. Humphreys Peak is on the ridge in the background, which exposes in cross-section lava flows that moved outward from the central vent, now collapsed or blown away.

To the north you can see Gray Mountain, a cascade of gray Permian lime-stone along a monoclinal fold; a bit to the right is Shadow Mountain, the north-ernmost volcano of the San Francisco field. In the middle distance you can make out the perfect black cinder cone (associated with basalt flow) of SP Mountain (Hike 16), at 71,000 years old one of the youngest volcanoes of the field.

Far to the north-northeast rises the dark hulk of Navajo Mountain, 10,346 feet high and another sacred landmark for native peoples. This mountain is a *laccolith*, formed when the subterranean intrusion of magma inflated the over-lying Jurassic Navajo sandstone into a great dome.

To the right of Navajo Mountain is Black Mesa, capped by Cretaceous Mancos shale and Mesa Verde sandstone, which contain coal being mined for the Four Corners power plant near Page, Arizona. Nearer at hand is the broad, open, mature valley of the Little Colorado River, outlined by the pink-to-red cliff bands on its north side. This valley is typical of the valleys of the Colorado Plateau before canyon-cutting started less than 5.5 million years ago.

In the distance to the east you can see the dark basaltic buttes of the Hopi volcanic field. These extraordinary volcanoes were formed by lavas highly charged with water vapor, which explosively drilled funnel-shaped vents.

Colorful Sunset Crater is conspicuous in the middle distance. You can identify it by the road on its north side. Sunset Crater is the youngest volcano of the field: it erupted in 1066 to 1067 A.D., bringing great change to the life of the pre-historic Puebloan people of the region.

To the south, beyond Flagstaff, the surface of the Colorado Plateau is made up of basalt flows about 6 million years old and is dotted with small and medium-sized volcanoes. The plateau comes to an end at the Mogollon Rim. Beyond this great scarp is the Arizona Transition Zone, which once consisted of a lofty mountain range towering above the plateau. During the Miocene Era, these mountains were rifted, collapsing into the ranges and intervening basins we see today. The nearest basin is the Verde Valley, and the nearest range is the Black Hills beyond it. In the far distance and to the left of the Verde Valley are the Mazatzal Mountains, culminating in Four Peaks near Roosevelt Lake. These are composed of ancient Precambrian rocks between 1.6 and 1.7 billion years old.

In the middle distance to the west are large volcanoes that tower above their surroundings. From right to left, these are Kendrick, Sitgreaves, and Bill Williams Mountains. They define a belt of large dome-cluster volcanoes that trends southwest as seen from here. Farther west you may make out the abrupt shape of Picacho Peak, a volcanic butte, and, more to the right, the gentler humps of the small Mount Floyd volcanic field. Between the two, on the far horizon, are the Hualapai and Peacock Mountains near Kingman, now in the Basin and Range Province, but once part of the mountain range that rimmed the Colorado Plateau.

Hike 14

KENDRICK MOUNTAIN TRAIL

A fine trail takes you to an outstanding view at the summit of the second highest mountain in the San Francisco volcanic field, a volcano made up of clustered dacite domes.

LOCATION ■ Kendrick Mountain Wilderness, Kaibab National Forest
DISTANCE ■ About 4.5 miles one-way
ELEVATION ■ 7710 to 10,418 feet
DIFFICULTY ■ Moderately strenuous
TOPOGRAPHIC MAPS ■ Kendrick Peak, AZ, 1:24,000; Flagstaff, AZ, 1:100,000
GEOLOGIC MAPS ■ 14
PRECAUTIONS ■ Snow in winter, lightning in summer, and high winds any time
INFORMATION ■ Kaibab National Forest

Landscape and Geology: Kendrick Mountain is the second highest volcano in the San Francisco volcanic field. The high mountains in this field are either *composite volcanoes* (stratovolcanoes), represented by Humphreys Peak, or combinations of lava domes and lava flows. Kendrick Mountain is a good example of a lava dome volcano.

Lava domes are large blobs of viscous lava that were forced to the surface by high pressure. Often, the lava blobs issue from more than one vent, produc-

The top of Kendrick Mountain. Ahead is the andesite cone with the fire lookout tower.

ing clustered domes. Elsewhere, lava breaks out from the cooled and hardened shell of a dome, producing several lobes. In either case, the result is a mountain with a lumpy surface. Bill Williams Mountain, Sitgreaves Mountain, Kendrick Mountain, and Mount Elden near Flagstaff are all good examples. Most domes are composed of silica-rich viscous lava, such as *dacite* and *rhyolite* at Kendrick Mountain, but flows of silica-poor rocks such as *andesite* and *basalt* may also be part of a volcano made up primarily of domes.

Bill Williams, Sitgreaves, and Kendrick Mountains are all aligned on a northeast trend along Mesa Butte fault. This is a high-angle normal fault, the product of pull-apart forces. Faults like this tend to concentrate volcanic vents along them because

Humphreys Peak in the San Francisco Mountains (Hike 13)

A bomb is a blob of magma erupted into the air, where it freezes into a shape as large as several feet across (Hike 16).

Previous page: *View west into the Grand Canyon, from the top of the Redwall limestone along the Kaibab Trail*

The Heart of Rocks area gives you fine views of the columns and spires that are typical of erosion working upon welded tuffs. Cochise Head is on the right skyline (Hike 34).

The forces of erosion at work near Redwall Cavern in Marble Canyon

Looking north from the rim of the SP Mountain crater, you can see where lava flows have issued from the cone (Hike 16).

Opposite: *A graben visible along the Colorado River from the Tanner Trail (Hike 3)*

View south toward the Pinal Mountains from near the Coon Butte Spring trailhead (Hike 21).

Opposite: *Keet Seel (Hike 8)*

Interior of Red Mountain (Hike 15)

Lake Mead, at the mouth of the Grand Canyon (Hike 6)

View north into the Grand Canyon from the Tanner Trail (Hike 3)

The heart of a cinder cove (Hike 15)

Opposite: *The Aztec Peak hike offers a spectacular view of Workman Creek Falls, shown here forming an ice stalactite/stalagmite in winter (Hike 18).*

Looking at the Colorado River in Glen Canyon from the highest point on the Spencer Trail (Hike 2), you can see the Navajo sandstone in the walls of the canyon.

Logs in the Petrified Forest (Hike 9)

Opposite: *Flood country, Matkatamiba Canyon—a tributary of the Grand Canyon*

The Santa Catalina Mountains form part of a metamorphic core complex. This photo shows one of the complex's three parts, a lower plate composed of the metamorphic rock gneiss that has been sheared and folded (Hike 37).

Columnar zone in tuff, Aravaipa Canyon (Hike 27)

Tilted tuffs in Sycamore Canyon (Hike 41)

they represent the path of least resistance for the rising magma.

Trail Guide: From Flagstaff, take US 180 toward the Grand Canyon. Just beyond the turnoff to the Snowbowl, the highway crosses the meadows of Fort Valley, then climbs onto an old basaltic shield volcano to reach aspen country at 8000 feet. After passing the Nordic Center, turn left (west) at MP 233 onto dirt road FR 193. Set your odometer to zero. This road can get muddy, but otherwise it is passable for passenger cars if driven with care. At 3.1 miles, turn right onto FR 171 toward Kendrick Mountain. At the junction with FR 100 at 5.1 miles, bear right toward Pumpkin Center and immediately turn right onto FR 190, marked by a trail sign. The trailhead at 5.6 miles boasts a fence, parking area, outhouse, and trash disposal bin.

Note that much of Kendrick Peak was burned during a devastating forest fire in the summer of 2000. The trail logged here escaped relatively unscathed.

The first one-half mile of the trail was added by a Forest Service relocation of the trailhead. The uninspiring forest here is composed of second-growth ponderosa pines; the trail is in basaltic cinders and colluvium. Outcrops of basalt show up near the wilderness sign. Basalt and cinders are from nearby East Newman Hill, a *cinder cone* shown on the topographic map.

The forest opens up after reaching an old jeep trail at one-half mile, which leads through increasingly diverse forest that includes Douglas fir and limber pine. After several switchbacks, you reach a saddle about 1100 feet higher than the trailhead. One of the switchbacks exposes cinders with a weathered soil layer at the top.

At the saddle, the trail proper begins. It passes through aspen groves and open meadows with fine views, reaching the flat top of the mountain after sixteen switchbacks (hairpin curves), counting from the saddle. Count the switchbacks as you climb to keep track of where you are.

Initially, the trail is in colluvium that contains boulders of *dacite*, a lava with moderate to high silica content. After switchback nine, the trail traverses the south face of the mountain, which provides fine views to the south. You can see outcrops of purplish flow-banded dacite. A hand lens will help you see white to glassy crystals of plagioclase feldspar and a few black needle-shaped crystals of the mineral hornblende. This dacite is part of a volcanic dome.

Switchback ten is at a dike of dark, finely vesicular *andesite* (lava with moderate to low silica content) with whitish aggregates of plagioclase crystals and dark crystals of the mineral pyroxene. Several more wall-like dikes are visible downslope from farther up the trail. They are all part of the plumbing along which andesite magma rose to the surface, helping to make the volcano.

The light-colored soil on the trail beyond switchback fourteen is rich in *pumice*—solidified volcanic froth. It is part of a breccia unit that contains blebs of dark-gray *obsidian*, a black glass formed by the very rapid cooling of rhyolite lava. A *breccia* is a rock composed of angular fragments.

The flattish top of the mountain is in meadows punctuated with dwarf juniper, spruce, and fir. The eastern part is underlain by obsidian from a rhyolite dome that probably filled a summit crater of the mountain.

The fine old cabin on the top was built around 1910 and used as a residence by fire lookouts. The Bull Basin trail, a way of climbing the mountain from the north, joins our trail here.

The final 300-foot climb takes you to the fire lookout tower, which is built on a small cone of dark vesicular (pitted) andesite. The cone sits on top of the dacite that forms much of the mountain. The cone was fed by the andesite dikes, which cut through the dacite. Taken together, these relationships show you that the andesite eruptions were the final phase of volcanism on Kendrick Mountain.

A helicopter pad near the tower is an excellent place to rest and eat lunch. The view is inspiring, even though pollution from Las Vegas and southern California increasingly obscures the landscape.

To the south, the platform of the Colorado Plateau, dotted with small volcanoes, comes to an end along the Mogollon Rim, beyond which are Verde Valley and Mingus Mountain, both in the Arizona Transition Zone. Ancient Proterozoic rocks on Mingus Mountain are higher than the younger Paleozoic rocks on top of the plateau. This is a measure for the amount of uplift of the Mogollon Highlands, the ancient mountains that once formed the plateau's south edge.

The view southwest from the top of Kendrick Mountain includes Sitgreaves and Bill Williams Mountains, which (like Kendrick Mountain) are composed of clustered domes.

The lumpy Sitgreaves and Bill Williams Mountains to the southwest are composed of clustered domes, like Kendrick Mountain. You can see that they line up. If you look northwest, you can see a break in the rocks, with a dark cinder cone directly at the break. This break is Mesa Butte fault, which controls the alignment.

The volcanic Mohon Mountains are far to the west, and to the right of these, you can make out the dark mass of Mount Trumbull, about 100 miles away and part of the Uinkaret volcanic field near the south edge of the Colorado Plateau.

To the north, you can see the Kaibab Plateau, looking rather like the back of a whale and cut by the gash of the Grand Canyon. To the northeast is the dark cone of SP Mountain (Hike 16), with a lava flow issuing from its base.

To the east, you have a fine view of the broken cone of the San Francisco Peaks, whose Mount Humphreys (Hike 13) is the highest point in Arizona at 12,633 feet elevation. With your eyes, follow the slopes of this volcano upward to imagine where the summit was before the top of the mountain was destroyed a few hundred thousand years ago. You can see why geologists think that the mountain once reached the lofty elevation of 16,000 feet, higher than present-day Mount Rainier.

Just to the right of the San Francisco Peaks are the prominent cinder cones of Wing and A-1 Mountains, and behind them the more distant Mormon Mountain. You should also be able to make out the scarp along Oak Creek fault.

RED MOUNTAIN TRAIL

This short walk to the interior of a cinder cone takes you to a secluded world of fantastic natural sculptures—a photographer's paradise.

LOCATION ■ Coconino National Forest

DISTANCE ■ About 1 mile one-way

ELEVATION ■ 6750 to 7050 feet

DIFFICULTY ■ Easy

TOPOGRAPHIC MAPS ■ Chapel Mountain, AZ, 1:24,000; Ebert Mountain, AZ, 1:24,000; Cameron, AZ, 1:100,000

GEOLOGIC MAPS ■ 15

PRECAUTIONS ■ Smooth rock slopes covered by a thin veneer of loose cinders can be dangerous.

INFORMATION ■ Coconino National Forest, Peaks Ranger District

Landscape and Geology: The San Francisco volcanic field includes hundreds of basaltic cinder cones, typical of other fields along the southern margin of

Red Mountain, a cinder cone

the Colorado Plateau. In spite of this abundance, you can seldom see the interior structure of cinder cones because most are little eroded, and talus mantles the slopes of those that are. Red Mountain is a great exception. Erosion has sliced through this 740,000-year-old volcano, exposing its interior layering.

As the volcano was erupting, the *pyroclastic* products of the eruption—ash, cinders, bombs—were ejected from the vent and fell around it, forming a cone. Wind greatly influences this process: the cone builds up in symmetrical fashion if there is no wind during an eruption. If there is wind, or if the vent is angled to one side, more material is deposited on one side than the others, forming an asymmetrical cone. Red Mountain is asymmetrical.

Cinder cones generally do not erupt continuously but in spurts. In this cone, each spurt produced a layer of debris, so it started small and gradually grew to its present size. Each spurt is now represented by a bed of cinders dipping radially outward from the center.

At times during the eruption, fluids and gases oxidized the iron-rich minerals produced by the eruption, giving the cinders a red color. At other times, there was no oxidation, leaving the minerals dark gray to black. Both colors can be seen at Red Mountain.

The cinders of Red Mountain are consolidated into rock, instead of being loose. This is why the cinders can be eroded into the cliffs, gullies, and pinnacles that give Red Mountain its fascinating shapes.

Trail Guide: Take US 180 northwest from Flagstaff toward the Grand Canyon. At MP 247 turn left (south) onto dirt FS 9023V, passable for a normal passenger vehicle when dry, but too muddy when wet. Go about 0.4 mile to a parking area at the fence. The trail starts here, in pinyon-juniper country.

The material underfoot is *alluvium* (material deposited by water) composed of cinders and basalt fragments. As you walk, you can glimpse the gash in Red Mountain through the trees and see how the beds dip away from the center of the cone. At about three-fourths mile, the trail descends into a wash that it follows a short way to a small dam in a constriction created by a wall of gray

Cinder beds inside Red Mountain

cinders. Watch for dark rounded blebs in the sand of the wash. They are composed of the mineral hornblende and not obsidian, as you might think; the light-colored crystals are feldspar.

Scramble up the path to the right of the dam, which takes you to a little pass. Indurated cinders covered by a thin veneer of loose ones make for tricky footing here. This is also true anywhere you clamber around on the indurated cinders: be careful! From here, you get a photogenic view of the amphitheater carved into the cone.

Beyond the cinder wall, you enter a fairy world of pinnacles, cliffs, gullies, and sensuous shapes reminiscent of the sculptures of Henry Moore, all highlighted by large ponderosa pines and brilliant green bushes. Many of the pinnacles are the result of erosion along joints; others are true *hoodoos*—spires in which the soft cinders are protected by a caprock of gray basalt. These basalt blocks are mostly volcanic *bombs* and are embedded in the cinders like raisins in a cake. Examine one that is in easy reach: your hand lens will reveal black crystals of hornblende (and maybe pyroxene), white to glassy feldspar, and green *olivine*, a mineral common in basalt.

Most beds consist of cinders up to 1 inch across embedded in a finer-grained matrix. Some beds are considerably coarser grained, testimony to more violent phases of eruption.

Take a good look at the dip of the beds around and above you. You will see that they do not dip away from the amphitheater in which you are standing. This means the amphitheater is not the ancient crater, as you might think. The beds in the high wall still dip toward you, showing that the crater is on the other side of the wall.

The many caves in the wall were probably formed by the dissolving of the mineral material that held the cinders together. Seeps near a cave relatively low in the center of the wall support this notion. If the light is right, you may also see some small aligned holes below this cave. These holes may be footholds and handholds carved by prehistoric inhabitants of the Colorado Plateau.

You may wonder why this particular cinder cone was breached to produce the spectacular amphitheater, while many other cones are not. One possible explanation is related to *hydrothermal fluids*, mineral-laden water derived from and heated by magma. Red Mountain is on the trace of the Mesa Butte fault, a normal fault that could have served as a conduit not only for magma but also for these fluids. Minerals deposited by these fluids as they percolated through the cinders may have created the "cement" needed for hardening of the steep walls. At the same time, the pressure of the fluids may have fractured the rock, making it easier for blocks of cinders to fall off the walls. This would greatly speed up erosion. The small wash here is most likely the result of the amphitheater, rather than its cause.

SP MOUNTAIN

This steep but scenic hike up a young volcano shows you how a cinder cone looks shortly after activity ceases.

LOCATION ■ San Francisco volcanic field

DISTANCE ■ About 3 miles round trip

ELEVATION ■ 6240 to about 7000 feet

DIFFICULTY ■ Moderate to strenuous; a short but steep climb up a loose slope

TOPOGRAPHIC MAPS ■ SP Mountain, AZ, 1:24,000; East of SP Mountain, AZ, 1:24,000; Cameron, AZ, 1:100,000

GEOLOGIC MAPS ■ 16

PRECAUTIONS ■ Avoid snow in winter and thunderstorms in summer. Walking sticks are an asset on this steep slope with loose cinders.

INFORMATION ■ SP Mountain is on state land in a grazing preserve.

Landscape and Geology: SP Mountain is one of the most northern and, at 71,000 years old, one of the youngest volcanoes of the San Francisco volcanic field. Most of the younger volcanoes are in this active part of the volcanic field, indicating that volcanic activity has shifted northeastward with time. Thus, the next eruption will probably be in the area of the Little Colorado River.

SP Mountain is a classic cinder cone, of which there are hundreds in the San Francisco volcanic field. Cinder cones are composed of several sizes of volcanic debris that fell out of the air during the eruption: *ash* (small, light particles of basalt), *cinders* (particles from a fraction of an inch to several inches), and *bombs* (chunks of basalt up to several feet long). Bombs, being

View of the crater from the south

135

larger, cool more slowly and remain plastic in flight. Many spin, acquiring the shape of a spindle or football, while others show evidence of plastic deformation. Yet others have a cracked surface rather like that of bread crust and are called "bread crust bombs." These form when the surface of a bomb cools enough to become brittle while the inside is still deforming like taffy.

Most of the material ejected falls only a short distance from the vent, building up a *rim* surrounding a central *crater*. This rim grows with time as more material accumulates.

Material on the outside of the rim settles down at the *angle of repose,* which is the maximum angle (measured from horizontal) that is possible for a slope built in unconsolidated material. The angle for a slope made of cinders is about 32°. A slope that begins to build up to a steeper angle will collapse, reestablishing this barely stable angle. This is why it is hard to walk up the side of SP Mountain: with each step, material moves downslope, taking the hiker along. Note that the walls of the crater are steeper than the outer slope of the cone because the cinders in the crater were hot enough to become welded together.

A basalt lava flow emerges from the base of the cone on the north side. Many cinder cones have such a flow. The surface of the flow is composed of rough and blocky lava, known by the Hawaiian name *aa*.

The cone joined to the southwest side of SP Mountain is an older crater against which the cinders of SP were banked. Colton Crater, also known as Crater 160, is about 3 miles due south. This crater is of interest because it brought up to the surface fragments of material from a depth of 30 miles or more within the earth. This material is from the Earth's *mantle*, the hot, plastic layer beneath the outer brittle *crust*. These fragments enable geologists to see the composition of the mantle.

Many cinder cones are visible to the south. Beyond them looms the mass of San Francisco Mountain, the highest part of the volcanic field and the highest mountain in Arizona.

Few volcanoes are present to the northwest, where instead you see the aptly named mass of Gray Mountain, composed of Paleozoic Kaibab limestone. The east slope of the mountain is a fold in the rocks called a *monocline* (see figure 5) that in places becomes a fault. Just right of Gray Mountain is Shadow Mountain, another volcano, and behind it the indistinct cliff line of the Echo Cliffs, another monocline. A little to the right of these, the dark hump of Navajo Mountain can sometimes be seen low on the horizon on clear days. This mountain, sacred to the Native Americans and long a landmark for travelers, was formed when molten rock intruded and bowed up sedimentary rocks.

In the middle distance to the north and northeast is the subdued valley of the Little Colorado River. This is a *strike valley* that follows the trend of the rock's structure; it gives a good feel for what the old pre-canyon landscape

136

The rim of the crater is composed of blocks, bombs, and cinders welded together.

looked like. The flat terrain north of SP is underlain by lava flows and cinder deposits.

Trail Guide: Take highway US 89 north from Flagstaff. Travel about 24 miles from the junction with the Townsend–Winona road, which is at the north end of town and marked by a traffic light. Look for milepost 445. Just about 1 mile after this milepost, turn left onto a wide dirt road where milepost 446 is in sight and Hanks Trading Post is about 200 yards to the north. Set the trip odometer to zero.

Pass two water tanks and a large power line, then go between two hills. Turn left at mile 5.1 onto a well-traveled dirt road that passes between SP Mountain and Hill 6666 to the east. At mile 7.0, a dirt track takes off to the right, aiming for the saddle between SP Mountain and an older cone to its south. A sign in the middle of the track indicates that it is closed. Park near this sign.

The track starts on an old lava flow, recognizable mainly by the lava squeeze-ups. Most of this flow is mantled by cinders. The slope of SP Mountain ahead is at an angle of about 32°, the *angle of repose.*

As you start climbing toward the saddle, you can see deep trenches along a former location of the track. This kind of severe erosion is why driving up these steep slopes in loose material is a bad idea.

SP Mountain is best climbed from the highest point of the saddle, where vague tracks zig-zag up the hill. The going is rough, but it's not far.

The more resistant rock that forms the rim of the crater is composed of blocks, bombs, and cinders that are welded together to form a steeper ledge. This happens because the material falling here is still hot enough to be soft. A welded rim like this grows upward with time as the cinder cone grows. If you look at freshly broken rock from the rim with a hand lens, you will see green crystals of the mineral *olivine.* The lava that built SP Mountain is an *olivine basalt.*

At 1.2 miles, you are on the rim, where you can peer down into the crater about 400 feet. This is the throat of the volcano, from which glowing gases and fountains of molten rock were ejected to heights of hundreds of feet. It must have been quite a sight.

I recommend walking around the rim—it's only about three-fourths mile and there is much to see. Many interesting bombs litter the ground. Some are almost 10 feet long but were broken into several pieces upon landing. Some are spindle-shaped, while others show the classic bread crust surface. You can see evidence for plastic deformation in the form of ropy lava or folds in the layering. Many remind me of sculptures.

The north and northeast part of the rim is a good place for looking at the crater below, the San Francisco Peaks to the south, and Colton Crater in the middle distance. From here you can also see the basalt flow that issued from the base of SP Mountain. You should be able to make out the lateral *levees*, arc-shaped transverse ridges that formed when lava at the edge of the flow cooled faster than lava in the middle.

Going down the mountain is easier than climbing up. But take it easy with the "scree skiing," which accelerates erosion.

Once back at the car, you may wish to take a look at the flow issuing from the base of the crater. To do this, drive back 0.9 mile to the junction with the main road, turn left, then left again after about 1.5 miles where the road Ts into a wide dirt road. This road crosses the flow. In the opposite direction (northeast), it takes you back to US 89.

Hike

17

VULCANS THRONE

This combination drive and hike to see lavas cascading into the Grand Canyon is one of the best geologic and photogenic sites in Arizona.

LOCATION ■ Grand Canyon National Park, Toroweap Valley

DISTANCE ■ 0.7 mile one way

ELEVATION ■ 4520 to 5102 feet

DIFFICULTY ■ Moderate; a short but steep climb up a loose slope

TOPOGRAPHIC MAPS ■ Vulcans Throne, AZ, 1:24,000; Mount Trumbull, AZ, 1:100,000; Fredonia, AZ, 1:100,000.

GEOLOGIC MAPS ■ 17 and 18

PRECAUTIONS ■ Have properly inflated tires, an inflated spare, and a full tank of gas for the 60-mile drive on a dirt road. Bring plenty of water and food.

INFORMATION ■ Grand Canyon National Park

Landscape and Geology: At Toroweap Overlook, the Grand Canyon looks quite different from what people see at the South and North Rims, the viewpoints visited by most people.

View from Toroweap Overlook, looking downstream. The dark masses cascading into the canyon on the right are ancient lava flows. The white water some 3000 feet below is Lava Falls Rapids, the biggest in the Grand Canyon.

Instead of the typical wide, intricate canyon, here you will see a two-tiered effect—a precipitous inner gorge, less than 1 mile wide but 3000 feet deep, cut into a broad flat-floored upper valley about 4 miles wide with walls 2000 feet high. Toroweap Point, the ridge directly north of the lookout and identified on the topographic map, is part of the upper wall. Toroweap Overlook is on the esplanade—the floor of the valley.

The floor of the broad upper valley is a platform cut on the Esplanade sandstone, the upper formation of the Supai Group of late Paleozoic age.

The walls of the upper valley are in Permian beds that include the red Hermit shale at the base, then the white Coconino sandstone, and finally the gray cliff-forming Toroweap Formation and Kaibab limestone at the top.

The inner gorge is cut into the platform. Its walls expose Paleozoic rocks ranging in age from Cambrian Tapeats sandstone at the bottom to the Pennsylvanian and Permian redbeds of the Supai Group at the top.

Looking upstream, you can see the flat-floored upper valley and its rims for a considerable distance. This is not the case downstream, where the strata—including the platform-forming Esplanade sandstone—are dropped down to the west along two faults.

The Toroweap fault is the eastern one of the two. It offsets the Vermilion Cliffs near Pipe Springs, then continues southward, forming a linear scarp just east of the road on which you drive to Toroweap. Vulcans Throne is right on this fault, which continues south of the Grand Canyon, where it is marked by down-to-the-west displacement along Prospect Valley.

The second of the two faults is Hurricane fault, one of the major faults of the Colorado Plateau. It is 8 miles west of Toroweap Overlook.

Toroweap is an *extensional* (pull apart) fault that provides an easy conduit for molten rock to rise to the surface. This explains why Vulcans Throne and several young cinder cones on both sides of the Grand Canyon are along Toroweap fault. One of these cones is prominent across the canyon, about 2 miles downstream from the viewpoint. This cone is being destroyed by gradual erosion of the canyon rim.

Vulcans Throne and its neighboring cones are very young geologically and are thus little eroded. One recent study gives an age of 74,000 years.

Many vents in this field produced basaltic lavas that flowed southward into the Grand Canyon. Can you imagine what this would have looked like while it was happening? Fiery red molten lava cascading into the canyon, then into the Colorado River, with great boiling and hissing of steam, a river of lava meeting one of water.

The lavas made great dams that impounded the Colorado River, creating lakes that extended far upstream into the Grand Canyon. Many of the lavas also flowed far downstream from the dams. All this happened repeatedly in the Uinkaret volcanic field between about 1 and 0.5 million years ago.

Lavas in this region tell us much about when the Grand Canyon was cut. Those at the bottom of the canyon prove that it was as deep 0.5 million years ago as it is today because lavas of that age flowed down a channel that was only about 100 feet above the present one. Contrast this with lavas on the Shivwits Plateau, about 20 miles west of Toroweap Overlook. The basaltic lavas that cap this plateau flowed over a nearly flat landscape with no signs of incision, even where it is right next to precipices that today plunge down several thousand feet into the canyon. The Grand Canyon did not exist when these lavas flowed 8.0 to 6.0 million years ago.

Trail Guide: Topographic maps are really helpful on this trip. They keep you from getting lost and tell you what you are looking at.

In Fredonia, turn west on Arizona Highway 389. After 8 miles, turn south onto a wide well-signed dirt road to Toroweap. Set the trip odometer to zero. From here, the drive is about 60 miles; stay on the main road and follow signs to Toroweap at junctions. The country is open grassland with vast views. In spring, it can be quite green with lots of flowers.

After a while, you will see a limestone scarp east of the road. This scarp is along the Toroweap fault. The highest mountain to the southwest is Mount Trumbull, in the Uinkaret volcanic field. Once you get to Toroweap Valley, you will see how ancient lava flows from this field cascaded into the valley.

The Park Service Ranger Station is at 54.6 miles. At 58 miles, the track to Toroweap Lake and Vulcans Throne branches off to the right (southwest). Note the turnoff for future reference, but don't go that way for now. To go to Toroweap Overlook, stay on the main road, which now enters intricate slickrock country carved out of the Esplanade sandstone (*slickrock* is a Colorado Plateau term for bare sandstone rock). A branch road to the left leads to a pleasant but primitive campground with picnic tables and pit toilets but no water. But continue on to the viewpoint parking area at 61 miles in slickrock dotted with pinyon and juniper trees. There are two primitive campsites here in addition to those at the campground. The viewpoints are a few hundred feet beyond the parking area. Be careful at the rim: there are no restraining devices here, the most precipitous drop that can be reached by car anywhere in the Grand Canyon and the most spectacular view of the Colorado River far below.

Do you have a feel for how wide the river is way down there? It is difficult because there is nothing to give a sense of scale. The first white people to see the Colorado River in the Grand Canyon had the same problem. Captain Cárdenas and his men, all members of the great Coronado expedition of 1540, reached the rim of the canyon to the east of here in the fall of that year. They thought the river was about a fathom wide (6 feet) and not too far down. But the topographic map tells us that the Colorado River is about 3000 feet below Toroweap Overlook and 400 to 500 feet wide!

Perhaps the most photographed point is a few hundred feet to the east along the rim, beyond some ledges. Here is a spectacular view up canyon and a breathtaking one straight down to the river, framed by a startling red wall. From here you can also get a good feeling for how the inner gorge slices through the flat-floored upper valley.

You can reach an even more unique view by walking a few hundred feet west along the rim. Far below, a wisp of white water on the Colorado River makes a faint noise barely audible on a calm day. This wisp is Lava Falls Rapids, the most renowned rapids in the entire Grand Canyon. At river level, the noise is deafening, the waves gigantic. The rapids are created by sediments dumped into the river by *debris flows* coming out of Prospect Canyon. The clay, sand, and rocks carried in these muddy flows partially dam the river, creating a constriction that speeds up the water. Impressive standing waves and "holes" occur near submerged boulders. Most rapids in the Grand Canyon are formed by constrictions caused by debris coming out of side canyons.

The black rock you can see on the north wall is lava that has cascaded into the canyon. Most issued from vents in the Uinkaret volcanic field, filling Toroweap Canyon and Whitmore Canyon to the west. Remnants of lava are visible at the bottom of the canyon. One of these flows went down the canyon for 85 miles from here. Vulcans Throne, beautiful and vaguely sinister, rises

1 mile to the west, directly on the Toroweap fault. A dissected cone is visible across the river on the west side of Prospect Canyon.

The surface of the sandstone on the rim contains shallow depressions. After rain or snow, these depressions fill with water and are important to the wildlife of the area. The dark material you see in them are plants and lichens that secrete organic acids. These help dissolve the calcite cement that holds the sandstone together, deepening the depressions over time.

To go to Vulcans Throne, get back in your car and drive to the junction of the previously noted track with the main road. Turn left onto the track and go 1 mile to a shallow saddle just beyond Toroweap Lake. This track is rough and rocky but passable for a regular car if you drive with care. The "lake" here is actually a *playa*, a shallow depression sometimes occupied by an ephemeral lake. Vulcans Throne gives you a more wide-ranging view than you get at Toroweap Overlook. Park the car at the shallow saddle just beyond the lake.

Walk cross-country along the saddle to the base of the cone, then angle to the right, following grass to the highest point you can. The grass stabilizes the cinders and makes walking a little easier. Avoid walking in single file, which produces unwelcome trails. Eventually, you'll have to grunt straight up the rubbly slope for about 400 feet. Along the way, notice the cinders and bombs that make up the cone.

Once on top, turn right and head for the western peak. Go down the slope a little ways toward the canyon for the best view. The lava cascades are spectacular from here, as is the dissected cinder cone on the other side of the canyon. You can also figure out the location of the Toroweap fault on the south side of the canyon by the offset of strata and topographic benches developed on the same geologic layer.

Looking north from the top of the cone, you can see how Toroweap Valley is controlled by the fault and how lavas have flowed into the valley from the Uinkaret Mountains, whose highest point is the 8000-foot Mount Trumbull, 13 miles to the northwest.

The skyline far to the west is the Shivwits Plateau, at the western edge of the Colorado Plateau. Its top is formed by 8.0 to 6.0 million-year-old lava, which rests on a smooth surface that extends for miles. There is no evidence of lava cascading into the canyon there, as it did at Vulcans Throne. The bump sticking above the skyline is Price Point, a volcano that is now cut by the edge of the canyon. Carving of the canyon must have happened after this volcano was formed.

In roadcuts near Workman Creek Falls, gray and unbedded basalt (below) comes in contact with bedded, purple Troy quartzite (above).

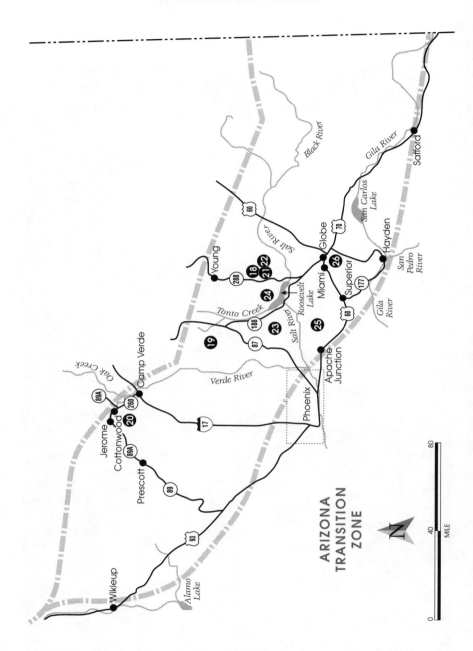

The Arizona Transition Zone gets its name because it is geologically partway between the Colorado Plateau and the Basin and Range Province. On one hand, the sedimentary layers, or strata, tend to be flat-lying as they are on the Colorado Plateau, instead of tilted as they are in Basin and Range. On the other hand, the region is broken up into the typical basins and ranges of that province, which are absent from the plateau.

The Arizona Transition Zone began as the Mogollon Highlands, a belt of mountains created at the end of the Cretaceous Period during the *Laramide orogeny,* a major mountain-forming event. The mountains formed the rugged south rim of the Colorado Plateau, over which they rose and onto which they drained and shed sediment. Because of the uplift that formed the mountains, rocks were brought to a high position relative to that of the same rocks on the nearby Colorado Plateau.

In Miocene time, the Mogollon Highlands were broken up by tectonic pull-apart forces and collapsed into the mountain ranges and linear valleys that we see today, creating the Arizona Transition Zone. This collapse was accompanied by volcanic activity. The old stream drainage to the north was disrupted and replaced by generally southward drainage, toward the Gila River.

Even after the collapse, rocks in the Arizona Transition Zone are still higher than on the Colorado Plateau, giving some idea of how high the Mogollon Highlands must have been originally.

One of the most interesting geologic features of the Arizona Transition Zone is the Apache Group (see Hike 18), a middle and late Proterozoic sequence of strata deposited in shallow sea water. The strata are invaded by many sills of *diabase,* a coarser grained equivalent of basalt. The Apache Group is roughly equivalent to the Colorado Plateau's Grand Canyon Supergroup, but with differences in detail.

Hike 18

AZTEC PEAK TRAIL

A pleasant, well shaded trail leads to a breathtaking view of some of the most rugged country in the state.

LOCATION ■ Sierra Ancha Wilderness, Tonto National Forest

DISTANCE ■ 2.7 miles one way

ELEVATION ■ 6400 to 7750 feet

DIFFICULTY ■ Easy

TOPOGRAPHIC MAPS ■ Aztec Peak, AZ, 1:24,000; Seneca, AZ, 1:100,000

GEOLOGIC MAPS ■ 19

PRECAUTIONS ■ Watch for snow and cold in winter, and lightning on the peak in the summer.

INFORMATION ■ Tonto National Forest, Pleasant Valley Ranger District

Landscape and Geology: At nearly 7800 feet, Aztec Peak is the highest point in the beautiful and remote Sierra Ancha, which means "the wide range." Because it is both high and isolated, the mountain affords a sweeping view of much of the Arizona Transition Zone and the neighboring Mogollon Rim.

Well-exposed along the trail is the Apache Group, one of the most interesting geologic features of the Arizona Transition Zone. These Proterozoic sedimentary rocks were deposited in a shallow sea. The strata are invaded by many sills of diabase, a coarse-grained intrusive equivalent of basalt. The Apache Group is about the same age as the Colorado Plateau's Grand Canyon Supergroup.

The top of Aztec Peak is capped by a small remnant of Cambrian sandstone. This happy circumstance enables geologists to pinpoint the unconformity (missing gap in the geologic record) between Proterozoic and Paleozoic rocks at about 7700 feet elevation here. In the Grand Canyon, the same unconformity is at 2800 feet. This difference of about 5000 feet is evidence for the ancient belt of uplift—the Mogollon Highlands—that once occupied the present Arizona Transition Zone.

The mountains of the original Mogollon Highlands were much higher than the present-day Aztec Peak from which nearly all Paleozoic rocks have been eroded. It is likely that the ancient mountains were more than 12,000 feet high (see figure 16).

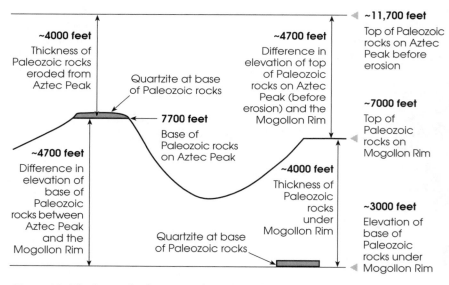

Figure 16. The base of Paleozoic rocks on top of Aztec Peak is at 7700 feet. On the Mogollon Rim, the same layer is in the subsurface at about 3000 feet, or 4700 feet lower. This is a measure of the uplift of the ancient Mogollon Highlands relative to the Colorado Plateau. If we restore the 4000 feet of Paleozoic rocks eroded from the top of Aztec Peak but still present on the Mogollon Rim, we find that the mountains were at least 12,000 feet high, towering some 5000 feet above the nearby Colorado Plateau.

Trail Guide: From Roosevelt Lake, travel north on Arizona Highway 288, the Young Road. Set the odometer to zero at the junction with the A + road, where the pavement ends (as of 2001). Beyond this point, AZ 288 is a well-graded gravel all-weather road that gradually climbs the south face of the Sierra Ancha.

After climbing in Tertiary gravel deposits for a few miles, the road suddenly confronts a cliff of purplish *quartzite* (metamorphosed sandstone). You have just crossed the Armer Mountain fault, one of the range-front faults that form Tonto Basin, which contains Roosevelt Lake. The cliff is the lower member of the Dripping Spring quartzite of Proterozoic age (see figure 17).

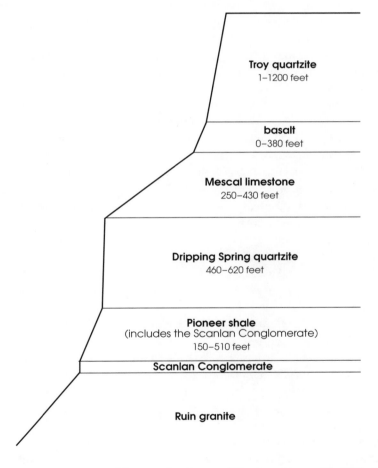

Troy quartzite
1–1200 feet

basalt
0–380 feet

Mescal limestone
250–430 feet

Dripping Spring quartzite
460–620 feet

Pioneer shale
(includes the Scanlan Conglomerate)
150–510 feet

Scanlan Conglomerate

Ruin granite

Figure 17. Formations of the Apache Group of Proterozoic age. The Ruin granite is below the group. Diabase sills intrude all parts of this section. Rocks shown here with a vertical edge form cliffs; those shown with a sloping edge are less hard and form slopes.

Above the cliff, the road takes advantage of open country formed by a thick and easily eroded *diabase sill* intruded into the quartzite. Outcrops of the dark diabase along the road provide an opportunity to examine this rock type, which is chemically like basalt but contains larger crystals because it was intruded at some depth. It thus cooled more slowly, allowing the crystals to grow larger. The needle-like light-colored crystals are *feldspar*, and the dark groundmass is the mineral *pyroxene*. Note the *spheroidal weathering*—the tendency of the homogeneous rock to weather into rounded boulder-like masses. At mile 10.4, the road crests in pretty ponderosa pine country. At mile 13.6, turn right onto FS road 487, marked by the sign "Workman Creek Recreation Area, Sierra Ancha Wilderness." The road is passable to a passenger vehicle. At mile 16.2, park at a gate with the sign "Road closed December 15–March 31 annually" or in nearby Falls Recreation Area. This is the start of the hike. Note that the vegetation along this trail was hard hit in 2000 by the Coon Creek Fire, but the trail is fine. Near the gate, you can see exposures of a well-bedded yellow-gray siltstone. Farther up the road, the cuts show a greenish gray shale and a light gray limestone. All are in the upper part of the Proterozoic Mescal limestone. This "limestone" is actually mostly *dolomite*, a sedimentary rock similar to limestone but containing magnesium as well as calcium. The light color is due to "cooking" by the overlying diabase sill. The fine, wavy laminae in the limestone are called *stromatolites*, ancient algae that were one of the earliest forms of life. The algae formed sticky mats on the shallow sea floor, which trapped sediment. In places the lamination is deformed into conspicuous folds.

Less than one-half mile up the road, you can see a prominent cliff above a metal bridge. The cliff is composed of dark gray rock that weathers reddish brown. This is an altered basalt that is found in places at the top of the Mescal. Spheroidal weathering and *vesicles* (pits or holes from gas bubbles) typical of lava flows are much in evidence. The basalt ledge forms Workman Creek Falls, which you can see from an unprotected lookout. In winter, the falls form a remarkable ice cone.

The contact between the basalt and the overlying Proterozoic Troy quartzite is exposed on the north side of the road just above the falls. This quartzite is pinkish, cross-bedded in places, and contains pebbles near its base. The pebbles and the low-angle cross bedding show that this is a water-laid, not a wind-laid, deposit (see figure 12).

From here on, the road is in subdued rolling terrain with no rocks to view. You are now walking on an area underlain by a diabase sill that intrudes the Troy quartzite. Diabase weathers easily, so tends to form subdued terrain with few outcrops.

Shortly after the road crests a hill, a brown sign marks Trail 151, which goes left (north) and is indicated by the sign "Aztec Peak 2 miles." Take this woodsy

148

Looking east from the top of Aztec Peak across Cherry Creek and the Salt River canyon in the middle distance. Quartzite is in the foreground.

trail, which is marked by rock cairns and climbs gently toward the peak, which you can glimpse from an old apple orchard in a clearing.

About 500 feet before reaching the top, you can see along the trail outcrops of a fine-grained light-gray to purplish-white quartzite with low-angle cross bedding. This is again the Troy quartzite, here above the diabase that intruded the middle of it. A few hundred feet farther, nearly at the top, conspicuous outcrops of purple-brown cross-bedded coarse-grained pebbly sandstone form the top of the mountain. This is a Cambrian sandstone, equivalent to the Tapeats sandstone of the Grand Canyon. Between the sandstone and the quartzite below—but not easily visible here—is an erosional unconformity that represents hundreds of millions of years.

A fine place to rest is on the sandstone ledges on the east edge of the mountain. Take a look at the sandstone: the coarse grains, pebbles, and low-angle cross beds all tell you that this rock was deposited in a high-energy environment. This was the beach sand of the Cambrian sea that advanced over the ancient, worn-down Proterozoic rocks some 600 million years ago.

The view is spectacular. Right below you is the deep valley of Cherry Creek. The intricately dissected country farther east, underlain by Tertiary gravel and lighter-colored volcanic sediments, includes an ancient channel carved there by water that once flowed northward from the Central Arizona Highlands onto the Colorado Plateau. Farther back you can make out the canyon of the Salt River, and to the southeast, the dark hump of the Pinaleno Mountains. The subdued mound of the Mount Baldy complex (Hike 12), a Tertiary shield volcano in the White Mountains, rises above the horizon far to the northeast.

Looking north from the fire tower, you can see the intricate country of the Sierra Ancha and, farther back, the light-colored scarp of the Mogollon Rim with the Colorado Plateau at its back. This is Zane Grey country. To the west, the Mazatzal Range lies beyond Tonto Basin, and to the southwest, the spires and turrets of the Superstition Mountains emerge from the Phoenix smog.

BARNHARDT TRAIL

On this rugged and picturesque hike, see striking deformation of ancient Precambrian rocks that were deposited 1700 million years ago at the growing edge of the North American continent.

LOCATION ■ Mazatzal Wilderness, Tonto National Forest

DISTANCE ■ 6 miles round trip

ELEVATION ■ 4200 to 5850 or 6000 feet

DIFFICULTY ■ Moderate

TOPOGRAPHIC MAPS ■ Mazatzal Peak, AZ, 7.5' quadrangle; Payson, 1:100,000.

GEOLOGIC MAPS ■ 20

PRECAUTIONS ■ Carry plenty of water. Spring is the best time to hike here; summer brings heat and storms and winter brings snow.

INFORMATION ■ Tonto National Forest, Payson Ranger District

Landscape and Geology: The North American continent had been growing outward for more than a billion years from its ancient core in the Canadian Shield when its edge reached what is now central Arizona some 1700 million years ago. We know that here the continent was growing out toward the southeast because progressively older rocks are found northwest of the Mazatzal Mountains. These early rocks were typical of those at continent margins and were deposited under water in or near *island arcs*, the volcano-studded archipelagos, such as the Japanese Islands, that parallel subduction zones.

The early Proterozoic rocks of the Mazatzal Group were laid down near the margin of the newly consolidated continent. Some were deposited in shallow water on the *continental shelf* near the shore, others by rivers on land. The sediment was derived from the continent to the northwest. Cross bedding and pebbly layers tell us that it was deposited in water that was full of energy.

The Mazatzal Group is composed of several different *formations* or rock units. Going upward in the stratigraphic "layer cake," these are the Deadman quartzite, the Maverick shale, and the Mazatzal Peak quartzite, the latter subdivided into a lower red member and an upper white member. All are visible on the hike. The quartzite was apparently deposited as sand on a stable but slowly sinking continental shelf.

This peaceful state of affairs came to a violent end during the Mazatzal *orogeny* (mountain-building event), when these sedimentary rocks were shoved northwestward toward the continent in great thrust faults such as the Barnhardt Thrust. The tectonic stresses that accompanied the thrusting were not kind to the rocks, crumpling them into the folds well displayed along this trail. Even the end of thrusting brought no peace because then north-trending high-angle normal faults produced *grabens*—downdropped blocks in which the Mazatzal Peak quartzite was preserved. The Barnhardt Trail area is in one such graben.

Chevron folds, Barnhardt Canyon

About 1400 million years ago, the broken and folded rocks were disturbed again, this time by the intrusion of granite that is not visible on the hike, but forms much of the southern Mazatzal range near Four Peaks. This event was followed by erosion, which for a few hundred million years did its best to smooth and level the land. Then, renewed deposition brought the middle Proterozoic Apache Group, which has been eroded from the Mazatzals but is still present in the Sierra Ancha range east of Tonto Basin. After another few hundred million years of erosion, the seas swashed back onto the eroded land starting about 590 million years ago, depositing the Paleozoic strata that record the blossoming of life on Earth. These strata have also been eroded from the Mazatzals, but are still visible in their full glory on the Mogollon Rim to the north.

Peace and tranquillity were broken once more at the end of the Mesozoic Era about 65 million years ago when another compressive mountain-building event was unleashed by crustal plates crashing together, this time to the west. One result was uplift of the Mogollon Highlands, including the area where the (much younger) Mazatzal Mountains are now. Sediment eroded from these mountains was shed northward onto the then-low Colorado Plateau in the form of the "rim gravels" which contain material derived from the south.

Collapse of the mountains in Miocene time formed northwest-trending basins such as Tonto Basin and Verde Valley, which are key features of the Arizona Transition Zone. This event interrupted deposition of the rim gravels and caused development of other drainage networks, including the one that deposited gravel along the upper parts of this trail. Volcanic activity accompanied the faulting, producing rocks such as the basalt exposed near the divide.

Trail Guide: Take Forest Road 419 which branches west off State Route 87, just north of milepost 239 and about 1 mile south of the Rye Creek store. The turnoff to the trailhead is signed "Barnhardt Trail Head."

Drive about 5 miles on FR 419 to the trailhead. The road is quite rocky in places, but passable for passenger cars with a little care. The road is built on a pediment surface that becomes moderately wooded near the end of the road at about 4200 feet. The trailhead has plenty of parking space but no other facilities. The trail takes off directly uphill from the parking lot. After a few paces, a sign marks the junction of Divide Trail on the left with Barnhardt Trail, #43, on the right. Take the Barnhardt Trail.

The mouth of Barnhardt Canyon ahead is in the Maverick shale. The prominent reddish cliffs up canyon are in the Mazatzal Peak quartzite, which there is above the Barnhardt Thrust. The red cobbles that litter the trail and make walking difficult are composed of the red member of the Mazatzal Peak quartzite. With a hand lens you can see the original glassy rounded grains of quartz sand embedded in more quartz that has grown in between them. These are known as *overgrowths,* deposited on and between the grains after the rock was formed. This hallmark of a quartzite gives the rock its outstanding durability.

Keep looking at the cobbles: in some you can see pebbles, including fragments of red chert or jasper. In others you can see low-angle cross bedding. These features tell you that the quartzite was deposited as sand in fast flowing water.

The trail climbs gradually along the south side of the canyon through a woodland of oaks, juniper, prickly pear, and agave. Along water courses you can see willows, as well as Arizona sycamore and walnut. Pinyon pines appear as you climb higher, then stands of ponderosa pine and even a few Douglas firs. Just before traversing a small side canyon about 1000 feet from the trailhead, the trail crosses a boulder field. Beyond this, the trail is cut into a new formation—platy light-gray to cream-colored siltstone and recrystallized shale that weather into splintery chips. You are in the Maverick shale, also visible across the canyon. Walking becomes easier here because this rock weathers readily into soil. The distant rampart of the Mogollon Rim, north of Payson, marks the southern edge of the Colorado Plateau.

Beyond a Wilderness sign, the bottom of the canyon has pools of water near Garden Spring at one-half mile. The shale crops out along the trail here and there. Then, at about three-fourths mile, the trail turns left around an exposed nose marked by a prominent outcrop of Maverick shale along the trail and adorned by a fine display of native cactus. This is a first-class geologic location, for which it is worth pulling out your geologic map and camera.

The gently sloping, parallel, rod-like structures on the surface of the outcrop

Mullions

are beautiful *mullions*, formed by the stretching and folding of a more resistant bed, in this case sandstone, encased within less resistant beds, in this case shale. Mullions typically occur on a fold, as you can see here.

The canyon wall south of the trail displays a train of folds, made conspicuous by light-colored beds. This is a spectacular textbook example of *chevron folds*, produced in weak rocks such as shale by compression at right angles to the folds. The general effect is like the bellows of an accordion. Similar folds are also visible in the north wall of Barnhardt Canyon, where a light-colored resistant layer also shows that rocks to the right (southeast) have been thrusted over rocks to the west. Features such as mullions, folds, and faults are used in geology to determine the past arrangement and directions of tectonic forces.

Once across the side drainage, just beyond the nose with the mullions, admire the nice fold in sandstone layers exposed in a cut along the trail. This fold also shows that rocks to the east overrode those to the west. An interesting feature here are the fractures parallel to the axis of the folds. This is called *axial-plane cleavage*, which is common in folded rocks and allows geologists to determine the configuration of folds even when exposures are limited.

About one-half mile up canyon from the mullion nose, the trail switchbacks up the south wall of Barnhardt Canyon following a side creek that has water in the spring and is graced by sycamore, velvet ash, and Arizona walnut trees. Pinyon pines make their appearance along the trail here.

Partway up the switchbacks, you have good views of the side canyon and the rugged wall beyond it—a good excuse to catch your breath. On this wall, the grayish slopes of the Maverick shale are overlain by the reddish cliffs of the red member of the Mazatzal Peak quartzite. Here, the two units are separated by the Barnhardt Thrust, a low-angle fault along which the upper block has ridden over the lower one.

Open parts of the trail give fine views of the Mogollon Rim to the north. The rim is near the north edge of the latest Mesozoic uplift that formed the ancient Mogollon Highlands. Today's Mazatzal Mountains did not exist at that time: the present range is the product of much younger faulting.

The trail crosses the Barnhardt Thrust just below one of the last switchbacks and below the base of a purplish cliff of quartzite at about 5100 feet. As you climb here, cuts in the trail show the Maverick shale, then a few feet of no rocks, which marks the location of the thrust fault, followed by reddish quartzite. Fracture fillings of white quartz are abundant in the broken rock of the quartzite cliff above the thrust.

Once over the quartzite cliff, the trail contours westward, passing a small canyon where water flows over bedrock in the spring. This is a great place for a rest. To the north, across Barnhardt Canyon, you can see a conspicuous unit that forms dip slopes as well as pinnacles. This is the Deadman quartzite, which overlies the Maverick shale and here is folded into a *syncline*, a trough-shaped fold.

After continuing along the trail a few hundred feet, you can see intense deformation in the quartzite to the north, across the headwaters of the side canyon. About one-fourth mile farther, the trail crosses a glade of ponderosa pine and approaches an impressive slot canyon that is cut into the quartzite and has water in the spring. Slot canyons generally develop in hard rocks. Just before the canyon, you can see preserved *ripple marks* in the quartzite along the trail. These tell us that the water in which the sand was deposited either had a current or was so shallow that the bottom felt wave action.

In another one-fourth mile, the trail rounds a prominent nose, beyond which is the subdued and scrub-covered upper part of Barnhardt Canyon. The nose gives a great view of the west-dipping Barnhardt Thrust and the red quartzite cliffs above it.

Beyond the nose, whitish quartzite fragments along the trail are from outcrops of the white member of the Mazatzal quartzite. Then, the quartzite gives way to rounded cobbles and pebbles of various rock types that include granite and a pebbly sandstone rather like the Tapeats of Cambrian age. The rounding of these gravels indicates that they were transported by a river. These Miocene gravels were deposited in an ancient valley that occupies the subdued country up valley and the notch in the divide at the end of the Barnhardt Trail.

You can end the hike here. If you continue, the trail crosses a charming glade of ponderosa pine, oak, and Douglas fir about 1 mile beyond the prominent nose.

These trees form a relict population that will vanish if the climate becomes even warmer or drier. During the last ice age, plants such as these were widespread at lower elevations, but were forced upward to maintain their habitat as the climate became drier and warmer. Now they are "island populations" and are found only on high mountaintops, their last refuge in this desert country.

Boulders of basalt containing green crystals of olivine become abundant at the far end of the glade. They come from Miocene basalt that crops out in the bluffs south of Mazatzal Divide. The divide is a little more than 6000 feet high and underlain by Miocene river gravel.

BLACK CANYON AND COLEMAN TRAILS

Hike 20

Proterozoic igneous rocks along this scenic trail provide a picture of what was going on at the edge of the growing North American continent 1800 million years ago.

LOCATION ■ Mingus Mountain, Prescott National Forest

DISTANCE ■ 7.7 miles one way

ELEVATION ■ 4120 to 7250 feet

DIFFICULTY ■ Strenuous day hike, moderate two-day backpack

TOPOGRAPHIC MAPS ■ Cottonwood, AZ, 1:24,000; Prescott, AZ, 1:100,000

GEOLOGIC MAPS ■ 21

PRECAUTIONS ■ This is a long hike; bring plenty of water. Snow is a danger in winter, lightning in summer. Heavy brush discourages wearing shorts.

INFORMATION ■ Prescott National Forest, Verde Ranger District

Landscape and Geology: The trail climbs up the east face of the Black Hills, aiming for a high point near Mingus Mountain. The face was formed by movement on the Verde fault, a down-to-the-northeast normal fault that has been active on and off since Proterozoic time.

Movements on Verde fault in Miocene time formed the Verde Basin, one of the basins typical of the Arizona Transition Zone. The basin was then partially filled by the Verde Formation, composed of Miocene and Pliocene lake beds and gravel. These beds were themselves cut by later movement on the Verde fault. We can get a measure of the amount of Tertiary displacement on the fault from the Hickey basalt of Miocene age, which caps Mingus Mountain. On the other side of the fault, in Verde Valley, this basalt is 2500 feet lower than on Mingus Mountain.

The northeast side of Verde Valley is the Mogollon Rim, a line of erosional cliffs that marks the edge of the Colorado Plateau.

Most rocks along the trail are Proterozoic basalt and *rhyolite* (a high-silica

155

lava) that were deposited on the southern margin of the North American continent. The continent had been growing outward from its ancient core in Canada for more than 1 billion years and had reached this area about 1800 million years ago. It grew by incorporating volcanic and sedimentary rocks derived from *island arcs* similar to the present-day Japanese archipelago.

In most places, these ancient rocks have been metamorphosed, making it difficult to identify their original character. Think of the dark schist and gneiss at the bottom of the Grand Canyon. In the Black Hills, however, metamorphism has been slight, enabling us to see many original features and to decipher what was going on in this area so long ago.

In the upper part of the trail, Proterozoic rocks are overlain by the Cambrian Tapeats sandstone, which is 590 million years old. The erosional surface (*unconformity*) between the two represents an interval of 1200 million years whose rock record has vanished without a trace. This is twice as long as the interval between the Cambrian, when life began to explode on Earth, and the present day.

Above the Tapeats are the Martin Formation of Devonian age and a few remnants of the Mississippian Redwall limestone, about 330 million years old. All are overlain by the much younger Hickey Formation (12 to 14 million years old), a thick sequence of olivine basalt and sediments. The contact between the Miocene Hickey and the Paleozoic strata is another erosional unconformity, which in this case represents more than 300 million years.

The basalt on the Colorado Plateau across Verde Valley is part of the San Francisco volcanic field and is much younger than the Hickey basalt on Mingus Mountain. This pattern occurs all along the south margin of the plateau, telling us that volcanism is migrating north onto the plateau over time.

In many parts of the world, basaltic volcanism is accompanied by *rifting*, the dropping down of large blocks along normal faults due to the crust being pulled apart. Volcanism has already migrated onto the plateau, so we infer that rifting will soon follow. The Arizona Transition Zone is eating its way into the Colorado Plateau.

Trail Guide: Turn south onto AZ 260 at the junction of Arizona 89A with AZ 260, 1 mile west of the bridge across the Verde River. After 2.9 miles, and just south of MP 209, turn west onto Ogden Ranch Road, a wide gravel road. Set the odometer reading to zero here. This road soon crosses the old highway, then gets smaller and potentially muddy and climbs increasingly steep pediments. Cross the trashed-out parking area at 4.5 miles and continue through the gate for 0.1 mile to a wider spot in the track to park. Scout around to find where the trail goes down to some large live oaks in the nearby wash. This is the unmarked start of the Black Canyon Trail, #114.

The trail climbs out on the west side of the wash, then meanders around on various pediment surfaces. Cottonwood trees and a water trough mark Quail Spring. About 1 mile from the start, after crossing several washes and a fence, the trail climbs southward around a prominent nose in gravel of the Verde Formation. This a good place to enjoy a fine view northeast across the Verde Valley to the Mogollon Rim near Sedona and the San Francisco Peaks on the skyline.

The trail crosses the Verde fault near a small wash just beyond the nose. The fault itself is not visible, but you know you have crossed it because you start seeing outcrops of the cream-colored, brecciated, and flow-banded Deception rhyolite of Proterozoic age, an amazing 1800 million years older than the gravel.

The "improved" trail ends beyond the wash and the Proterozoic Shea basalt begins. In the stratigraphic layer cake, this basalt underlies the Deception rhyolite. The basalt weathers pinkish-tan, is dark gray on fresh surfaces, and forms a subdued landscape with few outcrops. At some time in the past, minerals in this rock were altered chemically by hot fluids percolating through them. The fluids also deposited veins of quartz and pistachio-green *epidote,* a calcium-aluminum-iron silicate mineral. Nevertheless, you can still see flow banding and *amygdules*—vesicles filled with minerals such as calcite or quartz. These are the same things you would see in a geologically young rhyolite.

About one-half mile beyond the fault, you come to a second prominent nose marked by a conspicuous juniper tree and large rocks painted orange. From here you have views to the southwest of spectacular pinnacles in and near Black Canyon. These are made of the tough Buzzard rhyolite, which underlies the Shea basalt. During the runoff season, you can see inviting waterfalls and large pools here, but too far away across rugged country to be reached with any ease.

Across the canyon, the southeasterly trace of the Verde fault is marked by rounded humps of Verde Formation gravel to the left of the fault and by cottonwood patches near springs. The springs are there because fault *gouge*—ground-up rock—is impermeable to groundwater flowing downhill through the rocks, forcing it to rise to the surface.

Continuing on the trail, keep your eyes open for a conspicuous boulder-shaped outcrop to the right of the trail and a few tens of feet beyond the juniper tree. On its surface, you can see irregular blobs several inches across surrounded by grayish shells that have weathered below the surface of the outcrop. These blobs are *pillow basalt*, formed when red-hot lava flowed into water, creating pillow-shaped masses whose outer surfaces cooled rapidly and solidified into glassy rinds. The rinds are the shells you see here.

The process of molten lava hissing its way into the sea and forming pillows can be seen today in Hawaii and has been photographed in spectacular underwater movies. The pillows on this trail tell us that the processes we see today

Pillows in Shea basalt of Proterozoic age

were taking place 1800 million years ago. About one-half mile beyond the juniper tree, the trails enters the Proterozoic Buzzard rhyolite, a glassy and almost black rock that weathers tan, and forms many outcrops because it is so tough. Contorted *flow banding* and *flow breccia* are common in this volcanic rock; both formed when the cooling lava was flowing like taffy.

About 1.25 miles farther, you cross two branches of a major wash. Both have water in the spring. Brush makes the going heavy here as the trail climbs around a prominent nose. About 400 feet beyond the nose, the trail enters the Proterozoic-age Gaddes basalt, in which it remains until near its junction with the Allen Spring road. This rock weathers pinkish tan and is gray but not glassy on fresh surfaces. Conspicuous flow banding and breccia are absent.

So far, you have been going *down* in the stratigraphic section (that is, the formations are getting older) even though you have been climbing *up* on the ground. How can this be? The answer is that the formations dip more steeply toward Verde Valley than the slope of the topographic surface (see figure 18).

About one-half mile from the wash, you enter a new world: leaving dry brushy slopes, you drop into Black Canyon, a pleasant, well-forested valley with a stream. This is a good place to rest in the shade.

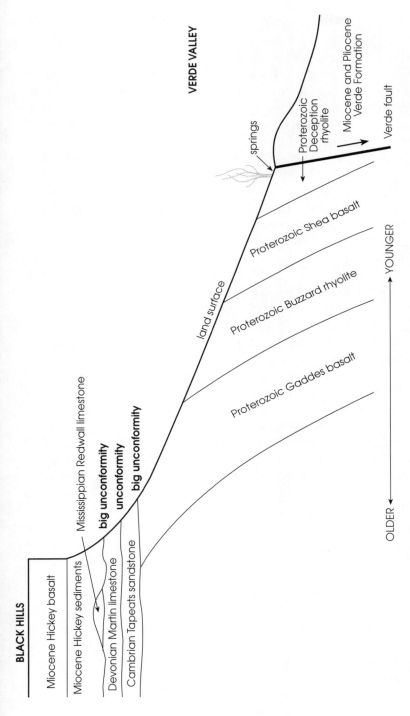

Figure 18. Schematic cross section showing how you get into older and older Proterozoic rock units as you walk up the slope toward the Black Hills. The dip of these units is exaggerated to make the point clearer. The Cenozoic rocks that cap the Black Hills cut across the Paleozoic units.

At one-half mile after entering Black Canyon, the trail turns north into Gaddes Wash, graced by water flowing from a fine spring. Here you can find water-polished outcrops of Gaddes basalt. Brown cobbles and boulders of coarse sandstone become noticeable in the wash debris. This is the Cambrian Tapeats sandstone, which crops out on the flanks of the valley, but not along the trail. About 1 mile upstream from Black Canyon, the trail becomes a track, which then turns west, crosses the wash, and intersects FR 413 (Allen Spring Road) on which you turn right.

After crossing Gaddes Wash again, you can see outcrops of well-bedded light gray dolomitic limestone with sandstone and shale interbeds. This is the Devonian Martin limestone, which here rests directly on the Tapeats sandstone; the Cambrian Bright Angel shale and Muav limestone of the Grand Canyon are missing. A little farther along are outcrops of conglomerate containing rounded pebbles of Paleozoic limestone. This is the sedimentary part of the Miocene Hickey Formation.

About one-half mile from the crossing of Gaddes Wash, turn left onto the Coleman Trail, #108, marked by a brown sign. The trail starts out in the Martin Formation, which soon gives way to slope wash covered by chaparral. Outcrops of vesicular basalt begin partway up the slope. This is the Miocene Hickey basalt, with abundant olivine crystals altered to the rust-colored iron-rich mineral *iddingsite*.

After cresting in a low saddle, turn right, leaving the trail and keeping to open ground to reach a scenic viewpoint about 1500 feet to the southeast on a spur of Mingus Mountain. From here you have a splendid view across Verde Valley of the edge of the Colorado Plateau at Sedona's red cliffs and of the mountains of the San Francisco volcanic field.

The thick basalt of Mingus Mountain is 13 to 15 million years old and was formed before the Verde Valley. In contrast, the unfaulted basalt platform that you can see across the valley and the cinder cones near Flagstaff are between 6 million and 1,000 years old. This gives you a visual impression of how volcanism has been migrating northeastward with time. Faulting is sure to follow soon, so you can have fun visualizing another trough like the Verde Valley where Flagstaff is now. Residents of Flagstaff who wish to move to a warmer climate need only stay put and wait a million years or two!

In this area, the contact between the relatively flat-lying Paleozoic rocks and the Proterozoic rocks beneath them is at about 6500 feet elevation. At the Mogollon Rim across Verde Valley, the same contact is far below the surface of the Colorado Plateau. This is a graphic illustration of the once lofty height of the ancient Mogollon Highlands uplift, of which the Black Hills and Mingus Mountain are a part.

COON BUTTE SPRING TRAIL

This undemanding hike through the Proterozoic Apache Group leads to a perennial spring near the headwaters of Coon Creek.

LOCATION ■ Sierra Ancha Wilderness, Tonto National Forest

DISTANCE ■ 2.75 miles one way

ELEVATION ■ 5000 to 4400 feet

DIFFICULTY ■ Easy

TOPOGRAPHIC MAPS ■ Aztec Peak, AZ, 1:24,000; Seneca, AZ, 1:100,000

GEOLOGIC MAPS ■ 19

PRECAUTIONS ■ Snow and cold in winter, lightning and heat during summer. A four-wheel-drive vehicle is recommended.

INFORMATION ■ Tonto National Forest, Pleasant Valley Ranger District

Landscape and Geology: This hike is on the south face of the Sierra Ancha mountain complex. You will have the opportunity to look at part of the Proterozoic Apache Group (see figure 17) and to see how rock type influences the landscape. Much of the hike is in the lower part of the Mescal limestone. This rock unit was originally a *dolomite* (a sedimentary rock made of calcium-magnesium carbonate), but here it has been metamorphosed ("baked") into *limestone* (calcium carbonate) by the heat from intrusions of molten igneous rock. Throughout the Apache Group, these intrusions created nearly horizontal sills of diabase, the intrusive, coarser grained equivalent of basalt.

The upper part of the Mescal includes siltstone, *argillite* (hard claystone), and beds of finely laminated limestone rich in *stromatolites,* fossils of ancient algae.

The Dripping Spring quartzite is a hard, reddish, cross-bedded sandstone that is under the Mescal and forms a massive cliff below the trail. The trail contours on top of this cliff for about three-fourths mile, then descends into the canyon, giving you the opportunity to examine the rock in the cliff. The Dripping Spring quartzite cliff is a prominent feature of the landscape in the Sierra Ancha.

Trail Guide: Traveling north on Arizona Highway 288, the Young Road, cross the Salt River and turn right near milepost 265 onto all-weather dirt FS 203, marked by a brown sign for Coon and Cherry Creeks. Reset the odometer to zero.

The road meanders through diabase, granite, and light-colored volcanic sedimentary rocks. At mile 9, bear right across pretty Coon Creek, with trees and perennial water, following the brown sign "Rd 203." At the pass between Coon and Cherry Creeks, mile 10.5, turn left onto a road marked by a sign for Bull Canyon Road and Sierra Ancha Wilderness.

This road starts out harmlessly enough in Proterozoic granite country, but washouts soon make it impassable to passenger cars. Much of the road is steep and narrow, and on an exposed sidehill, so exercise caution. After climbing a sidehill in granite, the road brings you magnificent exposures of Proterozoic rocks between miles 12.3 and 13.3. It is worth stopping to look, if you can find a place to park the car.

At mile 12.3, directly above the granite, you can see a small bench underlain by conglomerate containing rounded pebbles. This is the Scanlan Conglomerate Member of the Pioneer Formation at the base of the Proterozoic Apache Group.

The Pioneer Formation forms the cliffy exposures above the conglomerate. It is a reddish and cross-bedded feldspar-rich sandstone. A diabase sill is intruded into the middle of the formation.

Another conglomerate with rounded pebbles—the Barnes Conglomerate Member of the Dripping Spring quartzite—crops out at about mile 13.1. From here to about mile 15, the road is in the Dripping Spring quartzite, mostly reddish and cross-bedded.

For the last 1.6 miles to the trailhead at mile 16.6, you drive on a bench developed in the lower part of the Mescal limestone. There is a parking area at the trailhead but no other facilities. Note that the vegetation near Coon Butte Spring was affected by the Coon Creek Fire in 2000.

The trail is marked by a Sierra Ancha Wilderness sign. After walking about one-fourth mile across a gentle saddle, turn left at the trail junction marked by a sign for Coon Spring and Coon Creek Trails. The trail is an old jeep road on the Mescal limestone.

At one-half mile from the junction, the trail turns north and goes up a gentle slope to a saddle, ahead and to the right of which are ledges of whitish rock in the upper part of the Mescal. This part of the formation has been stripped from the bench on which you have been walking.

Well-bedded, finely laminated Mescal limestone crops out along the trail in the downgrade beyond the saddle. The wavy lamination is typical of *stromatolites*, which are fossils of ancient algae. The fibrous mat formed by the algae on the shallow sea floor was a good trap for fine sediments, thus creating the fine layers.

The trail next follows a bench on top of the cliff made by the upper part of the Dripping Spring quartzite. The bench was made by erosion of the softer Mescal from the top of the very hard and resistant Dripping Spring. High at the head of the canyon you can see the whitish cliffs of the Troy quartzite, which is above the Mescal and forms the top of the Proterozoic-age Apache Group. The bench on top of the Troy is carved into a diabase sill that intruded the quartzite. The part of the Troy above the sill is near the top of Aztec Peak (Hike 18).

Notice that formations resistant to erosion and weathering, such as the Pioneer, Dripping Spring, and Troy, form cliffs, whereas softer units such as the Mescal limestone and the diabase form the more subdued terrain of slopes and benches. This property is helpful when trying to sort out the geology of an area from a distance.

After walking on the bench for about 1 mile, you switchback down into Coon Creek past excellent outcrops of the upper part of the Dripping Spring quartzite. This unit is made of finely laminated, cross-bedded, white to purple quartzite. With a hand lens, you can see rounded grains of quartz, as well as the quartz *overgrowths* that fill the voids between the grains and make this into a very hard rock, the reason for the cliff. The cross beds have a low angle, and they are scooped-out or troughshaped instead of being parallel. These characteristics tell you that the sand that originally formed this formation was deposited in moving water rather than being a fossil dune.

Quartzite cliffs along Coon Creek Canyon

Once below the cliff, you can see a disturbed zone of rocks along the trail: this is a block of Mescal limestone dropped down against the Dripping Spring by a small fault. Most of the white material is limestone "cooked" by a diabase intrusion, which you can see above and below the disturbed zone. The rest of the way down the slope to the creek you walk on diabase mantled by scree, or talus.

There is a spring at the bottom of the canyon in a magnificent copse of live oaks and sycamores. It is developed and provides perennial flow out of a pipe.

DEEP CREEK TRAIL

This trail in the Proterozoic-age Apache Group meanders through open chaparral and savannah country to a remarkable viewpoint.

LOCATION ■ Sierra Ancha Wilderness, Tonto National Forest

DISTANCE ■ 5.25 miles one way

ELEVATION ■ 5000 to 5500 feet

DIFFICULTY ■ Moderate

TOPOGRAPHIC MAPS ■ Aztec Peak, AZ, 1:24,000; Sombrero Peak, AZ, 1:24,000; Seneca, AZ, 1:100,000

GEOLOGIC MAPS ■ 19

PRECAUTIONS ■ Snow and cold in winter, heat and lightning in summer

INFORMATION ■ Tonto National Forest, Pleasant Valley Ranger District

Landscape and Geology: This hike, on the open south slope of the Sierra Ancha mountain complex, illustrates how the physical properties of rock formations in the Proterozoic Apache Group influence the landscape. The soft, poorly resistant Mescal limestone and diabase intrusions form subdued, open country, whereas the very hard and erosion-resistant Troy quartzite at the top of the group forms imposing cliffs. Even the quality of the trail depends on the rock type: walking is easy in the Mescal and diabase but difficult in the talus, or *scree*, below the Troy cliffs.

The hike ends at a remote viewpoint that provides an awesome view of the wild and intricate country of the Arizona Transition Zone and the edge of the Colorado Plateau.

Trail Guide: The trailhead for Deep Creek Trail #128 is the same as that for the Coon Butte Spring Trail. See Hike 21 for the directions to the trailhead. Be sure to take a look at the great exposures of the lower part of the Apache Group along the road.

The trail is mostly in rolling open terrain formed by the Mescal limestone, whose resistance to erosion is relatively low. The cliffs to the north are Troy quartzite, as is most of Coon Butte to the west. This formation is *well-indurated* (hardened) and holds up cliffs wherever it is exposed.

Cross-bedded sandstone in the lower part of the Mescal is exposed on the other side of the shallow saddle just north of the trailhead. Less than one-fourth mile beyond that you come to the junction with the Coon Creek Spring Trail; go straight, as indicated by the sign for Deep Creek and Moody Point Trails.

The trail climbs and descends gently here through manzanita chaparral and an attractive savannah of alligator juniper. The trail is good in the flat parts, but rocky on the slopes, which are littered with *chert* (microcrystalline silica) nodules that have eroded out of limestone.

About 2 miles from the trailhead, you cross Deep Creek in a nice grove of live oaks, junipers, and a few ponderosa pines just above exposures of the Dripping Spring quartzite. You then grunt up the north side of the creek valley until you contour on a talus slope littered with pieces of light-colored Troy quartzite and a scattering of boulders of purplish conglomerate, also from the Troy.

The walking is not easy here below the Troy cliff because quartzite makes no soil. You will enjoy easier footing when you get on soft dark soil derived from a diabase intrusion upslope from the trail and below the quartzite cliff. As you can see, geology has a direct impact on your hiking pleasure.

The trail eventually cuts across the *sill* (a nearly horizontal intrusion) for a short distance, as you can see from outcrops of tan-colored weathered diabase. If you examine a fresh exposure with your hand lens, you can see the characteristic texture of diabase—needles of light-colored feldspar in a dark *groundmass* (background) of the mineral pyroxene. *Diabase* is the coarse-grained intrusive equivalent of basalt. Slower cooling at deeper depths gives the crystals a chance to grow larger, thus creating the coarser texture.

Now here is a little geology quiz for you. Locate the dark-colored boulders along the trail just beyond a small wash. Examine one using your hand lens. Can you identify this rock? Note that it is dark, fine-grained, pitted (vesicular), and with no layering. This indicates that it is not sedimentary, is most likely igneous, and that it cooled near the surface since it has no crystals. If you answered basalt, then you are correct. The only problem is that the geologic map shows no basalt here! But you can see a distinctive dark layer if you look upslope toward the base of the Troy cliff. This layer is indeed a basalt between the Mescal limestone and the Troy quartzite, presumably the same one that forms Workman Creek Falls along the Aztec Peak Trail (Hike 18). The dark layer is certainly in the right place in the layer cake for this. We may have made a new contribution to geologic knowledge of this place, and this is fun.

For about the next mile, the trail becomes indistinct; keep your eyes open to avoid losing it. Eventually you cross a fork of Deep Creek, which is along a down-to-the-west fault that drops the upper part of the Mescal against the lower part. The trail now switches back up a ridge, near the top of which it Ts into the Moody Point Trail, #140. Go left on trail #140.

Go a few hundred feet to the crest of the ridge. Now you must abandon the trail and go south cross-country along the ridge to the top of a small rise. You have now arrived at the end of the hike and can rest, enjoying the spectacular view. The gray limestone on the rise is a small remnant of the upper Mescal. The fine and wavy lamination is characteristic of *stromatolites*, fossil mats of algae that were an early form of life.

The deep valley immediately to the west is that of Cherry Creek. The Moody Point Trail works its way down into this valley along the slope just below you. Most of the cliffs on this slope are of Dripping Spring quartzite; some are held up by the Pioneer Formation. The geology of the slope is complicated by faults and folds that run about parallel to the slope.

The intricately dissected country east of Cherry Creek is underlain by Tertiary-age basin beds, volcanic sediments, and river gravel, which crop out in places as whitish exposures. Geologists have shown that the gravel is part of a river system that once drained north from the Mogollon Highlands onto the Colorado Plateau.

The lowest subdued cliff in the higher ground north of the basin beds is held up by the Pioneer Formation. The bench above it is in diabase, and the overlying cliffs are in the Dripping Spring quartzite. The Troy quartzite holds up the

View of the Cherry Creek valley from near the Moody Point Trail. Tertiary basin beds and silicic volcanic rocks are exposed in the low area east of Cherry Creek.

166

higher wooded mountains to the northeast. Far to the northeast you can glimpse the Mogollon Rim, which is the edge of the Colorado Plateau. The subdued rise to the east on the far skyline is the Mount Baldy complex in the White Mountains, about 75 miles away. Mount Baldy is a shield volcano (Hike 12).

The low terrain east and southeast of you is the valley of the Salt River, beyond which rises the dark hump of the Pinaleno Mountains, nearly 100 miles away. The Pinal Mountains south of the town of Globe form the high mountain complex on the skyline to the south. If you now look in the middle distance to the northwest, you can see the prominent Troy cliff at whose foot you have been hiking. Beyond it rises Aztec Peak, capped by Cambrian sandstone (Hike 18).

FOUR PEAKS, AMETHYST, AND BROWNS TRAILS

Hike 23

The drive to the trailhead is as spectacular as the hike itself, which is in a cool forest with great views and reveals the top of an ancient pluton.

LOCATION ■ Four Peaks Wilderness, Tonto National Forest

DISTANCE ■ About 4.3 miles round trip for the loop

ELEVATION ■ 5700 to 6860 feet

DIFFICULTY ■ Easy to moderate

TOPOGRAPHIC MAPS ■ Four Peaks, AZ, 1:24,000; Theodore Roosevelt Lake, AZ, 1:100,000

GEOLOGIC MAPS ■ None

PRECAUTIONS ■ Snow in winter, lightning in summer

INFORMATION ■ Tonto National Forest, Tonto Basin Ranger District or Mesa Ranger District

Landscape and Geology: The Four Peaks are near the south end of the rugged Mazatzal Range. They are a landmark easily recognized from afar and owe both their height and distinctive shape to roof pendants of Proterozoic-age Mazatzal quartzite and Maverick shale engulfed by 1500 million-year-old granite. *Roof pendants* are remnants of the *country rock* (the surrounding or preexisting rock) into which an igneous pluton is intruded. They occur at the top, or roof, of the intrusive mass.

At the contact between intrusion and country rock, both rocks are altered by *contact metamorphism.* The intrusive granite near the contact is cooled rapidly, resulting in smaller crystals (fine grains) and is usually banded, or *foliated.* The foliation is produced by shearing or friction within the moving plastic granite magma near the contact. The country rock is "baked" and altered by fluids coming from the magma. The altered rock may be so fine-grained that no

Looking north along the axis of the Mazatzal Mountains; in the foreground is quartzite.

grains are visible. This is called a *hornfels*, the bane of geology students who think they are alone in not being able to identify these rocks.

The rugged massif of the Four Peaks stands in sharp relief because the Mazatzal quartzite, of which it is made, is a very hard rock, made even harder here by recrystallization and the addition of *silica* (quartz) near the granite intrusion.

Trail Guide: Turn east from Arizona Highway 87 (Phoenix to Payson) onto paved Arizona Highway 188. Just north of milepost 255, turn west onto El Oso Road, FR 143. Set the trip odometer to zero. El Oso Road is dirt and very steep in places, but should be passable for normal passenger cars under dry conditions. The road climbs about 3500 feet from Tonto Basin, and the views eastward into the basin and across Roosevelt Lake to the Sierra Ancha are breathtaking and well worth a stop or two.

After 8.9 miles on El Oso Road, you reach El Oso Divide and the junction with FR 422. Bear left (south), staying on FR 143. At mile 10, bear left again onto FR 648, and follow this road past Pigeon Spring trailhead to the trailhead at Lone Pine Saddle, mile 11.4.

The trailhead is in a forest of ponderosa and pinyon pine, alligator juniper, and oak. These trees once grew at much lower elevations, but are now restricted to the mountaintop by the present climate, which is much drier and warmer than it was some 12,000 years ago at the end of the last ice age. If the climate gets any warmer and drier, this island population will have nowhere to go and will eventually disappear.

In the road cut just north of the parking lot, you can see granite so eroded and weathered that it is recognized as bedrock only by the quartz veins that cut through it. Such weathering of granite produces *grus*, a coarse sand composed of quartz and feldspar grains.

The large boulders surrounding the parking area are mostly of Mazatzal quartzite with fine, wavy bedding. Look at this rock, which is a metamorphosed sandstone, with your hand lens: notice that fresh surfaces look glassy. You can see the faint outlines of rounded quartz grains, the original sand grains before the sandstone was metamorphosed. Much later, the mineral silica (SiO_2) was deposited around the quartz grains, filling the voids between grains; it was then recrystallized. The result is *quartzite*, an exceptionally hard and durable rock.

Some of the boulders around the parking lot are made of fine-grained granite. One boulder on the east side is of coarse-grained granite containing large crystals of pinkish orthoclase feldspar and smaller black hexagons of the dark mica *biotite*. This is the 1500 million-year-old granite that intruded the quartzite.

The granite erodes, or *exfoliates*, in characteristic rounded forms along the Four Peaks Trail, #130, which contours on the east side of the divide. Exposures of the granite come to an end after walking about 1 mile and crossing a couple of gullies. At this point, you can see a banded *gneiss* (a metamorphic rock) that formed near the margin of the granite intrusion.

About 1000 feet beyond the gneiss outcrops, turn right onto Amethyst Trail, #253, which is deeply worn, showing the effects of erosion on a trail that is too steep. The rocks exposed along this trail are quartzite and nondescript fine-grained metamorphic rocks best classified as *hornfels*, which were originally Maverick shale. They are near the contact zone between the granite intrusion and the quartzite country rock.

After 1 mile and a 1200-foot climb, you reach Browns Saddle, just north of Browns Peak. Outcrops along the ridge toward Browns Peak consist of dark, banded, fine-grained hornfels. Quartzite crops out on the shoulder of the peak. The peak itself is a large mass of quartzite.

You will find no easy and non-technical way of climbing the peak from here, but you can scramble around on its north shoulder. If you wish to walk a little farther before turning back, you can continue on the Amethyst Trail, which contours around the west side of the peaks for a couple of miles.

Return to the parking lot from Browns Saddle on Browns Trail, #133, which stays near the crest of the ridge. After about 15 minutes of walking back, you reach a prominent switchback, beyond which the trail goes back into granite and the typical pleasant landscape of rounded outcrops. No large crystals are visible at the contact zone, but they gradually increase in number as you walk away from it. Dark inclusions of mafic rock are common, most standing out in relief because they are more resistant to erosion than the granite.

JUG TRAIL TO SALOME CREEK

The granite dells carved out of the Proterozoic-age Ruin granite along Salome Creek are one of my favorite places.

LOCATION ■ Salome Wilderness, Sierra Ancha, Tonto National Forest

DISTANCE ■ 2.2 miles one way

ELEVATION ■ 3320 to 2680 feet

DIFFICULTY ■ Easy

TOPOGRAPHIC MAPS ■ Armer Mountain, AZ, 1:24,000; Greenback Creek, AZ, 1:24,000; Theodore Roosevelt Lake, AZ, 1:100,000

GEOLOGIC MAPS ■ 19

PRECAUTIONS ■ The trail is very hot in the summer. Tonto Creek is often impassable during spring floods.

INFORMATION ■ Tonto National Forest, Tonto Basin Ranger District

Landscape and Geology: The Sierra Ancha and nearby Mazatzal Mountains are part of the Laramide orogenic belt of uplift that formed the ancient Mogollon Highlands. The *Laramide orogeny* was the major mountain-building event at the Cretaceous–Tertiary boundary. Because of the uplift, Proterozoic rocks, normally far below the surface, are now exposed here at the surface by erosion.

The oldest rock exposed along Salome Creek is the Ruin granite, which is 1400 to 1500 million years old. Directly above the granite is a *sill*, a nearly horizontal tabular mass intruded into preexisting rock; it is made of Proterozoic diabase. Above it is the Proterozoic Apache Group (see figures 17 and 19).

Several formations that make up the Apache Group are *quartzite*, a metamorphosed sandstone that is very resistant to erosion. Because of this, the quartzite forms cliffs, which are much in evidence on the flanks of Dutchman Butte, directly east of Salome Creek. In contrast, rocks such as *diabase* (the coarse-grained equivalent of basalt), composed largely of iron- and magnesium-rich minerals, weather easily. These rocks tend to form slopes.

At Salome Creek, the lowest sill is intruded just below the contact between granite and the lowest part of the Apache Group. Proterozoic rocks above this level were at least 1400 feet thick. When the sill was intruded, it had to lift the entire weight of this column of rock above it. Calculating the weight of this rock column, you find that the diabase magma was intruded at a pressure of at least 1600 pounds per square inch.

The hike is on the west flank of the Sierra Ancha, near where the range ends. One of the range-front normal faults responsible for the transition from the range to Tonto Basin is exposed near Salome Creek, where it drops geologically young Tertiary gravel against very ancient Proterozoic Ruin granite. South of Dutchmans Butte, this fault has an offset of about 1000 feet.

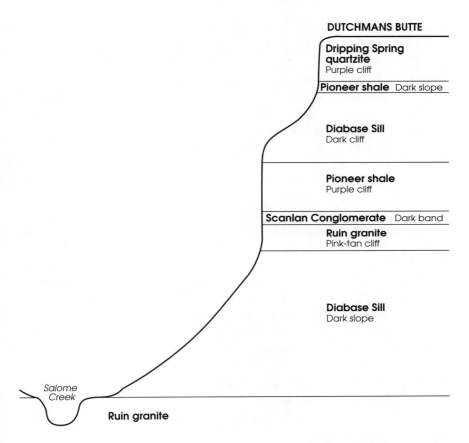

DUTCHMANS BUTTE

Dripping Spring quartzite
Purple cliff

Pioneer shale   Dark slope

Diabase Sill
Dark cliff

Pioneer shale
Purple cliff

Scanlan Conglomerate   Dark band
Ruin granite
Pink-tan cliff

Diabase Sill
Dark slope

Salome Creek

Ruin granite

Figure 19. Rocks of the Apache Group exposed on the west side of Salome Creek. The vertical parts of the section represent cliffs and the sloping ones represent slopes. The prominent slopes are underlain by diabase sills, one of which intrudes the top of the Ruin granite, the other the top of the Pioneer shale. (Note that the Ruin is not part of the Apache Group.)

Trail Guide: Turn east from AZ 87 (Phoenix to Payson) onto the paved AZ 188. At milepost 255, turn east onto a dirt road marked by "A + cross road" sign. Set the odometer to zero. After about 1 mile, you will see the brown sign "Salome 15 mi" and the ford across Tonto Creek. Do not attempt to ford if the water is high.

At the junction at mile 1.5, go straight on the paved road indicated by the "Salome Creek" sign. At the 2.5-mile junction, bear left onto a dirt road marked by the A + road sign. This road is graveled and passable to passenger vehicles, but at about mile 4.5 it might be muddy after a rain.

The road reaches a saddle at mile 9.6 after a long climb that gives you fine views of Roosevelt Lake and the Four Peaks across the basin (Hike 23). The saddle has a cattle guard across the road and Cactus Butte to the south. About 1 mile later, just where the road starts following a narrow ridge, park in the dirt parking area marked by the "A + trailhead" sign. This is the start of Jug Trail, #61, which takes you into the Salome Wilderness and to Salome Creek.

The old jeep trail that you walk on winds around in the intricate landscape developed in Tertiary river gravel. This kind of topography is characteristic of poorly consolidated conglomerate and gravel and is helpful to identify areas underlain by such deposits. You can see cobbles of many rock types, some angular, some rounded, in a fine-grained mud background, or *matrix*. Note the occasional white crust of *caliche,* calcium carbonate deposited near the surface by soil-forming processes. The amount of rounding of the cobbles in the gravel indicates they were transported quite far. This could not happen just from movement of talus on a slope, so the deposit must in part be reworked from preexisting river deposits.

At 1.25 miles, after a third major reentrant (gully), the trail suddenly enters an area underlain by granite, which weathers into rounded knobs and forms granite sand called *grus*. Saguaro cacti become abundant here. They evidently prefer bedrock to gravelly slopes. You have crossed the range-front normal fault that places Tertiary gravel against Proterozoic granite. The same fault goes through the saddle south of Dutchmans Butte on the other side of Salome Creek.

It is worth stopping near here to look at the fine exposure of the lower part of the Apache Group on the flank of Dutchmans Butte. This group is roughly the same age as the Unkar Group of the Grand Canyon.

The granite you are standing on forms the gorge of Salome Creek. This is the coarse-grained Ruin granite of Proterozoic age. Normally, the Pioneer Formation is directly above the granite, from which it is separated by an erosional *unconformity* (gap in the geologic record) that represents several hundred million years. Here, however, the slope above the granite gorge

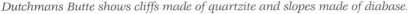

Dutchmans Butte shows cliffs made of quartzite and slopes made of diabase.

Weather-smoothed Ruin granite along Salome Creek. Large boulders of granite and diabase litter the channel, as well as a few boulders of conglomerate.

is underlain by a thick sill of Proterozoic diabase, and more granite is at the base of the cliff halfway up the slope (see figure 19).

The main part of the lower cliff across the valley consists of bedded and purplish Pioneer Formation. The distinct dark band at its base is the Scanlan Conglomerate Member of the Pioneer Formation (see Hike 21). This conglomerate is at the base of the Apache Group and rests on the Ruin granite, as you see here. The line between conglomerate and granite is the erosional unconformity.

The dark-gray top of the cliff is composed of a second sill of diabase, which also forms the overlying slope. The skyline cliff is composed of the reddish Dripping Spring quartzite, with a thin layer of Pioneer at the base, which you cannot make out from here. The sill was intruded near the top of the formation rather than at the contact between one formation and another, which is what you might expect. One explanation is that the sill intruded itself in whatever rock happened to be present at the level where the pressure of the magma was the same as the weight of the overlying rock column. This is where the sill was able to make room for itself by lifting the rocks above.

After crossing a gate, you are walking on a ledge floored by the granite, with diabase to your left (west). The ledge marks the intrusive contact between the two rock types. It is there because the more easily eroded diabase is removed from the top of the granite.

About 1000 feet beyond the gate, you enter a flat, grassy area. This is a good place to leave the trail and go right a short distance to the creek in its beautiful sculptured gorge.

The water-polished rocks here are a photographer's paradise. Once you have satisfied that urge, and maybe taken a dip in one of the nice pools if the weather is warm, take a good look at the granite and the dark boulders of diabase as well. It is not often that you get to see diabase this fresh. With your hand lens, you can see the classic *ophitic* texture, with white needles of plagioclase feldspar in a dark groundmass of the mineral pyroxene.

Hike

25

PERALTA CANYON TRAIL

This popular loop hike, with its great views of well-known Weavers Needle, shows you impressive sheets of welded tuff produced by a great volcano in the famous Superstition Mountains.

LOCATION ■ Superstition Wilderness

DISTANCE ■ About 6 miles round trip (via Peralta Canyon and Geronimo Cave)

ELEVATION ■ 2400 to 3850 feet

DIFFICULTY ■ Moderate to strenuous

TOPOGRAPHIC MAPS ■ Weavers Needle 7.5' quadrangle; Mesa 1:100,000

GEOLOGIC MAPS ■ 22

PRECAUTIONS ■ Carry plenty of water in the summer, or hike this trail in cooler months. Trail-finding abilities and scrambling on sloping bare rock are required for this hike.

INFORMATION ■ Tonto National Forest, Mesa Ranger District

Landscape and Geology: The geologic character of this area was shaped by events in Oligocene and Miocene time (about 25 to 15 million years ago), when volcanic activity formed several *calderas*. These were created when so much volcanic material erupted that the roofs of the now-empty magma chambers collapsed downward, forming large circular depressions.

The erupting magma was so charged with gas that it created a glowing froth, capable of traveling great distances at high speed. After coming to rest, the froth solidified into *ash-flow tuff*, the hottest parts of which became welded by the heat. The tuff erupted while the calderas were collapsing, so it accumulated to great thicknesses within the deepening calderas.

Eruptions that produce ash-flow tuffs and calderas are the most violent volcanic phenomena known. One of these calderas, in the western Superstition Mountains, is the focus of this hike.

The Superstition volcanoes were built up on an old and geologically complex foundation made up of igneous and metamorphic rocks of early Proterozoic age, as well as middle Proterozoic sedimentary and intrusive igneous rocks of the Apache Group. These rocks are exposed in the bottom of the Grand Canyon and in the Sierra Ancha, respectively.

Pinnacles weathered out of welded tuff along Peralta Canyon

The Proterozoic rocks here are fractured and relatively easy to erode, thus forming the low terrain south of the Superstition Mountains in the Peralta and Coffee Flat Valleys. In contrast, the welded ash-flow tuffs in the caldera are resistant to erosion and form the rugged high ground of the Superstition Mountains.

The abrupt south flank of the Superstition Mountains coincides with the south margin of the caldera. In the Peralta Canyon area, the margin is made even more visible by a steep east-west fault This fault probably represents renewed activity of the old fault that formed the caldera long ago. The old fault dropped down the block to the north, producing the depression of the caldera, but the younger movement is in the opposite sense, up to the north. This helped lift the western Superstition Mountains above the surrounding plains.

The original caldera can no longer be seen directly. Just north of the Peralta trailhead, its edge is revealed by an abrupt thickening of tuffs as you cross the inferred margin.

Trail Guide: Drive southeast about 9 miles from Apache Junction on US 60/89. Exit at the Peralta Road sign. Peralta Road is a well-traveled dirt road roughed by "washboard" but suitable for normal passenger cars. After about 6 miles on this road, you come to a junction. Follow the left fork, signed "Peralta Trailhead" and "Dons Camp." Continue about 2 more miles to the trailhead. Do not stop at the first Forest Service parking lot, but go to the one at the end of the road, where there is an outhouse but no water. You will be greeted by a ranger who collects parking fees.

This is the start of Peralta Trail, a good trail with moderate elevation gain. The vegetation includes mesquite, catclaw, jojoba, sumac, cottonwood, saguaro, and scrub oak, locally in thickets. The prominent and rugged cliffs to the left (west) are a mass of intrusive *rhyolite* (fine-grained equivalent of granite) whose brecciation is visible even from a distance. The *breccia* (rock broken into angular fragments) was formed during intrusion.

A little farther up the canyon, at about one-fourth mile, you pass into a world composed exclusively of ash-flow tuffs. You have entered the ancient caldera.

Examine the tuffs at the first crossing of the wash, where their surfaces are fresh. Look at the large boulder in the middle of the wash to the left of the trail. You can see dark inclusions of squashed *pumice*, solidified glassy froth. The still-hot clots of pumice were squashed by the weight of overlying rock, producing the dark, lens-shaped masses called *fiamme* that you see in the boulder. Also note the lens-shaped cavities that are gas bubbles or maybe pumice that has weathered out.

Now look at the surface of the boulder with your hand lens. You can see crystals of the black mica biotite, milky feldspar, clear quartz, and the glassy mineral sanidine, which typically has a rounded shape and shows a play of color. *Sanidine* is a high-temperature feldspar rich in potassium. These minerals are typical of the Superstition tuffs. You have more opportunities farther up the trail to look at the tuffs again.

Looking up the canyon, you may be impressed by the many pinnacles visible on the skyline. These are typical of welded tuffs. Welded tuffs crack when they cool, forming vertical fractures, or joints, with many intersecting orientations. Erosion works preferentially along the joints, leaving behind the solid rock between the joints as columns or pinnacles.

As you walk, you may be pleased by the easy footing on the sandy soil of the trail, which may remind you of walking in granite country. Interestingly, granite and rhyolitic welded tuff

Welded tuff. The darks blobs are "fiamme," clots of pumice that were squashed while they were still hot.

have the same composition. Both are rich in quartz, with the quartz eventually weathering out of the rock and concentrating in the sandy soil.

After crossing the wash a second time, the trail goes through some good outcrops of tuff, where you can see conspicuous elongated cavities. Many contain remnants of squashed pumice. Now look toward the east. This is a good place to see how vertical and horizontal joints give rise to the pinnacles, slabs, and blocks that are characteristic weathering shapes for welded tuffs.

At the next crossing of the wash, about 1.5 miles from the trailhead, look down the canyon. You can see a prominent layer of yellow tuff on the east side of the wash. Surprisingly, the color is due primarily to lichens. Note that the yellow tuff is mostly unfractured and weathers into rounded shapes, whereas the tuff on the west side of the wash is jointed and weathers into sharp pinnacles. The difference is due to the degree of welding: the tuff west of the canyon is more welded than the yellow tuff. More-welded tuff tends to crack more, thus forming joints. The degree of welding of a tuff sheet depends on its temperature when it stopped moving. The center is the hottest, so the most welded. A thin zone near the bottom is cooled by the underlying terrain, and a thick zone at the top is cooled by contact with air.

Outcrops farther along the trail give you the opportunity to get close and personal with the yellow tuff. Note that it is full of *lithic* fragments—angular fragments of preexisting rock plucked from the walls of the conduits along which the magma rose or picked up from the surface over which it flowed.

You can also see reddish alteration zones produced by gases and fluids circulating through the tuff.

Just before reaching Fremont Saddle, take a look at the dark blobs of volcanic glass at the base of the unit above the yellow tuff. The unit is a brecciated rhyolite flow that is at the top of the sequence of Superstition volcanic rocks in this area. This rock forms the rise east of the saddle. Now you get your reward for climbing here, about 2.3 miles from the trailhead. Rest, eat your lunch, and enjoy the view. Ahead of you is Weavers Needle and the ruggedly intricate country for which the Superstition Mountains are famous.

The saddle is a good place for thinking a bit about structural geology. The topographic map and the landscape in front of you show that Peralta Canyon lines up with East Boulder Canyon, the canyon north of the saddle. Alignments like this often flag a fault; erosion tends to follow the belt of weak, gouged up rocks along a fault. Sure enough, what you see here is a fault that strikes northwest and dips to the northeast. The movement of the fault is *normal*, that is, the block on the northeast ("above" the fault plane) has moved down relative to the one on the southwest.

How do we know this? Look down Peralta Canyon. On the east side of the canyon, you can see that the yellow tuff lies above the pinnacle-forming tuff. But on the west side, the pinnacle-forming tuff is at the same elevation as the yellow tuff on the east side. The pinnacle tuff was brought up against the yellow tuff because the west block was lifted up along the fault, which runs down the canyon.

To return by completing the loop, continue the hike by going east over the rise composed of the reddish, brecciated rhyolite flow. Follow the trail, marked by cairns, as it wends its way southeast along the ridge. In places, the trail is poorly marked, so keep looking for cairns. Be careful as you make your way down steep slickrock slopes on this stretch.

Near Geronimo Cave, at three-fourths mile from the saddle, the trail follows a bluff at the base of which is a tuff unit that contains pumice and chunks of rhyolite. This tuff is at the base of the rhyolite flow. The contact between the two is well exposed right at the cave. You can also see cross bedding that was probably formed by a *base surge*. Base surges are masses of gas and debris hurled outward at great speed and near ground level from an explosion. If you have ever seen a movie of an atomic bomb exploding, you have seen a base surge: it is the whitish ring that spreads out from the base of the mushroom cloud. Volcanic eruptions can do the same thing.

Before moving on, look up Peralta Canyon: the fault contact between the pinnacled tuff to the west and the yellow tuff to the east is nicely displayed here.

About 1 mile beyond the cave, the trail joins the wider Dutchmans Trail. Turn right at the junction. The trail drops steeply off the ridge near the end of the hike. Here, it crosses splays of the fault along the southern boundary of the caldera. Hunt for these in the area near the section number "29" on the topographic map (you have it along, right?). The fault brings tuff up against the purplish-red intrusive rhyolite that forms the gnarled cliffs across Peralta Canyon near the trailhead. The rhyolite is hard, fractured, and contains inclusions of other rocks, including a rounded granite boulder smack in the middle of the trail. This boulder originally must have been picked up by the rhyolite. The rhyolite is also full of masses of volcanic glass.

As the trail sidehills down toward Peralta Canyon, the bluff to the right (north) of the trail is composed of brecciated rhyolite. One splay of the bounding fault is at the foot of this bluff.

SIXSHOOTER CANYON TRAIL

This well-shaded hike takes you to the top of Pinal Peak, giving fine views along the way and displaying some of the oldest rocks in the Arizona Transition Zone.

LOCATION ■ Pinal Mountains

DISTANCE ■ 5.75 miles one way

ELEVATION ■ 4840 to 7850 feet

DIFFICULTY ■ Moderately strenuous

TOPOGRAPHIC MAPS ■ Pinal Peak, AZ, 1:24,000; Globe, AZ, 1:100,000

GEOLOGIC MAPS ■ 23

PRECAUTIONS ■ This trail can get snowy and cold in winter. Lightning on the peak is a hazard during the summer.

INFORMATION ■ Tonto National Forest, Globe Ranger District

Landscape and Geology: This is one of the classic areas of Arizona geology. Geologic mapping was done here at the turn of the century because of the Globe copper district, which was discovered and began to be mined in 1874. The mapping was undertaken by the great early geologist Frederick L. Ransome, who named many geologic formations after geographic features in this area—Pinal, Dripping Spring, Mescal, Barnes, Scanlan, Pioneer, Ruin, and Whitetail. He also defined the Apache Group, which includes most of the Proterozoic formations.

The Pinal Mountains are a relatively isolated dome-shaped mountain complex that provides fine views of the Basin and Range mountains to the south, the Arizona Transition Zone mountains to the east and west, and the edge of the Colorado Plateau to the north.

The Pinal Mountains are underlain by irregular masses of Madera quartz diorite, a gray, coarse-grained granite-like intrusive igneous rock composed of quartz, plagioclase feldspar, and the dark mica biotite. The diorite, which is 1600 to 1700 million years old, intrudes the even older Pinal schist, the oldest rock in this area.

Rocks near the contact between the Madera and Pinal are more resistant to erosion than the same rocks away from the contact because these rocks were "baked" and thus hardened by the intruding diorite pluton. The Pinal Mountains are high because they include an abundance of metamorphosed contact rocks. This hike explores the quartz diorite, the schist, and the metamorphism along the contact between them.

The Madera and Pinal are part of the Proterozoic *basement* of the area—the substrate on which the oldest sedimentary rocks were deposited. Finding the basement rocks at 7850 feet on top of the mountain tells you that the Mogollon Highlands—an ancient mountain range that once existed here—must have been quite high in its time. Even now, after rifting, the top of the Paleozoic rocks would be at about 16,000 feet or more. This figure is estimated by adding to the top of Pinal Mountain the rocks that once were there but have been eroded away.

Trail Guide: Travel east through Globe on US 60. Just after crossing the viaduct over the valley and railroad, turn right at the red Pinal Mountain Recreation Area sign. Set the odometer to zero here. Negotiate various stops and turns, following signs for the Pinal Recreation Area. You eventually cross the railroad tracks, then go east up the valley. After crossing a bridge at mile 1.2, turn right onto a paved road that goes up the side valley. At the stop sign (mile 3), go straight onto Pioneer Road and FS 112. The road to the right takes you to the top of Pinal Peak.

You are driving through coarse basin-fill deposits of Tertiary age, called the Glance Conglomerate by Ransome. The pavement ends at mile 5.1. At mile 5.6, you come to a junction with the road going left to Icehouse Picnic Area, the official trailhead for the Sixshooter Canyon Trail. However, you can save about 1 mile and 300 feet of climb in shadeless country by continuing up the road to the bridge over Sixshooter Creek at mile 7.1. Park your car here just below the bridge and pick up Trail 197 about 100 yards up the road. Turn uphill onto the trail at the sign.

At first, the trail goes up near the floor of the canyon, close to the intrusive contact of the Madera quartz diorite into the Pinal schist. The "diorite" here is actually a relatively fine-grained gneiss with contorted mineral banding, or *foliation*. The "schist" has been metamorphosed (altered) into a light gray gneiss with conspicuous large silvery flakes of the light-colored mica *muscovite*. The rest of this rock consists principally of quartz and feldspar. Both Madera and Pinal are metamorphosed near the intrusive contact.

Boulders of Madera quartz diorite in the bed of Sixshooter Creek

Along the trail are occasional small exposures of a foliated or banded rock. This is Pinal schist that has not been metamorphosed to gneiss. Crossings of the wash show many large rounded boulders of coarse-grained granitic rock containing quartz, gray plagioclase, and black biotite mica. This is unmetamorphosed Madera quartz diorite that has been carried down the wash from outcrops far away from the contact zone.

Eventually, the trail leaves the canyon and enters country underlain by the quartz diorite. You climb through fine woods of oak, ponderosa, alligator juniper, Douglas fir, and even maple. Open spots give you views to the north, where you see the town of Globe, the canyon of the Salt River, the Sierra Ancha, and the Mogollon Rim far in the distance.

At about 3.5 miles and an altitude of about 7000 feet, you reach an old jeep road that you follow downhill to the right. You soon pass a junction with Telephone Trail #192, then reach the Ferndell Trail, #204, after another three-fourths mile. Follow Ferndell Trail to Pinal Peak, another three-fourths mile away.

Pinal Peak is composed of quartz diorite with minor outcrops of Pinal schist. The peak itself is disappointing because it bristles with antennas and other installations. You can get a decent view to the east by going to the easternmost cluster of towers and looking for a metal ladder that climbs up a huge diorite boulder behind the tower compound. The view to the south is spectacular. You can see it from the southernmost cluster of towers or by walking down the road several hundred feet west to a small cleared rise.

In the Ajo Mountains, Organ Pipe Cactus National Monument

Part 3
BASIN AND RANGE PROVINCE

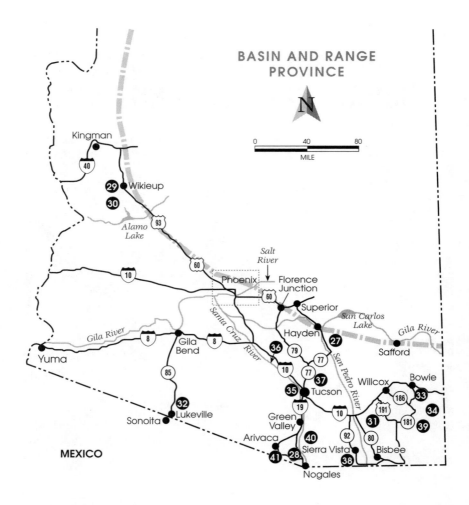

The Basin and Range Province occupies the southern third of the state, the lower elevations of which are Sonoran desert. In contrast, the tops of the ranges, the aim of most hikes in this section of the book, are in subalpine to alpine forest.

The faulting that gave this province its distinct character and name occurred in Tertiary time, which is quite youthful in a geologic sense. Before then, this area was underlain by a complex assortment of rocks of all kinds and ages. Two ancient events in particular had a great influence on this country.

The first was a long episode of *subduction* (see figure 6) off the coast west of the continent, which was then in or near Arizona. The subduction started in Mesozoic time and continued into the Tertiary. It had three effects of interest to us.

One was a tectonic effect—the colliding plates produced compressive forces that here resulted in thrust faults and uplifts such as the Mogollon Highlands.

Another effect was igneous—material from the oceanic plate, together with deep-sea sediments and material scraped off the edge of the continent, was *subducted* or carried down far below the continent, where the great heat caused some of it to melt. Magma then rose. Some cooled within the crust, forming plutons. Other magma rose to the surface, creating volcanoes, many of which were made up of rocks high in silica (SiO_2) content. Some of these resulted in the eruption of enormous volumes of welded tuff and the formation of great calderas.

The third effect was economic—the magma was associated with fluids that contained valuable elements and minerals in solution. When the rocks cooled, these were concentrated by various means into valuable deposits that have been mined and for which Arizona is well-known.

In Miocene time, the compressive aspect of subduction came to an end and the much-abused crust of the continent was able to relax, bringing about the second major ancient event. At first, the relaxation came about through enormous stretching (or extension) of the upper part of the crust along low-angle faults, maybe to twice its original width. This was accompanied by heating, metamorphism, and volcanic activity. Later, the extension changed, becoming more deep-seated and occurring along high-angle faults. Stretching of the crust was much less than before, but produced the magnificent basins and ranges that are a hallmark of so much of the West today.

To get a good sense for the geology and landscape of the Basin and Range Province, read John McPhee's wonderful book by the same name. McPhee is a nongeologist writer who understands and appreciates geology better than some professionals in the field. He can certainly write about it with more lucidity and greater flair than most.

ARAVAIPA CANYON TRAIL

Hike 27

This, one of the premier hikes in Arizona and a photographer's and bird-watcher's paradise, takes you through a rugged canyon cut into welded tuff and ancient Proterozoic basement.

LOCATION ■ Aravaipa Canyon Wilderness

DISTANCE ■ About 5 miles one way

ELEVATION ■ 2600 to 2850 feet

DIFFICULTY ■ Easy, but some route-finding skills and a map are needed

TOPOGRAPHIC MAPS ■ Brandenburg Mountain, AZ, 1:24,000; Mammoth, AZ, 1:100,000

GEOLOGIC MAPS ■ 24

PRECAUTIONS ■ This canyon is subject to extreme floods during spring and summer; consult weather forecasts before hiking. A permit is needed to hike here (see Trail Guide section below).

INFORMATION ■ Bureau of Land Management, Safford Office (for permits), or West Aravaipa Ranger Station (for information)

Landscape and Geology: Aravaipa Canyon is carved across the Galiuro Mountains, one of the northwest-trending ranges in the Basin and Range Province.

Proterozoic igneous and metamorphic rocks of the Pinal schist are exposed at the western end of the canyon, as well as *diabase* (the coarse-grained equivalent of basalt) and sedimentary rocks of the Proterozoic Apache Group. Brandenburg Mountain, which looms to the north of the mouth of the Canyon, is capped by Paleozoic rocks ranging in age from Cambrian to Mississippian. These rocks were stripped from the country to the east along the axis of the range before the Miocene Galiuro volcanics were laid down. The volcanics consist mainly of rhyolitic *ash-flow tuff* and lava and andesite flows, all resistant enough to form impressive cliffs and canyons. These volcanic tuffs are products of eruptions in which highly gas-charged silica-rich magma flowed over the landscape at great speed, covering large areas and finally solidifying into enormous sheets.

Tuff sheets include horizontal zones created by different degrees of welding of the tuff. The degree of welding depends on the temperature of the tuff when it stopped moving. The center is the hottest, so it becomes the most welded. A thin zone near the bottom is cooled by the underlying terrain, and a thick zone at the top is cooled by contact with air.

Aravaipa Canyon is ideal for viewing Pinal schist, diabase, and various components of ash-flow tuffs because all these rocks are wonderfully exposed along the canyon.

Trail Guide: A permit is required for hiking in the canyon. It can be obtained by calling the BLM Safford Office at (520) 348-4400 no more than 13 weeks before the planned date of your hike. You will be mailed an Aravaipa Canyon Wilderness (ACW) number, which you must use when registering at the trailhead.

Turn east off Arizona Highway 77 at the sign to Central Arizona College, just north of milepost 124. The road is paved for 4.6 miles, after which it is all-weather dirt.

The road initially goes through hills of conglomeratic basin fill, then along scattered outcrops of Proterozoic igneous and metamorphic basement rocks. For the last several miles, the road is mostly in gray Proterozoic diabase. The road ends at 12.8 miles in a small dirt parking lot with a primitive toilet, trash barrel, and information kiosk. The kiosk tells how to register using your

ACW permit and how to deposit the fee ($5 per person per day). Camping is allowed here, but no fires. Dogs are not allowed in Aravaipa Canyon, the maximum party size is ten, and the maximum length of stay is 3 days and 2 nights. You will find neither an official trail nor signs in the wilderness. A topographic map is indispensable to keep track of where you are and to identify the geologic features described here.

You will be walking in water much of the time, so appropriate footwear is needed. Wear old boots and carry some duct tape for emergency repairs. You can also try hiking sandals, but you may find that sand and pebbles collect in them.

The trail initially descends to the river from the parking lot along a gully cut into conglomeratic basin fill. Just a little way upstream, you pass outcrops of Proterozoic diabase with prominent horizontal joints on the west side of the river.

A cliff of purplish conglomerate with a conspicuous band of white tuff

Pinal schist and welded tuff sheets in the narrows of Aravaipa Creek

in the middle soon comes into view upriver. This is the Tertiary Whitetail Conglomerate, which is older than the Galiuro volcanics on the skyline above. The Whitetail comes down to the river's edge about 1.3 miles upstream, beyond the first major bend to the right. Just before this bend, the outcrops of diabase come to an end and those of the Pinal schist begin.

The Pinal schist is a tough rock, as befits its great age of more than 1700 million years. This hard metamorphic rock has been carved out to create narrows that are one of the most beautiful places in the canyon. The exposures are great, so it is easy to see that it is a *foliated* (mineral banded) medium-grained pinkish rock. The foliation is nearly vertical. Because of its orientation, the foliation is best seen going downriver on the return trip. The rock is shot through with veins of white quartz that fill tension cracks and are folded.

If you look straight up canyon from the mouth of Hells Half Acre Canyon at 1.6 miles, you can see a wall topped by a massive cliff composed of one ash-flow tuff. Beneath it is another ash-flow tuff that contains a whitish zone with columnar joints. This zone was hotter initially, resulting in better welding and thus became harder. The less-welded zones in tuffs like these tend to form slopes and rounded shapes, whereas the better welded zones form cliffs and sharp angular shapes.

At about 2.8 miles, you may find the walking rather difficult for a stretch owing to a jumble of large boulders that choke the canyon. These are part of a large rockfall that originated on the walls of the canyon.

The mouth of Javelina Canyon is at 3.1 miles, after which the Pinal schist dives below the surface at 3.6 miles. One of the ash-flow tuffs forms the floor of the canyon for the rest of the hike. This tuff is full of holes 0.5 to 2 inches in diameter, which are filled with microcrystalline silica (SiO_2) called *chalcedony*, which is similar to chert. These holes, or *vugs*, were originally filled with gases and are characteristic of the so-called vuggy zone of ash-flow tuffs.

The floor of the canyon becomes wider once you are in the tuffs upstream from the Pinal schist, showing that the tuffs erode more easily than the Pinal. The severity of floods is less in this wider stretch, so river terraces are preserved here, along with the park-like vegetation of large trees that grows on them. This area is a favorite camping spot for backpackers.

The hike ends at the confluence of Horse Camp Canyon with Aravaipa Canyon, about 5 miles from the trailhead. This is a good distance for a day hike. If you are keen on exploring more, you should consider backpacking in and setting up camp in this area. The next day, you can walk with a light pack to the eastern end of the canyon, also about 5 miles from here. That part of the canyon is carved into conglomeratic basin fill, which gives rise to intricate shapes and narrow slots. You can then return to the trailhead on the third day.

Columnar zone in tuffs in Aravaipa Canyon

ATASCOSA LOOKOUT TRAIL

Hike 28

This little-known gem leads through a Miocene caldera complex to a summit with a 360° view that embraces Mexico.

LOCATION ■ Trail 100, Atascosa Mountains, Coronado National Forest

DISTANCE ■ About 2.4 miles one way

ELEVATION ■ 4700 to 6249 feet

DIFFICULTY ■ Moderate to easy

TOPOGRAPHIC MAPS ■ Ruby, AZ–Sonora, 1:24,000; Atascosa Mountains, AZ–Sonora, 1:100,000

GEOLOGIC MAPS ■ 25

PRECAUTIONS ■ Heat and lightning in summer

INFORMATION ■ Coronado National Forest, Nogales Ranger District

Landscape and Geology: The Atascosa Mountains are composed mostly of Miocene rhyolite lava flows, air-fall tuffs, and ash-flow tuffs. These volcanic rocks may be part of an ancient caldera complex, now so deeply eroded that its original *morphology* (shape) is no longer evident. In places, volcanic flows are banked against eroded tuffs, and in other places, tuffs are deposited against flows, giving clues about the shape of the land surface when the volcano was erupting.

Trail Guide: Turn west off Interstate 19 at the Peña Blanca/Ruby Road, Arizona Highway 289, Exit 12. Follow the road 9 miles west to Peña Blanca Recreation Area where the pavement ends and becomes the Arivaca–Ruby Road, FR 39. Continue about 5 miles west to the parking area on the south side of the road at the trailhead. This is easy to miss, so watch closely. The trail starts at the brown post on the north side of the road.

The gray and reddish rock near the trailhead is a *rhyolite flow*, a silica-rich lava. The red color is due to iron oxides. The yellowish parts of the flow are volcanic glass that has been altered over time, or *devitrified*. Rhyolite cools rapidly, thus forming glass. With time, the glass slowly alters to finely crystalline masses of silica. The rock also contains substantial crystals of potassium feldspar, six-sided crystals of the dark mica biotite, and rounded grains of quartz and probably *sanidine*, a glassy, high-temperature form of potassium feldspar.

The butte straight ahead as you round the first nose is capped by well-bedded volcanic tuffs. The chaotic unbedded rocks south of the butte are rhyolite flows.

Bedding characteristics give you a good clue about what you see from a distance. In general, rhyolite flows have no bedding, but might show contorted *flow banding*, formed when the hot, taffy-like rock was still moving. Many rhyolite flows are *brecciated*, meaning they contain broken rock fragments. *Air-fall tuff* is very well bedded because it is the product of volcanic ash settling out of the air onto the ground, much like snow. *Ash-flow tuff* has little or no internal structure if it is thin, but has a simple horizontal zonation if thick. These tuffs form as a highly gas-charged froth of incandescent lava that flows out of the vent down the slopes of the volcano. The zones are due to differences in characteristics such as welding which affect the degree of hardening.

A reddish *flow breccia* crops out between the gate and the 0.5-mile post. This breccia (rock composed of angular fragments) forms when partially solidified rhyolite at the surface of a flow is broken up and incorporated in the still-moving lava.

Outcrops of rhyolite just before the 1-mile marker show flow banding. As the trail flattens out, the large yellowish-white boulders on either side of the trail are unbedded ash-flow tuff that broke off outcrops higher up on the slope. The tuff contains lots of crystals like those of the rhyolite lava, as well as angular rock fragments that were either brought up from depth by the rising lava, or were swept up from the ground over which the tuff flowed. The well-bedded rock just beyond the 1.5-mile marker is air-fall tuff. Here you can see how it differs from the ash-flow tuff. The layers rich in fragments are tuff mixed with debris eroded from preexisting volcanic rocks at the surface.

A prominent saddle gives you a good view of the mountain with the lookout on top. As you pass the 2-mile marker, the trail enters the wooded northeast side of the mountain through a medium-gray rhyolite flow that is also visible on the saddle about one-half mile to the northeast. You can recognize it at a distance by its gray color and lack of prominent layering.

The rest of the climb to the top is through tuff and tuffaceous sedimentary layers, with a few rhyolite flows. Tuffaceous sediment consists of eroded volcanic tuff that was mixed with other kinds of rocks, then deposited.

The spur jutting south from the lookout mountain is composed predominantly of tuffs and is capped by a massive layer of ash-flow tuff. You may well wonder why there is a difference between the section on the spur and that below the lookout, with its rhyolite flows. They are so close that you would be justified in thinking that they should be the same. A likely explanation is that the tuffs of the spur are banked against the rhyolite flows under the lookout. Rhyolite flows are very *viscous* (thick) and form bulbous, steep-sided domes and ridges. Later air-fall and ash-flow tuffs then butt against these small hills or thin over them.

Right after you crest the ridge and go through a fence, you walk on light-colored rock that is the ash-flow tuff capping the south spur. Look at this rock with a hand lens: the crystals are composed of black biotite, glassy quartz, potassium feldspar, and possibly *sanidine*, another potassium-rich feldspar that is recognized by its *chatoyance*—a play of colors. You will also see rock fragments and yellowish fibrous masses that are *pumice* (frozen rhyolite froth).

Just below the lookout, the trail clambers over an outcrop of dark purplish gray fine-grained rock which displays platy weathering, vugs (holes), stubby crystals of some dark mineral, and large crystals of feldspar. This kind of rock is difficult for a field geologist to identify because a microscope and chemical analyses are needed. This is most likely a dacite or andesite that is part of a lava flow.

The lookout tower is old and no longer maintained, but it contains extracts from the diary of Edward Abbey, author of *The Monkey Wrench Gang,* written when he was stationed here years ago. It makes good reading. His rather plaintive tone suggests that he was not in the best of spirits during his stay at the lookout.

The view is exceptional. The peak in the middle distance to the north is Atascosa Peak, to the right of which rises the dark hump of the distant Catalina Mountains (Hike 37), visible above the Tucson smog. To the northeast are the Santa Ritas (Hike 40) and to the east are the Santa Cruz River valley and the Patagonia and Huachuca (Hike 38) ranges behind it. To the south is Mexico. To the southwest

From the Atascosa Lookout Trail, looking north toward Atascosa Peak, Rhyolite tuffs (bedded) and flows (unbedded) are visible.

you can see Sycamore Canyon (Hike 41), and to the west, the grassy plains near Arivaca. The tooth of Baboquivari Peak, sacred to the Tohono O'Odham tribe, looms to the northwest. You are looking at many thousands of square miles.

Before going back down, look at the flanks of Atascosa Peak to the north. If you remember how to distinguish between rhyolite flows, ash-flow tuffs, and air-fall tuffs, you should be able to work out that some units were banked against a hilly topographic surface developed on older rocks. This supports our "banking" hypothesis for the south spur.

AUBREY PEAK ROAD

This short hike leads to a sweeping view and provides a lesson on how to make sense of the complex rocks of the Proterozoic basement.

LOCATION ■ Hualapai Mountains

DISTANCE ■ About 1 mile one way

ELEVATION ■ 4300 to 5078 feet

DIFFICULTY ■ Easy: steep but short

TOPOGRAPHIC MAPS ■ Wikieup NW, AZ, 1:24,000; Bagdad, AZ, 1:100,000

GEOLOGIC MAPS ■ None

PRECAUTIONS ■ Heat and lightning in summer

INFORMATION ■ None

Landscape and Geology: Aubrey Peak is part of the Hualapai Mountains, the first range in the Basin and Range Province west of the Colorado Plateau in this area.

The Hualapais are made up of metamorphic and igneous rocks that are 1400 · to 1700-plus million years old. The rocks record complex episodes of intrusion and metamorphism and form the ancient geologic "basement" on which Paleozoic and Mesozoic strata were later deposited.

Tectonic plate collisions to the west at the end of Mesozoic time produced a belt of uplift, the northwest continuation of the Mogollon Highlands of central Arizona. The uplift brought about the erosional stripping of the Paleozoic and Mesozoic rocks from most of the area.

Refer back to the section on the Basin and Range Province in "The Making of Arizona" at the beginning of this book. This will help you make sense of the geology here.

In Miocene time, about 27 million years ago, a series of events began that resulted in the creation of several metamorphic core complexes along what is now the lower Colorado River. These collectively formed the extraordinary Highly Extended Terranes, where the crust was stretched to perhaps twice its original width by extension. During the stretching, rhyolitic and basaltic volcanoes were active, blocks of crust were tilted, and sediments of various kinds were deposited (see Hike 30). The volcanic activity resulted from heating of the Earth's crust and the *mantle* beneath it, suggesting that the extension was related to the heating and thus ultimately to processes going on in the mantle. In contrast to all this activity in the Basin and Range Province, nothing much was happening on the nearby Colorado Plateau at this time.

Later in Miocene time, strong extension was replaced by deep-seated but less severe extension along widely spaced high-angle *normal faults* that gave rise to classic basin and range features such as the Big Sandy Valley and the

Hualapai Range (see figure 7). This is when the edge of the Colorado Plateau was defined by faulting, forming the Grand Wash, Aquarius, and Cottonwood Cliffs. Basalt flows that erupted at this time pooled in closed basins, giving rise to the various pancake-shaped "black mesas." This shows that through-flowing drainage of the lower Colorado River had not yet formed at that time.

Trail Guide: Turn off US Highway 93 at the north end of Wikieup, between mileposts 123 and 124, near the north end of the lane separator. Turn onto the Chicken Springs road, marked by a green street sign and blue Arizona Department of Transportation (ADOT) sign. This road is paved for one-third mile. At 0.4 mile, go left at the junction onto the Yucca Alamo Lake road, identified by a green sign. Climb steeply for about 8.7 miles to a pass at the crest of the Hualapai Mountains. Park the car out of traffic's way at the pass. The walk is up the track on the ridge south of the road, leading to the microwave towers at the top of Aubrey Peak. Do not drive on this track, which is in private property belonging to a nearby ranch. The ranch allows walking on the track, but not driving.

Bring along a hand lens and a pair of binoculars. You are about to play detective. What kind of rock types are present here? How were these rocks formed? What are their ages relative to one another? These are the kinds of questions geologists try to answer when they work in country like this.

The most common rock in the cuts along the track is a gray medium- to coarse-grained granitic rock that contains large crystals of the mineral feldspar and weathers into rounded forms. In most places, it is *foliated*, meaning it has streaks and bands composed of different minerals, so it is properly called a *granite gneiss*. This is a metamorphic rock. The unfoliated parts are granite.

Notice that the degree to which the rock is foliated ranges from strong to none. One way to explain this is that we are at the margin of a granite *pluton*, a large underground intrusion of igneous rock. Here, relative movement between the cooling pasty magma and the *country rock* (preexisting rock) gave rise to flow-banding made evident by the concentration of minerals into bands. Thus, this foliation is an expression of *contact metamorphism*. This interpretation is supported by noting that several rock types are not foliated. If this were *regional metamorphism* rather than the intrusion of a pluton, we would expect all rocks to be foliated.

The granite gneiss includes chunks of dark gray, medium-grained, unbanded rock composed of dark minerals and plagioclase. This rock is probably *diorite* (a coarse-grained equivalent of andesite) and is part of the country rock into which the granite was intruded. The diorite weathers more easily than the gneiss, so now is present in low relief.

The third major type of rock along the track is pink to white unfoliated veins that cut across all other rocks. Some are coarse-grained, with large crystals of

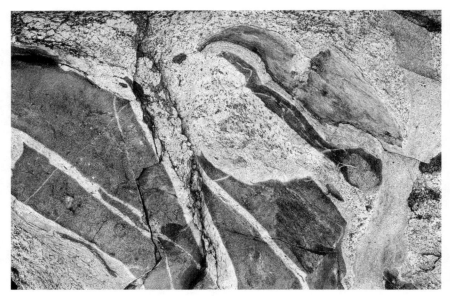

Granite gneiss (light) intruding diorite (dark)

feldspar that flash in the sun; this is *pegmatite*, similar to a granite but with much larger crystals. Others veins consist of fine-grained, light-colored granite composed of quartz, two kinds of feldspar, and almost no dark minerals. Yet others are white and composed mostly of quartz. All represent the material that crystallized last out of hot solutions when the magma of the pluton was in the late stages of solidification.

After you have walked less than one-fourth mile, you can see cuts on the left side showing zoned veins. Pegmatite is on the outside, quartz in the center, and light-colored granite in between. This shows the sequence of crystallization. The quartz at the center crystallized last. One reason why miners look for quartz veins is because the hot solution out of which quartz crystallizes sometimes also contains gold, which comes out of solution along with the quartz.

The prominent outcrop on the left, just before the saddle, shows granite gneiss that incorporates diorite inclusions. The gneiss has a fine-grained "chilled" margin at the contact with the diorite. Chilled margins indicate rapid cooling of magma near cool country rock. You can also see diorite incorporated within veins of the fine-grained, light-colored granite.

What we have seen so far enables us to make a few deductions about the geology. We know that the granite gneiss was hot and plastic when it was emplaced here. We also know that the diorite is older than the granite because it is intruded by it. And we know that the veins are the youngest of all because they cut all other rocks. What we see farther up the track will tell us whether we are on the right path for sorting out the events that happened here nearly 2 billion years ago.

Outcrops on the right between the saddle and the first switchback show stringers of diorite that are folded, as well as veins of pegmatite and quartz that cut across each other in a complex fashion. The relative ages of the veins can be determined by observing what cuts what—the vein that is cut is older than the one doing the cutting. Similar observations can be made farther up this leg, where veins and dikes of light-colored granitic rock cut each other and the diorite.

Halfway up the second leg, beyond the first switchback, an outcrop on the left shows dike-like bodies of diorite that seem to cut the granite. This would blow away our notion that the granite intrudes the diorite. But look more closely. Notice the fine stringers of granite that clearly intrude the diorite. The "dikes" of diorite are merely screens caught between masses of intruding granite. Can you understand why geologists sometimes have trouble dealing with the complexities of nature?

Note the well-formed folds in the granite gneiss on the left just before the power line. The rock here is gray and coarsely *porphyritic*, having large crystals in a groundmass of smaller ones. It is composed of glassy quartz, pink orthoclase feldspar, white plagioclase feldspar that shows crystal faces, and small crystals of biotite recognized by its brilliant black flashes on crystal faces.

At the top, hasten by the ugly towers to the south ridge, where you can find good places to sit and enjoy the views. Three different geologic terranes are present here for viewing: the Colorado Plateau to the east; the Hualapai Mountains, a classic range of the basin and range type (under your feet); and the jumbled hills and dome-shaped mountains of the Highly Extended Terranes to the south, southwest, and west.

The dark layer at the edge of the plateau is a Miocene age basalt that rests directly on ancient basement rocks. Notice how the basalt steps down along several faults into the Big Sandy Valley. These faults collectively create the edge of the Colorado Plateau here. Just north of the basalt and barely visible on the skyline is the volcanic complex of the Mohon Mountains. Just south of the basalt is another volcanic complex that includes rhyolite. You can still see part of the original shape of this volcano. The white patch to the south is the tailings pond of the Bagdad Mine. The Big Sandy Valley is a classic basin and range valley, formed when a block was dropped down along high-angle normal faults. These faults were also responsible for such ranges as the north-trending Hualapai Mountains, on which you are sitting, and the McCracken range to the southwest.

Most of what you see in the Highly Extended Terrane country are ridges in the "upper plate," a sheet of rock above the detachment fault that underlies

Looking west from Aubrey Peak toward basin and range country

much of this area. The ridges are formed by blocks that rotated along northwest-striking faults of small displacement (see figure 3). If the visibility is good, you may be able to see one of these tilted blocks near the tooth-shaped Artillery Peak, to the south.

Rhyolite volcanoes are typical of this extended country. Two are visible from here—the light-colored Aubrey Hills, just poking up behind the McCrackens, and the tooth-like volcanic plugs of the Castaneda Hills, in the distance behind the McCrackens. A *plug* is the resistant lava filling of the conduit at the core of a volcano, left standing after the weaker material around it has been eroded away.

To the right of the Castaneda Hills, you can see one of the black mesas formed by late-stage basalt flows. The Mohave Mountains are to its right. On the distant skyline, you can see a large hump with a spire on its south side. These are the Whipple Mountains of easternmost California, near the western margin of the Highly Extended Terranes. The broad mass on the southern skyline is the Harcuvar Mountains. The Whipples and Harcuvars are dome-like uplifts, and both are metamorphic core complexes whose upper plate and detachment fault once arched over these domes, but have been eroded (see figure 7). This left metamorphic rocks exposed at the core of the mountains.

Many geologists think that the entire highly extended terrane in front of you is a single structural entity, everywhere underlain by the same enormous detachment fault.

196

CENTENNIAL WASH

This drive and walk through remote and beautiful Sonoran desert country is a field trip to the remarkable geology of the "upper plate" of a metamorphic core complex.

Hike 30

LOCATION ■ Centennial Wash

DISTANCE ■ 4.8 miles round trip

ELEVATION ■ About 240 feet elevation change

DIFFICULTY ■ Easy

TOPOGRAPHIC MAPS ■ McCracken Peak, AZ, 1:24,000; Centennial Wash, AZ, 1:24,000; Bagdad and Alamo Lake, AZ, 1:100,000

GEOLOGIC MAPS ■ 26

PRECAUTIONS ■ A four-wheel-drive vehicle is highly recommended. Beware of loose sand. Carry plenty of water in this remote desert country.

INFORMATION ■ Bureau of Land Management, Kingman Field Office

Landscape and Geology: The geologic features seen on this hike are not simple, but if you persevere, the reward is an understanding of some of the most remarkable geology to be found anywhere. It would be helpful to refer to the Basin and Range Province section in "The Making of Arizona" at the beginning of this book.

At the town of Wikieup, you are near the southwest edge of the Colorado Plateau, which here is defined by the scarp east of the valley. Beyond the scarp, rocks of the plateau are nearly flat-lying and little faulted. The scarp itself is created by several faults that step down to the west. You can see these because they displace a sequence of basalt flows. The best place to view the edge of the Colorado Plateau and other features is from the pass across the Hualapai Mountains.

Wikieup is in the Big Sandy Valley, the first of the Basin and Range valleys (or basins). The Hualapai Mountains to the west are the first range. West of the Hualapais is another basin, and then a second range, the McCracken Mountains. All are classic basin and range type structures that are aligned roughly north-northwest and are the product of movement on high-angle *normal faults* along the range fronts. In this kind of structure, the block on one side of the fault moved relatively down to form a basin, whereas the block on the other side moved relatively up to form a range.

This orderly arrangement ends abruptly at the south end of the McCracken Mountains. To the south and west of these mountains is a jumble of small ridges and basins as well as hills that are eroded volcanoes. The Tertiary strata on the ridges everywhere dip southwest. In the distance rise some large dome-shaped mountains. All this is part of the geologically complex Highly Extended

Terranes of the Lower Colorado River corridor, which include several *meta-morphic core complexes.*

From your reading at the beginning of the book, recall that metamorphic core complexes are made up of three elements. The "lower plate," at the bottom, is composed of gneiss that deformed in plastic fashion, like taffy, when it was pulled apart. The "upper plate," at the top, broke into many blocks bounded by faults when it was stretched. This is called *brittle deformation,* analogous to breaking a piece of glass. In between is a horizontal "basal detachment fault," against which the blocks and faults of the upper plate end. These blocks are strongly tilted and generally dip in the same direction. Here, they dip southwest.

If you could see the detachment fault (which is mostly beneath the surface), you would discover that it is not flat but wavy, with blister-like upwellings here and there. The blisters correspond to the dome-shaped mountains in the distance. In each of these, the upper plate and the detachment fault have been eroded from the top of the blister, but are preserved on its flanks (see figure 7). What you see at the top are the metamorphic rocks of the lower plate, which form the core, surrounded by exposures of the detachment fault and rocks of the upper plate.

The upper plate consists of Miocene sedimentary and volcanic rocks that rest on a basement of Proterozoic granite similar to that found nearby on the Colorado Plateau. Many of the rocks were deposited while the detachment fault was active and the upper plate was breaking up into blocks.

The volcanic rocks basalt and rhyolite are notable components of the upper plate. The age of these rocks straddles those of the detachment fault and upper plate faults. This makes you suspect that the volcanic activity and faulting are related.

Volcanoes, especially those that produce mostly rhyolite, indicate that the crust has heated up because silica-rich magmas like rhyolite are what you get when you melt silica-rich crust. The most likely scenario is that the crust was simultaneously heated and stretched, and that, below a certain level, rocks were hot enough to stretch like taffy. This is the lower plate. Above that level, the rocks were not hot enough to be plastic, so were instead broken into pieces by brittle deformation. This is the upper plate. The boundary between the two is the detachment fault.

Trail Guide: This route starts in Wikieup on US 93 between Wickenburg and Kingman. Don't blink because it is easy to miss. Go to the north end of "town," look for the end of the lane separator between mileposts 123 and 124, and turn west onto the Chicken Springs road, marked by a green street sign and a blue Arizona Department of Transportation (ADOT) one. Set your trip odometer to zero.

The road is paved for one-third mile and has a pecan orchard on the left. At

0.4 mile, bear left at the junction onto the gravel Yucca Alamo Lake road, identified by a green sign. The road climbs steeply up the east slope of the Hualapai Mountains on ridges made of rocky sediment shed by the mountains. Ocotillo and yucca are abundant and so are spectacular views back toward the Big Sandy Valley and the edge of the Colorado Plateau. The road enters Precambrian granite gneiss country, then reaches the pass across the range at mile 8.3, about 2300 feet feet above the valley floor. It is worth stopping here to look around.

The jeep road going up from the pass to the repeater station to the south is the subject of Hike 29. To the east, you see the edge of the Colorado Plateau and the faults cutting through and displacing basalt. To the west, you look into Highly Extended Terrane country. The conspicuous "tooth" is Castaneda Peak, a rhyolite plug. The dome-like mountains in the far distance and to the right of a prominent spire are the Whipple Mountains of California, another metamorphic core complex.

Once over the pass, stay on the main road all the way to the T with Alamo Lake road at mile 15.3. Turn left and stay on the main road, going straight, making no turns. The junction with Signal Road (mile 25.7) has an overgrown dirt landing strip on the right and is not shown correctly on the 1:100,000 topo map. Go straight on the Alamo Lake road. At mile 30.1, you can see the windmill of Baker Well on the right, just before a power line crosses the road. This well is a source of emergency water. You are now on the upper plate of a metamorphic core complex.

At mile 30.3, turn right onto a small track that follows the power line. This track is poor; a high-clearance vehicle is recommended. The track meanders through weathered granite laced with white quartz veins. This granite is in the "upper plate" and is the foundation on which the Miocene sediments of the upper plate were deposited. Look for an outcrop of red conglomerate on the right (north) side of the wash. This is the lowest unit in the stack of Tertiary rocks here, deposited directly on the ancient Proterozoic granite and dipping steeply to the southwest. We will meet this conglomerate again.

At mile 31.7, the track leaves the power line and enters a bigger sandy wash with tracks. This is Centennial Wash. Drive down this wash for about 1 mile. A four-wheel-drive vehicle may be necessary here in the deep, loose sand.

At mile 32.6, follow the track to the left out of the wash, which here is barred by a cable and wilderness sign. The country to the west is the Aubrey Peak Wilderness. Aubrey Peak, the rugged, light-colored mountain down the wash, is an old rhyolite volcano. The road becomes firm again but locally washed out. Most bushes along the road are creosote. Take the right fork at mile 32.8. You can find good "wild" campsites along this stretch of the road.

It is worth parking and climbing the low hill to the right at mile 33.7 for a geologic overview and to admire the fine scenery. The hill is made of a peculiar *breccia* (rock made up of angular fragments) that you will see during the hike. It contains many pieces of metamorphic rocks—especially a shiny gray schist and sharp-edged fragments of hard quartzite.

Now look toward the gap made by Centennial Wash through the reddish ridge in front of you. The ridge is tilted southwest along a fault on the other side of the ridge, but the tilt is gentle. The red-brown conglomerate and light-colored rhyolite flows and tuffs of which it is made are the youngest rocks that were deposited while the faulting in the metamorphic core complex was going on. When you compare this tilt with the steep dip of the previously seen red conglomerate at the base of the section, you can deduce that all these rocks were deposited while the tilting was going on. The lower rocks experienced all the tilting, so are tilted the most, whereas the youngest experienced only the last of the tilting, so are tilted the least.

The rugged hills to the right (west) are the Aubrey Hills, made up of Miocene rhyolite flows and tuffs. The flows are altered, not bedded, and cream to gray in color. The tuffs are well bedded and yellowish. Binoculars help in distinguishing the two. A prominent reddish knob in the foreground is a *volcanic plug*, lava congealed in one of the vents from which the flows and tuffs issued. The lava that originally surrounded the vent has been eroded away.

Now look carefully toward the gap in the ridge. You can see that a thin layer of the red conglomerate that makes up the ridge crosses Centennial Wash and is interbedded with the rhyolite and tuff of the Aubrey Hills. In fact, it wedges out against these rocks. This small observation tells us a lot about what was going on here 13 to 14 million years ago. Because we can determine the age of the rhyolite, we can also "date" the red conglomerate interlayered with it and the late stages of faulting. Next, we can reconstruct in our mind's eye the landscape that existed here when the volcano was active and the conglomerate was laid down.

Visualize this scenario: on the right was the Aubrey Hills volcano, spewing out lava and ash. The lava flowed down the flanks of the volcano onto the surrounding country. All around the volcano, sand and gravel (which later hardened into the red conglomerate) was being deposited by many streams on a floodplain, but not on the high ground of the volcano, against which it banked. While this was going on, occasional earthquakes accompanied movement on the fault that slowly tilted this whole block to the southwest.

Continue down the track a short distance to the gate near the gap in the ridge and park here for the start of the hike.

Walk back upstream a few feet to a good outcrop of the red-brown conglomerate east of the track. You can see that it is well bedded, that sandy and cobbly layers alternate, and that the rock fragments, or *clasts*, are mostly angular and quite large. These characteristics tell you that the streams had a lot of energy (to carry big clasts) and the material was not transported very far (otherwise the clasts would have become rounded). The clasts include granite and gneiss like those in the Hualapai Mountains to the north, quartzite like that in the breccia, and weathered basalt. Now let's play detective again.

The breccia and basalt are units that are below the red-brown conglomerate in the layer cake of strata. So, how could they be at the surface to be eroded? The answer is that faulting and tilting exposed these rocks in ridges beyond the area where the conglomerate was being laid down. This is another piece of evidence to show that deposition and deformation occurred at the same time.

You can learn much about rhyolite lava in the narrows ahead. Walk downstream a little way along the east side of the wash to an outcrop of light gray and tan rhyolite, which here is mostly *devitrified* ("de-glassed"). Rhyolite is a relatively cool lava, which chills rapidly at the surface, preventing crystals from forming and producing volcanic glass. Glass is unstable and is eventually replaced by small crystals, whose growth leads to devitrification.

Because of its low temperature, the outer parts of a rhyolite lava flow solidify while the inner parts are still flowing. The solidified parts then break up into fragments that are incorporated into the lava, producing a *flow breccia.* The viscous, taffy-like flow also produces *flow banding.* Both are visible here and in several places down the wash.

In the narrows, you can see several flows that are partially black and glassy, like obsidian. This is rhyolite glass, with small crystals in a glassy matrix. This kind of rock is common at the base of flows, where the rhyolite cools rapidly. Also notice the cavities bounded by onion-like shells. Some are filled with *microcrystalline silica* or small quartz crystals, derived from fluids left in the lava after it solidifies. You can also see layers of yellow tuff, identified by the good bedding and by fragments of *pumice*, congealed rhyolite froth.

At three-fourths mile from where you parked, you emerge from the narrows abruptly where the ridge ends. The fault that rotated the ridge is under your feet, although you cannot see it. This fault dips northeast. Faults such as this are repeated again and again in the upper plate. They merge with, or butt into, the basal detachment fault.

Look southwest and locate a low hill about three-fourths mile away, capped by a dark resistant layer. Keep your eye on this landmark for navigation purposes. The hill is marked by the elevation 2174 feet on the Centennial Wash topographic map.

As you walk down the wash, look for outcrops of dark purplish gray, highly altered granite with coarse crystals of the mineral orthoclase feldspar. This is the basement upon which the Tertiary strata rests and the same rocks you saw under the basal conglomerate way up Centennial Wash. How did you go from the rhyolite, at the top of the section, into this granite, at its base? The reason is that you are now at the base of the next fault block tilted southwest. You got into this block when you crossed the fault at the end of the narrows.

When you are level with "hill 2174," stay on the west side of the wash and look closely for a cairn. This is a cue to look for a jeep track that takes off westward on the south side of hill 2174. The start of this track is hard to see from the wash because of vegetation. It is just north of a branch of the wash that has a wilderness post stuck into it and about 1200 feet north of the power line that crosses the wash.

Once on the track, follow it westward through rolling terrain about one-half mile to a substantial wash at the southwest end of hill 2174. The wash exposes a nice section of the basal conglomerate, dipping southwest as always. Down the wash, you find an almost complete exposure of the Tertiary section related to the metamorphic core complex, though broken up by many faults. You can't get away from faults around here, because the whole upper plate is shattered.

Up the wash about 1000 feet, you can find excellent exposures of the breccia, composed of angular clasts as much as 6 to 7 feet across. They are all of metamorphic rocks, which include shiny schist (originally a shale), quartzite, and greenish rocks with crystals, originally volcanic rocks of Mesozoic age. No rocks like this crop out in this area or to the north. This breccia must have slid off the bulge of a metamorphic core complex to the south, in the area of the Buckskin Mountains. This is the turnaround point for the hike.

On the way back, consider making the 200-foot climb to hill 2174. Get as close as possible to the hill on the track, then climb the western summit, which

Basal conglomerate in a wash

is less cliffy. The dark layer on top is a plate, or sheet, of reddish quartzite and highly altered gray limestone, both brecciated. These rock types are also found in the breccia. From the top, you have a fine view. To the north are the rhyolite flows and tuffs of the Aubrey Hills. Note the contorted flow banding in the flows. To the northeast is the tilted ridge that forms the narrows of Centennial Wash. East of the narrows, the ridge is made up of the red-brown conglomerate. To the south and southeast you can see many buttes, which are capped by plates of limestone and quartzite similar to the one on which you are standing, but larger. The buttes are near the south edge of the upper plate, on which you are standing here. Beyond the buttes is the high country of the Rawhide Mountains, which is composed of lower-plate gneiss and forms the core of the metamorphic core complex. The sheet-like plates slid off this core, which once was covered by Paleozoic and Mesozoic rocks. The detachment fault crops out between the buttes and the mountains, but is not visible from here. The Harcuvar Mountains form the skyline to the south. These mountains are also the lower-plate core of a metamorphic core complex.

The dark mesa to the southwest is Black Mesa. It was formed by a basalt that pooled in a basin after faulting had ended but before the Colorado River system was established here. This basalt originally occupied a topographic low but is now high because the basalt protected rocks beneath it from erosion while softer rocks beyond the basalt cap were stripped away.

Hike 31

COCHISE STRONGHOLD TRAIL

This pleasant hike goes through spectacular country carved into a granite stock, whose erosion has produced an intricate maze of knobs and gullies that are reputed to have sheltered the Apache chief Cochise during the Apache Wars of the 1860s.

LOCATION ■ Dragoon Mountains, Coronado National Forest

DISTANCE ■ 3 miles one way to Stronghold Divide

ELEVATION ■ 4920 to 5970 feet

DIFFICULTY ■ Easy to moderate

TOPOGRAPHIC MAPS ■ Cochise Stronghold, AZ, 1:24,000; Chiricahua Peak, AZ, 1:100,000

GEOLOGIC MAPS ■ 27

PRECAUTIONS ■ Heat and lightning in summer

INFORMATION ■ Douglas Ranger District

Landscape and Geology: The complicated geology of the Dragoon Mountains includes many thrust faults stacked on top of one another. The "plates" or

Intricately weathered Stronghold granite

sheets between these faults are made of Paleozoic and Mesozoic rocks. The faults were formed at the end of Mesozoic time by compression that resulted from a tectonic plate collision to the southwest. In Cenozoic time, granite intrusions invaded the thrust sheets. The latest of these is the Stronghold granite, which formed a *stock*, a medium-sized igneous intrusion, in Oligocene and Miocene time, about 22 to 28 million years ago. Erosion along joints in the granite has produced a topography so intricate that it is reputed to have provided an impregnable refuge for the great Apache chief Cochise in his wars with the U.S. Cavalry.

Trail Guide: Exit from Interstate 10 south onto US 191. At the north end of Sunsites, take Ironwood Road (FR 84) westward about 12 miles to Stronghold Canyon East and the Cochise Stronghold campground, where you park. Cross the wash on a bridge southeast of the toilets. Trail 5279 to Halfmoon Tank and Stronghold Divide starts just beyond the wash.

The trail is in coarse sandy soil (*grus*) produced by the disintegration of granite. Large rounded boulders of granite line the trail. Some of the rounding is probably produced by transport in a wash, but much results from spherical weathering called *exfoliation*, the erosion into rounded shapes that is typical of granite. You can see it in the granite outcrops along the trail.

The granite itself is best examined in the wash where water action has produced fresh surfaces. Using your hand lens, you can see that the granite is coarse-grained, light-colored, and contains quartz, orthoclase and plagioclase feldspar, and biotite. You can also see dark gray boulders of Proterozoic *amphibolite* in the wash. This rock is composed mostly of the dark iron-magnesium mineral *amphibole* (for example, hornblende is an amphibole).

The trail climbs steadily in live oak, juniper, pinyon, manzanita, yucca, and cholla. Sycamores are present in the wash. Just after the 1.5-mile mark, the soil in the trail becomes dark and clayey, and small outcrops show a fine-grained, dark gray rock that is not shown on the geologic map. This is probably a small intrusion of Tertiary or Cretaceous andesite.

The small lake at Halfmoon Tank has nice reflections of nearby granite knobs. The water attracts a lot of birds to this area. At Stronghold Divide, a short distance beyond the tank, you are rewarded with fine views of the Stronghold area to the north—a maze of granite knobs, ravines, and bouldery ridges. No wonder that Cochise and his band could disappear here, to the dismay of those who were trying to track him. The clefts and knobs are the result of weathering along *joints*, fractures in the rock along which there has been no slippage. Water is concentrated in the joints, leading to accelerated chemical weathering, as well as physical disintegration due to frost wedging.

In many places, the granite supports growths of brightly colored lichens. These are quite choosy about the chemical composition of the rocks on which they grow; different varieties like different chemicals. Because of this, lichens have often been used as an aid in prospecting for mineral deposits.

Hike

32

ESTES CANYON– BULL PASTURE TRAIL
Walk through the innards of an extinct volcano while enjoying wide-ranging vistas across the bajadas and ranges of Organ Pipe Cactus National Monument.

LOCATION ■ Organ Pipe Cactus National Monument

DISTANCE ■ 4.1 miles round trip

ELEVATION ■ 2400 to 3400 feet

DIFFICULTY ■ Moderate

TOPOGRAPHIC MAPS ■ Mount Ajo, AZ, 1:24,000; Ajo, AZ, 1:100,000

GEOLOGIC MAPS ■ 28 and 29

PRECAUTIONS ■ Carry plenty of water and watch for rattlesnakes during the summer. Best to hike in the spring.

INFORMATION ■ Organ Pipe Cactus National Monument

Landscape and Geology: The trail is on the west flank of the Ajo Mountains, a *fault-block range* formed by basin and range type normal faults that strike north-northwest. These faults are an expression of pull-apart forces, or *extension*, that occurred here in the Basin and Range Province. Other ranges in the area are formed by the same extension, which occurred mostly in Miocene time. Basin and range type faults create ranges that move relatively up and basins that move relatively down along the faults.

Vast gently sloping plains called *bajadas* form the sides of the basins. The bajadas are surfaces of downslope transport of sediment and are underlain by a thin veneer of debris that covers bedrock and obscures the faults. The debris is coarse, with lots of large boulders and cobbles, at the apex of the bajadas near the source mountains and becomes progressively finer-grained toward the bottom of the basin, where salts also concentrate. This characteristic has a major effect on vegetation: the coarser material at the apex retains water better and favors lush growth of large plants such as saguaro cacti and paloverde trees, whereas the fine and salt-rich soil of the basin bottoms has poor water retention and supports only a sparse scrub vegetation of creosote, bursage, and saltbush.

The Ajo Mountains are a volcanic complex composed mainly of Miocene silica-rich lavas that today are present as flows, tuffs, and intrusive masses such as nearly vertical *dikes* and filled conduits along which lava once reached the surface.

Erosion that started when the fault-block range was created gives you excellent cross section views of the internal structure of the volcano. This is a treat because such good exposures of silica-rich volcanoes are rare.

Trail Guide: You get to Organ Pipe National Monument on AZ 85. To reach the trailhead, turn east onto Ajo Mountain Drive just south of the monument headquarters and across from the road to the campground. The drive is a 21-mile dirt road passable to passenger vehicles. Most of it is one-way.

After several miles, the road climbs to a saddle. You can see a viewpoint with a picnic bench partway up. Stop here for a fine view and to look at the outcrop. This is a gray *flow-banded* rhyolite. The flow banding is created by the taffy-like rhyolite lava flowing. Your hand lens enables you to see shiny black crystals of the mica *biotite*, some with its characteristic hexagonal shape.

Beyond the saddle, the road descends gradually into a valley, then swings to a southward course at a picnic area and viewpoint of a natural arch. The trailhead is about 1.5 miles farther at a shaded picnic area.

The trail starts across the road from the picnic area near a large organ pipe cactus. The reddish-brown outcrop to the left at the trailhead is *latite,* a volcanic rock poor in silica and rich in potassium feldspar. Note the large, boxy crystals of feldspar and smaller greenish-black crystals of the mineral *augite*.

The trail starts by crossing Estes Wash. Take the right fork at the register just beyond the wash. At first, the trail goes up a small wash whose rocky north wall is graced by a fine stand of organ pipe cactus, then it switchbacks up a

Tuff breccia, Estes Canyon

slope beneath cliffs of latite. After cresting and turning north, the trail is in outcrops of yellowish *air-fall tuff* all the way along the ridge beyond the first saddle. The tuff is composed of volcanic ash that settled out of the air during an eruption.

The saddle gives you fine views to the northeast, where you can see yellow-white bedded tuffs near the bottom of the valley overlain by massive purplish-brown rhyolite flows, and finally by more yellowish tuffs near the skyline. The whole section is tilted northeast to east. If you look carefully, you can see rhyolite dikes on the mountain face to the north; an especially prominent one is near the west end of the face. The *dikes* are vertical sheets of intrusive igneous rock that cut the other rocks of the face.

The trail then contours beneath a prominent butte to the south, near a marked trail junction. This butte is made up of bedded *tuff breccia*, a sedimentary rock composed of tuff that contains angular fragments of gray and purple rhyolite, red-brown latite, and dark gray basalt. Beyond the junction, the trail climbs up a canyon along a fault contact between purple-brown latite on the left (east) and yellowish tuff on the right. The fault dips west about 45° and is marked by a band of red-brown *gouge*—rock ground up from movement along the fault. You can make out the smooth fault plane in several places.

At a second saddle three-fourths mile from the trail junction, you can see vertical dikes of gray rhyolite intruded into tuff at the east end of the butte. A few feet east of the saddle, the trail cuts through the fault plane near a concrete step. This is the fault which the trail follows as it climbs to the saddle. You can also see a subsidiary fault right on the trail just above the step. The fault plane has a shiny surface marked by horizontal grooves. These are called *slickensides*, which tell you the direction the fault moved (in this case, horizontally). From here, you can also see a prominent rhyolite dike across the canyon to the north.

The trail now climbs in yellowish tuff and rhyolite, the rhyolite forming the floor of the trail for hundreds of feet. A cut in the trail just before the third saddle is in dark gray rock. This is rhyolite glass, or *obsidian*, formed when volcanic magma is quenched by cooling very rapidly. This is common at the base and top of a flow and along the sides of a dike. Look at the obsidian: it contains round pink blobs about 1 inch in diameter with radial structures visible with your hand lens. These are called *spherulites*, formed by a complex process of alteration of the glass.

Continue beyond the saddle on the trail that winds up the ridge on the right for a few hundred feet, then find some easy way of climbing onto the ridge. This is the turnaround point of the hike and a good place to rest.

The views of ranges and bajadas stretch westward to the horizon and southward into Mexico. The imposing ramparts of the Ajo Range fill the view to the north and east. They are made up of rhyolite flows interbedded with ash, all beautifully exposed in cross section.

Rhyolite flows are viscous, so they flow only short distances and thin rapidly away from the vent, forming wedges when seen in cross section. Flows from different vents wedge into one another, with the result that they have an irregular appearance rather than being parallel. You can see this on the face of the Ajo Range. The most interesting feature on the face are the dike-like conduits along which the rhyolite rose to vents at the surface, cutting preexisting rocks. You can even see how the rhyolite, once at the surface, bends over into a surface flow. What you are seeing here is the cross section of the interior of a rhyolite volcano, an opportunity that does not come along every day.

The most obvious vent is directly north of you, along the prominent gulch. The conduit funnels upward from dikes near the bottom of the valley to a wide zone with vertical banding that cuts all visible layers, including the tuffs near the skyline. A connection between conduit and surface flows is not visible from here; the flows may be the ones forming the crest of the range, above the upper tuff layer.

A more complicated vent is exposed to the right, near Mount Ajo. The right side of the conduit is composed of vertically banded rhyolite that cuts across flows. The rhyolite of the conduit then bends over to the right and becomes the purple-brown flow beneath the tuff layer. This part of the conduit is thus older than the tuff. The left side of the conduit, however, is made of a brownish rock, possibly tuff breccia, that cuts across some of the tuff layer. This represents a later and more explosive phase of the volcanic activity along the vent.

You can see a third vent area near the western end of the ramparts. This one is made prominent by several conspicuous dikes. This is a complicated volcano that must have been quite a sight when it was erupting.

On the way back down, retrace your steps to the trail junction north of the tuff breccia butte, and take the north fork, which switchbacks down a steep slope composed of latite lava covered by slope wash of tuff breccia. Tuff is exposed in places on the slope. In Estes Wash, the trail meanders on densely vegetated and bird-inhabited alluvial terraces interrupted in one place by a bedrock rib to the right of the trail. This is a rhyolite dike that dips steeply to the west. The dike probably continues into the third vent, now visible on the canyon wall above you. You can also see a prominent dike that goes upward, like the tail of a tadpole, into a mass of rhyolite shaped like the cap of a mushroom. The rhyolite has contorted flow banding. This is a dike that "fed" the rhyolite dome above it—another perfect cross section of a small rhyolite volcano.

The trail crosses Estes Wash for the last time and returns to the purple-brown latite with coarse crystals where you started. At the trail junction, go right to the trailhead and enjoy the shade of the ramada.

Vent area: Here purplish rhyolite (on right) cuts older rocks and passes upward into surface flows. Brownish tuff breccia (on left) cuts older rock and passes upward into a tuff layer. This overlies the rhyolite flow mentioned earlier, so the tuff dike is younger than the rhyolite dike.

FORT BOWIE TRAIL

This easy little charmer takes you through beautiful country, then rewards you with a deeper understanding of Southwest human history and the influence of geology upon it.

LOCATION ■ Fort Bowie National Historic Site

DISTANCE ■ 3 miles round trip

ELEVATION ■ 4800 to 5000 feet

DIFFICULTY ■ Easy

TOPOGRAPHIC MAPS ■ Bowie Mountain North, AZ, 1:24,000; Willcox, AZ–NM, 1:100,000

GEOLOGIC MAPS ■ 30

PRECAUTIONS ■ Beware of flash floods and heat during the summer. Carry plenty of water. Best hiked in the spring.

INFORMATION ■ Fort Bowie National Historic Site

Landscape, Geology, and History: In parched southern Arizona, the area where Fort Bowie once stood has been of importance to humans since prehistoric times. It combines a reliable water source, Apache Spring, with Apache Pass, the low spot between the Chiricahua and Dos Cabezas Ranges. These attractions place it astride a major travel route.

The Apache, who first came to Arizona with their Navajo cousins in the 1400s and 1500s, once used this area to camp and hunt and as a watering place during their travels. The Spaniards, who arrived not long after, called the pass *Puerto del dado*, "the pass of chance." The Anglos, as always the latecomers in the Southwest, did not arrive until the mid-1800s; they came as explorers, prospectors, emigrants, ranchers, and soldiers. One of their efforts was establishment of the southern branch of the Butterfield Overland Mail in 1858, created to carry mail in 24 days over the 2800 miles separating Memphis and St. Louis from San Francisco. At that time, such breathtaking speed had something of the magic quality of today's electronic mail.

In 1861, the U.S. Army responded to a rancher's probably unjustified complaint about Apache activity in the area by sending a detachment under Lt. Bascom. His job was to stop the so-called depredation by the Apaches. In trying to do so, he unjustly threatened the great Apache chief Cochise, thus starting 10 years of intermittent strife.

In 1862, a Union army, en route to confront Confederate forces in Arizona and New Mexico, was ambushed by the still-angry warriors in the Battle of Apache Pass. This led to the establishment of an initial primitive Fort Bowie in 1862 under the command of Colonel Bowie. In 1868, a permanent and much larger complex was built nearby. Until 1886, this fort was the center of operations against the Apaches under Generals Crook and Miles.

Cochise came to terms in 1872, but in 1876 the Apaches were moved to an especially dismal part of the Gila River Valley. This was too much for several dozen Native Americans who, led by the formidable Geronimo, spent the next 10 years writing some of the most amazing pages in the history of warfare while fighting the U.S. Cavalry, ever in hot but fruitless pursuit. Geronimo and his braves eventually surrendered in 1886, thus finally ending the last of the nation's Indian wars. Its purpose over, Fort Bowie lingered on in genteel neglect until 1894, when the last troops were withdrawn. No sooner had the dust settled than the wooden structures were pilfered, leaving only the stone foundations visible today.

One reason why Fort Bowie could be established here is Apache Spring, a pleasant and abundant rivulet emerging unexpectedly from these dry hills.

Apache Pass and the irregular terrain to the northeast, all small hills and shallow washes, is underlain by Proterozoic granodiorite about 1375 million years old. *Granodiorite* is a coarse-grained igneous rock intermediate in composition between granite and diorite. Prominent hills south of Fort Bowie, such as Helens Dome and Bowie Mountain, are made of very resistant Precambrian *metaquartzite*, a hard metamorphic rock. The linear ridges north and northeast of the granodiorite terrain are underlain by a mile-wide sliver of tilted Paleozoic and Mesozoic rocks that are bounded by faults. Siphon Wash cuts through this ridge and was used by the track of the Butterfield line. This large wash has a sandy bed and is lined by large trees such as cottonwood, walnut, and ash, which indicate that water flows in the sand not far below the

Foundations of buildings at Fort Bowie

surface. The water comes from Apache Spring, which is along a strand of the ridge-bounding fault.

Trail Guide: You can reach the trailhead on Apache Pass Road from Willcox or from Bowie, both on Interstate 10. From Willcox, drive 22 miles southeast on paved AZ 186 to the graded dirt road that climbs northeast toward Apache Pass. Alternatively, from Bowie, drive south 12 miles on the partially paved Apache Pass Road.

The trailhead is at a dirt parking lot with toilet facilities and shaded picnic tables. The trail crosses a small wash, then passes by the site of an old building, which uses a rock outcrop as a wall. This rock is ancient Proterozoic granodiorite, here altered and sheared. Red *hematite* (iron oxide) staining is much in evidence. Notice the 1-inch-wide blobs in the rock—these are crystals of a potassium-bearing feldspar, characteristic of this unit. The rock weathers into a yellow-brown sandy soil.

After crossing another sandy wash, the trail climbs on surfaces that slope south from the ridge on your left. These are small *pediments* and *alluvial fans* made by sediment washing down the slope from the ridge. They are a favorite place for flowers to bloom in the spring. The trail then climbs onto an alluvial apron where the Butterfield stage station was built. This is a grassland dotted with live oak and mesquite.

After passing by the cemetery at three-fourths mile, the trail goes down into the large, sandy, richly wooded Siphon Wash, which it then abandons to go up a tributary to Apache Spring. The spring has been developed, so it does not have its original appearance. Exposures along the trail near the spring show you that granodiorite is present here. Bedrock at the bottom of the wash forces the water to the surface. If this were not the case, the water would flow within the sand instead.

Now you climb away from the spring, past the spur trail to the old fort. Pay attention to the nice outcrop of granodiorite near the "laundresses" building. Beyond this building, watch for the sudden appearance in the trail of light gray rock streaked with dark gray. This is the Permian Horquilla limestone, here sheared and recrystallized. You have just crossed the southern strand of the Apache Pass fault, going from the granodiorite into a fault-bounded sliver of Paleozoic and Mesozoic rocks. You can see the fault by looking north to the ridge beyond Apache Spring, where the shallow valley cut into the ridge shows the yellow-red of the granodiorite on the left side of the valley against the gray of the limestone on the right. This color contrast also makes the fault visible on the flank of the conical mountain south of the fort.

Apache Spring owes its existence to Apache Pass fault. The zone of crushed rock along a fault (*fault gouge*) contains much clay, so it is impermeable to water. Water flowing downward (to the west) in the subsurface encounters the gouge and is forced up, forming the spring. This single fact is responsible for human activity in this area since prehistoric times.

Apache Pass fault extends for tens of miles northwest and southeast from here. The dominant movement on this fault is *strike-slip,* or along the trend of the fault; rocks of the sliver have moved northwest relative to the granodiorite. Beds in the sliver are faulted and deformed, but their overall dip is southwest toward the fault. This causes groundwater to move downdip within the sliver toward the fault.

As you continue walking, you can see outcrops in the trail of finely laminated, recrystallized shale. Limestone is again exposed at the 1.5-mile post.

Stop to look at the walls of the powder magazine, north of the trail. You can see many blocks of dark gray limestone. Just below eye level on the left side of the doorway, one of these

Looking south at the site of the fault, marked by yellowish brown granodiorite on the right and gray limestone on the left

contains fossil stems of *crinoids,* ancient filter-feeding sea animals. In cross section, these are light-colored disks about 0.25 inch in diameter with a dark dot in the middle. In side view, the stems look like a miniature backbone consisting of stacked disks. The crinoid fossils tell you that the limestone was deposited in clear, shallow sea water. They also indicate that alteration of the limestone was not severe enough to destroy the fossils.

The turnaround point is the visitor center (open 8 A.M. to 5 P.M.), which gives a good account of the history of the fort, although no mention is made of the geology that was the cause of all the human activity here.

The foundations of the fort's buildings show which rocks were preferred for construction. Granodiorite is absent because it does not break naturally into rectangular blocks. Limestone was used, but the favored rock was a dark gray siltstone that contains small, elongated, lustrous black crystals some of which are *twinned,* meaning that they grow together as pairs. The crystals here are softer than the siltstone and tend to weather out, leaving cavities. These minerals are probably andalusite and biotite, indicating that the rock was metamorphosed.

The siltstone weathers into rectangular blocks and can also be worked easily to produce shapes useful for building. The rock is probably from the Cretaceous Cintura Formation, which crops out extensively nearby, just east of the fort complex.

The return trail starts just behind the visitor center. It follows the ridge instead of the valley and provides panoramic views of Fort Bowie and the San Simon Valley far to the north. At first, the trail is on a ridge held up by the Horquilla limestone. Just before the high point, you can find an outcrop a few feet north of the trail that shows folded banding in the limestone.

Once you get to the bench at the top of the ridge, you can see tilted sedimentary rocks of the fault sliver to the north and the trace of Apache Pass fault to the south, on the flank of the conical hill beyond the fort. Look for the gray of the limestone on the left and the tan-brown of the granodiorite on the right. You can also see nice crinoid stems in the outcrop of gray limestone streaked with brown about 10 feet east of the Fort Bowie plaque.

Apache Pass fault is nicely visible as you go down to the saddle on the ridge. At the unmarked trail junction, the left trail is a short spur leading to bouldery granodiorite outcrops from which Apaches ambushed U.S. troops during the battle of Apache Pass. The right fork is the main trail, which soon crosses the fault. From this point, the return trail switchbacks down from the ridge into Siphon Wash and rejoins the main trail near the stagecoach building.

HEART OF ROCKS– ECHO CANYON TRAIL

Hike 34

This great trail combines intriguing nooks and crannies carved into a classic ash-flow tuff with impressive distant vistas.

LOCATION ■ Chiricahua National Monument

DISTANCE ■ 7.25 miles roundtrip for the loop; 0.9 mile extra for the Heart of Rocks loop

ELEVATION ■ 5980 to 6860 feet

DIFFICULTY ■ Moderate

TOPOGRAPHIC MAPS ■ Cochise Head, AZ, 1:24,000; Rustler Park, AZ, 1:24,000; Willcox, AZ–NM, 1:100,000; Chiricahua Peak, AZ–NM, 1:100,000

GEOLOGIC MAPS ■ 31 and 32

PRECAUTIONS ■ Best hiked in spring or fall. Get an early start in the morning for this long trail.

INFORMATION ■ Chiricahua National Monument

Landscape, Geology, and History: The Chiricahua Mountains were part of the home range of the Chiricahua Apaches. In the mid-1800s, the Apaches attempted to protect their territory as the influx of miners and settlers swelled to a torrent. Led by their great chiefs Cochise and Geronimo, they held the U.S. Cavalry at bay for more than 25 years, using extraordinarily successful guerrilla tactics. But in the end, the inevitable happened: the Apaches were removed to distant places and settlers moved into their former territories. Among them were the Ericksons and the Staffords, whose homesteads still exist within the national monument and can be visited.

The Chiricahuas are a rugged mountain range rising above the surrounding desert plain to more than 9700 feet. The range is the product of basin and range type faulting that has taken place over the past 20 million years; the faulting produced the ranges and intervening basins that we see today. The rocks that compose the ranges, however, are much older than the formation of the ranges themselves.

About 1.7 billion years ago, the southwestern United States was the site of *island arcs*, offshore complexes of volcanoes near subduction zones. Sedimentary and volcanic rocks accumulated near the margin of the growing continent. Over time, the deposits were heated and metamorphosed into the Proterozoic-age Pinal schist, the oldest rock in the region. By 1.4 billion years ago, the schist was intruded by granites and the island arcs were welded to the continent, which had been slowly growing by this process from its ancient core in Canada.

In much of Arizona, these events were followed by an unimaginably long period of erosion—some 800 million years—which are now represented only by the *unconformity* (gap in the rock record) between the schist and the overlying Paleozoic rocks. The latter were deposited in a shallow ancient sea between about 600 and 250 million years ago, as life was evolving on Earth.

In Mesozoic time, a *subduction zone* was active in the Southwest. In this zone, an oceanic plate was thrust northeastward underneath the continental plate. As the material of the subducted plate reached great depths, it began to melt. The resulting magma rose toward the surface. Some never made it all the way but cooled within the crust, forming great igneous intrusions such as the granitic Sierra Nevada. Magma that reached the surface created volcanoes.

The closing event of this unrest was the *Laramide orogeny*, a major mountain-building event at the end of Mesozoic time marked by volcanism and the formation of most of the ore bodies in the southwestern United States.

Volcanism associated with subduction continued into Tertiary time. About 27 million years ago, a large mass of silica-rich *rhyolite* (the fine-grained equivalent of granite) was present in a magma chamber a few miles below the surface in what are now the Chiricahuas. The magma vented to the surface when the pressure in the chamber became more than the overlying rocks could bear. Because of the sudden drop in pressure, gases in the magma expanded explosively, causing the magma to become an extremely hot froth. More than 100 cubic miles of it

Joints in welded tuff form pinnacles and balanced rocks.

emerged from the volcano in several eruptions and flowed swiftly away in the form of ash flows.

Ponder a moment the enormity of this number—100 cubic miles. It is the volume of a cube nearly 5 miles on a side. Can you imagine this volume moving down a volcano in a very short time? By comparison, Mount St. Helens produced only 0.1 cubic miles in its 1980 eruption, and the great 1991 eruption of Mount Pinatubo in the Philippines produced about 1 cubic mile.

Almost instantaneously, the flows covered an area of 1200 square miles with hot pumice and ash. No human being has ever witnessed this kind of eruption. The catastrophe that buried Roman Pompeii was peanuts by comparison.

The *pumice* (frozen glass froth) and ash eventually stopped moving, forming large sheets of *ash-flow tuff*. We call this the *outflow tuff* because it flowed out of and away from the volcano's caldera. The hottest parts of the tuff were

216

welded by the heat when they stopped flowing. These parts of the tuff are called *welded tuff*.

The roof of the magma chamber then found itself unsupported because so much material was being removed from under it by the eruptions. It collapsed downward, forming a huge circular depression about 12 miles in diameter. This is the Turkey Creek *caldera*, a crater at the heart of the volcano. Since the caldera was collapsing while the ash flow was erupting, a lot of tuff pooled within the caldera, where it reached a great thickness. We call this the *intra-caldera tuff*, because it accumulated inside the caldera.

After these events, the volcano calmed down some but was by no means dead yet. First, the floor of the caldera was warped up into a *resurgent dome* (a dome that rises up again) by subterranean injections of *dacite*, a fine-grained volcanic rock midway in composition between rhyolite and basalt. Some of it reached the surface near the moat formed between the growing dome and the rim of the caldera, while some managed to flow beyond the rim. The dacite was more resistant to erosion than other rocks, so it remained while the other rocks were gradually worn away. The result of this *differential erosion* is that the dacite now caps high points such as Sugarloaf Mountain.

The sheets of welded tuff cracked as they were cooling, forming vertical *joints*. These joints enclosed polygonal columns of rock. Erosion then worked its way on the joints, gradually widening them. The end result is the picturesque columns so characteristic of welded tuffs in the Chiricahuas and elsewhere. Erosion also attacked any softer horizontal bands within the tuffs, producing the balanced rocks that are common in the monument.

The final burp of the expiring volcano produced small amounts of rhyolite within the moat. Then, long after the volcano stopped breathing, it suffered the indignity of being broken up by basin and range faulting. Part of the volcano became a range, the Chiricahua Mountains, and part was dropped down into basins and covered with sediment. The topography you see today is not that of the original volcano but the product of this later faulting.

Trail Guide: To reach Chiricahua National Monument, take the marked spur road that branches from AZ 186 southeast of Willcox. The entire drive is on paved roads. The monument has a visitor center and a campground with water and toilet facilities, which is filled early each day. There are no gasoline, food, or restaurant facilities in or near the monument. Once in the monument, take the park road toward Massai Point. Shortly before reaching this point, turn sharply right on a paved road to Sugarloaf Mountain. After 500 feet, turn left into a parking lot at the start of the Heart of Rocks–Echo Canyon Trail.

Just after you have started on the trail, take the left fork signed "To Massai Point."

The trail is on the Rhyolite Canyon tuff, the relatively thin outflow facies that

Heart of Rocks

spilled out of the Turkey Creek caldera. In contrast, the part of the tuff within the caldera is more than 5000 feet thick. The vegetation here is mostly pinyon pine, alligator juniper, live oak, and red-stemmed manzanita.

The trail soon enters a canyon tributary to Rhyolite Canyon. You can see outcrops of the welded tuff along the trail, many forming characteristic pinnacles eroded out along joints. The northern of two pinnacles close to each other shows *honeycomb weathering*. This feature often marks places where steam made its way to the surface along irregular vertical pipes while the tuff was cooling.

At the next trail junction about 1000 feet from the trailhead, go right toward the Heart of Rocks. The approach to Rhyolite Canyon gives you fine views of the columns and spires that are typical of erosion working upon welded tuffs. Note how the columns are shaped by the interplay of erosion along vertical cooling cracks and along horizontal variations in hardness of the tuff.

Douglas fir and tall three-needle pine thrive here in the cool, wet canyon, as well as on its north-facing side. You cross Rhyolite Canyon near its head, then climb about 600 feet along a splendid trail built by the Civil Conservation Corps (CCC) in the 1930s. Once past the junction with the trail to Inspiration Point, you find yourself on a plateau formed by the middle member of the outflow part of the Rhyolite Canyon tuff; the upper member is on the flank of Sugarloaf Mountain (to the north), and the lower member is at the bottom of Rhyolite Canyon. Each member is the product of an individual eruption, but all are part of a distinctive and mappable geologic unit.

Climb onto the top of a large outcrop of welded tuff south of the trail; from here, the views to the south are fine. The first large drainage is Pinery Canyon; Pine Canyon is beyond it. The mountains forming the distant skyline are within the caldera. Look at the rock on which you are standing. Gray areas are places where slivers have recently broken off, exposing fresh rock. Using a hand lens, you can see abundant boxy crystals that are glassy and commonly show a play of colors (*chatoyance*). This mineral is *sanidine*, a high-temperature potassium feldspar common in rhyolite welded tuffs. Sanidine is a good mineral to use for dating volcanic rocks by radiometric age methods.

Walk a short distance along the trail to a rise that gives you excellent views in all directions. To the northeast is the prominent light-colored mountain called Cochise Head. This is formed of welded tuffs older than those from Turkey Creek caldera. Can you make out Cochise's profile? His chin is to the left, as viewed from here. To the northwest you can see the double peak of Dos Cabezas ("two heads"), composed of tuff of latest Mesozoic age. To the west is Sulphur Springs Valley, containing Wilcox Playa. The valley was formed by basin and range faulting long after the eruptions of Turkey Creek caldera. Wilcox Playa is all that is left of the much larger Lake Cochise, which existed during the Pleistocene Ice Ages when conditions were much wetter than now.

Beyond the rise, you enter the intricately dissected and picturesque terrain that is the hallmark of Chiricahua National Monument. Balanced Rock, which is marked with a sign, clearly shows how the columns form by erosion along vertical fractures, whereas the indentations on the columns themselves result from faster erosion of less hardened parts of the column. Balanced rocks are no miracle. Given the thousands of columns present in the area, it is not surprising that a few weather in such a way that the rock is balanced. The other unbalanced ones simply topple over. Eventually all do, as shown by the toppled rock near Balanced Rock.

A few hundred feet west of the Balanced Rock sign, the trail goes through a slot in the bedrock. In the walls of the slot, you can see blobs of white, gray, and yellowish rock about 1 inch long and in the shapes of horizontal lenses. These are *fiamme* ("flame" in Italian) structures, clumps of pumice that were hot enough to collapse under the weight of the rock during and after emplacement of the welded tuff. *Pumice* is frozen glass froth.

A sign marks the Heart of Rocks loop, which adds 0.9 mile to the walk but is well worth the effort. This is a fantastically eroded and picturesque area carved into the middle member of the Rhyolite Canyon tuff. You can see good examples of the internal structures of the tuff and a lot of flattened pumice. The effect of erosion along joints gives rise to intricate country that is a photographer's paradise. You can also enjoy great views across Rhyolite Canyon to Cochise Head.

After completing the loop, you switchback down a barren south-facing slope into the pleasant and wooded Sarah Deming Canyon, which you follow to its confluence with Rhyolite Canyon, a drop of about 940 feet. In this stretch, the trail is in the lower member of the Rhyolite Canyon tuff, which is better welded and harder than the middle member. You can see this because it weathers into sharp edges instead of the rounded ones more typical of tuff. Horizontal and vertical joints in the rock result in big boxy blocks and large horizontal tables.

A break in the trees allows a fine view to the north across the canyon, where you can see the three members of the Rhyolite Canyon tuff. The lower member weathers into relatively angular columns, whereas the middle member has more rounded columns. Between the two is a light-colored band of mostly unwelded tuff. The upper member is exposed on the distant slope of Sugarloaf Mountain.

At Rhyolite Canyon, turn right on the trail toward Massai Point and Echo Canyon and cross the wash, noting the large boulders—evidence of past flash floods. Climb 400 feet, then turn left toward Echo Canyon. The parking lot is 1.6 miles away and 450 feet higher.

The trail re-enters the middle member of the Rhyolite Canyon tuff near the crossing of Echo Canyon, beyond which it climbs out and goes through a narrow cleft. A few hundred yards farther, fiamme structures are beautifully exposed in the tuff walls along the trail, as are sanidine crystals on fresh surfaces. The trail then goes through a narrow flat-floored corridor, which is interesting because the walls show smooth, almost polished areas, remnants of the joint surfaces along which the corridor was carved. The floor gives a plan view of the pumice fragments that form the fiamme structures—they look like roughly circular blobs here. This tells you that, in three dimensions, fiamme structures are lens-shaped.

Take a good look at the tuff walls on both sides of the trail just before it crests out. The abundant cavities, less than 1 inch to several inches across, are a common feature near the top of welded tuffs. These cavities mark *fumaroles*, places where water in the ground was brought to boiling by the hot tuff and the resulting steam forced its way to the surface of the tuff.

HUGH NORRIS TRAIL (WASSON PEAK)

Hike 35

This is a pleasant ridge hike through an ancient volcanic caldera with fine views within the lovely Sonoran vegetation of Saguaro National Park.

LOCATION ■ Tucson Mountains, Saguaro National Park
DISTANCE ■ 4.9 miles one way
ELEVATION ■ 2570 to 4687 feet
DIFFICULTY ■ Moderate
TOPOGRAPHIC MAPS ■ Avra, AZ, 1:24,000; Silver Bell Mountains, AZ, 1:100,000
GEOLOGIC MAPS ■ 33
PRECAUTIONS ■ Heat and lightning in summer
INFORMATION ■ Saguaro National Park, Red Hills Visitor Center

Landscape and Geology: The Tucson Mountains, of which Wasson is the highest peak, are a modest desert range typical of Arizona's Basin and Range Province. The range is in the Sonoran vegetation zone because it is at a relatively low elevation.

You cannot tell much about the origin of the rocks that form the range by looking at the topography. Nevertheless, geologists who have studied these rocks conclude that this was the site of a volcanic caldera at the end of Cretaceous time, one of many in Arizona formed as a result of a subduction zone off the continent's margin, not far to the southwest. Many of these *calderas*, which are large craters produced by the collapse of an empty magma chamber, are associated with the economic mineral deposits for which the area is well known. Let's play detective during this hike, following the example of the geologists.

Three groups of rocks exposed along the trail were involved in the history of the caldera:

Group 1. Pre-caldera rocks. These rocks existed in the area before formation of the caldera. They include an ash-flow tuff that erupted from an older caldera near Silver Bell, as well as overlying sandstone and shale that were deposited in lakes and in low-lying areas surrounding the lakes.

Group 2. Rocks within the caldera. These include deposits of ash-flow tuff and megabreccia—a jumble of large angular blocks of pre-caldera rocks. These two units are interbedded. The ash-flow tuffs are solidified froth of silica-rich lava that once flowed away from the caldera. They represent the expulsion of huge volumes of rock, which led to the collapse that formed the caldera; the megabreccia represents collapse of the walls into the caldera.

Group 3. Post-caldera igneous rocks. These rocks were created by igneous processes after the caldera had formed. They represent a late-stage renewal of igneous activity under the volcano. Most are plutons that intrude rocks within the caldera (group 2). These rocks have been metamorphosed by the heat and pressure from the intrusions.

Long after it had died, the caldera was broken up by faults and tilted. Part of the caldera was faulted up into a range—the Tucson Mountains—by Tertiary basin and range faulting; part was dropped down into the nearby basins and covered by basin fill. The original shape of the caldera is now gone.

Trail Guide: Take Exit 257 (Speedway) from Interstate 10 in Tucson and travel west. Speedway eventually becomes Gates Pass Road. At Kinney Road, turn right. Go past the Arizona–Sonora Desert Museum to Saguaro National Park and the Red Hills Visitor Center. Turn right onto gravel Hohokam Road 1.7 miles past the center. The trailhead for Hugh Norris Trail is 0.8 mile farther. This is a large built-up trail; the many erosion-control steps in the first part of the trail are annoying.

The trail starts on a *pediment* (a gravel-mantled slope at the foot of desert

Late-stage granite

mountains), but it soon climbs in a medium-grained granite containing quartz, feldspar, and biotite that is weathered into rounded shapes. This is the interior part of the Cretaceous Amole pluton (named after Amole Mountain), one of the post-caldera rocks (group 3). This *pluton* intrudes both the pre-caldera and the caldera-filling rocks and represents late-stage resurgent igneous activity.

The short climb ends at about 1 mile from the trailhead in picturesque granite outcrops, then follows a ridge. Fine-grained, light-colored igneous rocks with many quartz veins crop out at the end of the ridge. This is *aplite*, a part of the pluton that consists mostly of quartz and feldspar.

About 500 feet farther, near a saddle between two hills to the south, the trail enters outcrops of medium and light gray rocks, both of which appear fine-grained if you look casually. But if you look at the lighter colored rock with a hand lens, you can see rounded grains of quartz. This is sandstone; the darker stuff is shale. Both have been metamorphosed into rather nondescript rock by the Amole pluton. We walk on these Cretaceous pre-caldera rocks (group 1) all the way to where the trail reaches a major saddle in the ridge crest.

At the saddle, you can see a light-colored rock that contains fragments. This is an ash-flow tuff that came from the Silver Bell area about 20 miles to the northwest. Its composition is *rhyolite*, the fine-grained equivalent of granite. The tuff is overlain by the sandstone and shale you just went through and is also a pre-caldera rock (group 1). As you start up the gentle slope east of the saddle, you suddenly enter an area underlain by a jumble of blocks of all sizes and many different compositions, including easily recognizable conglomerate. You have crossed the margin of the ancient caldera and are now in the Cretaceous caldera-filling megabreccia of group 2. The breccia contains clasts of mostly Cretaceous rocks like the ones you just walked through, which form the caldera rim and wall. The breccia represents material that avalanched into the caldera from its walls while it was forming.

The trail now climbs gently on the north side of the ridge to a trail junction in one-fourth mile from the saddle. Just beyond, you can see yet another rock type—a medium gray, medium-grained *granodiorite* containing quartz, plagioclase, orthoclase, and biotite. This intrusive igneous rock has a composition midway between granite and diorite. It forms the outer margin of the Amole pluton, so it is part of the late-stage igneous activity of group 3 that intruded the caldera fill. You have just walked across the intrusive contact from the megabreccia into the granodiorite that intruded it. Contacts like this one show that the Amole pluton intrudes all other rocks of the caldera, which means that it is the youngest rock here and represents the most recent igneous activity.

The trail reaches a saddle directly south of Amole Peak after following the ridge for about 1 mile. Wasson Peak is now visible to the east. Shortly beyond this saddle, you leave the granodiorite and enter megabreccia again, as indicated by the jumble of blocks on the slopes. You have once again crossed the contact between late-stage intrusion and caldera fill. As you switchback up the grade, however, you can see that here the trail is in a narrow belt of cream-colored rock with irregular banding, many inclusions, and dark lenses of flattened *pumice*—frozen rhyolite froth. This is a densely welded rhyolite ash-flow tuff, which the trail follows all the way to the summit of Wasson Peak. The tuff also forms the tilted ridge to the south with the radio towers. The tuff is interlayered with the megabreccia in a complex fashion. Geologists interpret this to mean that material slid off the caldera wall into the tuff as the tuff was erupting and the caldera was forming.

Safford Peak, in the middle distance to the north, is a *neck* (lava congealed in the throat of a volcano) surrounded by rhyolite flows that issued from it. The whole edifice has been tilted northeastward by basin and range type faulting. This is the northernmost part of the Tucson Mountains caldera.

If air pollution is not too bad, you may be able to see the Superstition Mountains far to the north (Hike 25). To the east, the Santa Catalina and Rincon Mountains rise above the smoggy Tucson basin and the Whetstones to the right of the Rincons. The distinctive pyramid of Mount Wrightson (Hike 40) is conspicuous in the Santa Rita Mountains to the southeast, as are the distinctive tooth of Baboquivari Peak and the Kitt Peak astronomical observatory to the southwest.

HUNTER TRAIL (PICACHO PEAK)

Hike 36

Climb this unscalable-looking peak for a spectacular view and a look at altered volcanic rocks from the upper plate of a metamorphic core complex.

LOCATION ■ Picacho Peak State Park

DISTANCE ■ 2.1 miles one way

ELEVATION ■ 2000 to 3370 feet (net climb is 1830 feet due to a 460-foot descent along the trail)

DIFFICULTY ■ Moderate to difficult

TOPOGRAPHIC MAPS ■ Newman Peak, AZ, 1:24,000; Casa Grande, AZ, 1:100,000

GEOLOGIC MAPS ■ 34

PRECAUTIONS ■ Watch for heat and lightning in summer. Steep cliff edges make this trail unsuitable for those who fear heights.

INFORMATION ■ Arizona State Parks

Landscape and Geology: At first sight, the improbable-looking spire of Picacho Peak may appear geologically simple. It is a sequence of altered lava flows and interbedded sediments about 20 million years old (Miocene age) that dips moderately to the northeast. Geologists, however, have found that it is more complex than it seems. Picacho Peak is actually linked geologically to the Picacho Mountains, a few miles to the north across a desert basin. Together, Picacho Peak and the Picacho Mountains form a *metamorphic core complex*, one of many such enigmatic geologic features in Arizona.

These complexes were the result of extreme *extension* (pull-apart deformation), and they form a northwest-trending belt in the southwestern part of the state. The Santa Catalina and Rincon Mountains near Tucson, South Mountain near Phoenix, the Harcuvar, Harquahala, and Buckskin Mountains in western

Picacho Peak from the south

Arizona, and the Whipple Mountains in eastern California all are metamorphic core complexes.

The name "complex" is given to these features because they are three-tiered. At the bottom is a *lower plate*, which was deformed in plastic fashion, flowing like taffy without breaking. This plate is made up of metamorphic rocks such as gneiss. The *upper plate* is at the top. It was cooler and thus responded to extension by breaking rather than flowing, so it now is composed of many tilted blocks separated by faults. Its rocks are generally altered and mineralized. Between the upper and lower plates is a nearly horizontal *detachment fault*, called that because rocks of the upper plate were detached, or uncoupled, from those of the lower plate, allowing them to deform in a totally different manner. Furthermore, rocks of the upper plate were not originally where they are now, but were moved into that position along the detachment. No wonder all this has given geologists something to argue about.

The Picacho complex is even more "complex" because it consists of three plates rather than two. The lowest is composed of the Proterozoic Oracle granite, about 1400 million years old. It went through taffy-like deformation about 22 million years ago. Next is a *middle plate* composed of broken-up Oracle granite in which dark minerals have been altered to the greenish mineral *chlorite* by hot (*hydrothermal*) fluids. The upper plate is made of 20 million-year-old volcanic rocks and interbedded sediments, which have been rotated along northwest-striking faults and intensely altered by hot fluids, which added a lot of potassium.

Picacho Peak and the surrounding hills are part of the upper plate. The elongated shape of the hills is caused by the resistant volcanic rocks that have been rotated along northwest-striking faults to form the ridge.

Trail Guide: Leave Interstate 10 at Exit 219, Picacho Peak. Follow the signs to Picacho Peak State Park, which charges a $5 admission fee. Go to the trailhead

East side of Picacho Peak: massive flows of altered intermediate to basaltic lava

parking, which is quite small and may be full. This area is in the Sonoran vegetation zone and is especially adorned with wildflowers in early spring.

Follow the signed Hunter Trail, which crosses the ridge at the saddle visible straight ahead. It then drops about 460 feet on the other side before climbing to the top. The ridge ahead culminates in Picacho Peak at its southeast end. Most of the rocks you see are lava flows of intermediate to basaltic composition (poor in silica). The flows dip toward you, and the ridge is parallel to the strike of the rocks.

The trail starts out on a sloping *pediment,* a bedrock surface that slopes away from the mountains and is mantled by a thin veneer of gravel. Near the foot of the cliffs, the pediment gives way to a talus slope marked by large boulders that have fallen off the cliffs. You can see an exposure of *brecciated* (broken up) basalt on the outside of a switchback. This is *flow breccia,* formed when flowing lava cools enough on the outside to solidify, forming a thin crust that then breaks up and is incorporated into the still-moving lava. You can see breccia like this in many places along the trail.

Once you get to the base of the cliff, you can see that the lava is *vesicular,* that is, full of pits that once were gas bubbles. It also contains substantial crystals of feldspar. In general, these flows are so altered that it is hard to make out minerals.

Just before the saddle at about three-fourths mile, you can see a small cavern on the left that sports a smooth, polished surface, now unfortunately decorated with graffiti. The polished surfaces are *slickensides,* formed when fault movement grinds and polishes the rock along the walls of the fault.

The rock on the steep pitch beyond the saddle shows many fractures with a reddish filling, possibly calcite and iron oxide. These give you some idea of how much these rocks have been fractured and altered. At the base of the descent, you can see a classic slickensided surface on the left side of the trail as you go around a nose.

At one-fourth mile from the saddle, you reach the intersection of the Hunter and Vista Trails. Stay on the Hunter. Now the climbing gets serious, but it is not nearly as difficult as it looks from below.

You may be hard-pressed to pay much attention to the geology while negotiating the cliffs. Overall, the rock is similar to what has been seen before—altered and fractured basalt. You may notice filled vesicles that make the rock look like conglomerate, and veins of the pistachio-green mineral *epidote* that are further evidence of alteration.

A puzzle awaits you on top of the cliffs in the form of a patch of granitic rock surrounded by basalt. What is a block of granite doing on top of the basalt? The granite plates are supposed to be way down below the basalt. The most likely explanation is that this granite block was wrenched from the walls of the conduit through which the lava rose to the surface, then was rafted by the lava to its present position.

The view from the top is impressive. Most interesting from a geologic point of view are the Picacho Mountains to the north, which form the bulk of the metamorphic core complex of which Picacho Peak is part. Most of the mountain mass is formed by light-colored gneiss and granite of the lower plate, but a few darker-colored humps in the southeast corner are upper plate rocks like those of Picacho Peak. The reddish-brown hillock rising from the desert plain between the interstate and the aqueduct is another piece of the upper plate.

Hike

37

HUTCHES POOL TRAIL

This pleasant hike through Sonoran and riparian vegetation provides a close look at the lower plate of a metamorphic core complex and leads to a bedrock pool with fine swimming.

LOCATION ■ Pusch Ridge Wilderness, Coronado National Forest

DISTANCE ■ About 4 miles one way

ELEVATION ■ 3334 to 3860 feet

DIFFICULTY ■ Moderate

TOPOGRAPHIC MAPS ■ Sabino Canyon, AZ, 1:24,000; Tucson, AZ, 1:100,000

GEOLOGIC MAPS ■ 35

PRECAUTIONS ■ Heat in summer

INFORMATION ■ Coronado National Forest, Santa Catalina Ranger District

Landscape and Geology: The Santa Catalina Mountains, together with the nearby Rincon Mountains, are one of Arizona's largest *metamorphic core*

Looking west up the cross canyon formed by the Romero Pass fault. The cliffs on the right skyline are in upper-plate granite.

complexes. (Refer to the Basin and Range section of "The Making of Arizona" at the beginning of this book.)

In their classic form, these complicated and still-debated geologic features consist of three parts—a *lower plate* composed of the metamorphic rock *gneiss* that has been intensely sheared and has flowed like taffy; an *upper plate* which has broken up in a brittle manner along many parallel faults; and a *detachment fault* which separates the two plates and against which the upper plate faults end. The detachment fault is the boundary between brittle deformation above and plastic deformation below.

The complexes are in zones of extreme *extension*, or pull-apart. Many have been warped up into dome-like mountain ranges. In most of these, the upper plate and detachment fault have been eroded from the crest of the dome and are preserved only along the flanks. This is the case in the Catalina Mountains. Trails here provide a good opportunity to look at a lower plate and its characteristic gneiss.

Trail Guide: From Tucson, take Tanque Verde Road to Sabino Canyon Road, which you follow to the parking lot at the visitor center. From here, take the shuttle bus ($6 per person) to the trailhead. The shuttles run about every half-hour. The last one leaves the turnaround at the trailhead at 4:30 P.M. As you ride, you have a fine view of the gneiss in the canyon walls.

At the turnaround, take the signed trail that switchbacks up the canyon side to the intersection with Phoneline Trail. As you climb, take stock of the rocks along the trail. Some are gneiss that contains light-colored flakes of *muscovite* mica; others are a darker gneiss that contains flakes of black *biotite* mica.

If you look carefully, you can see two features typical of the gneisses along this hike and characteristic of sheared lower plate gneiss in general. The first feature, called *lineation*, consists of subtle parallel streaks or lines in the gneiss. They are produced by aligned minerals. The other has the charming name *augen*, a German word meaning "eyes." They consist of large feldspar crystals around which the mineral lines and bands seem to curve and flow. The result looks like eyes, hence the name. Both lineation and augen were formed when the rock was being sheared and flowed like taffy.

At the junction with the Phoneline Trail, turn left toward Trail #24, but first pause to look across the canyon, where you can see that the foliation (banding) in the gneiss dips gently to the right, or north. When you were coming up the canyon road, you may have noticed that the layering at the mouth of Sabino Canyon dips gently south. These opposing dips indicate an *anticline* (upward fold) in the foliation called the "Forerange anticline." From here you can also see large boulders at the bottom of the canyon. It is said that these boulders fell off the canyon walls in 1887 as a result of an earthquake of intensity 6.1 that occurred about 100 miles south of here in Mexico.

Sabino Canyon is carved approximately along the Sabino Canyon fault, a high-angle fault of relatively small displacement. The fault is not conspicuous, but it generally runs just west of Trail #24 and passes through a few saddles crossed by the trail. It is marked by reddish fault gouge.

As you walk along the trail, you can see outcrops of gneiss that contain both muscovite and biotite. These micas are present because the original rock that was altered into the gneiss was a *two-mica granite*. This granite was intruded into the Proterozoic Oracle granite in Eocene time in the form of thick *sills* (tabular intrusive masses that parallel layering). It was then converted into sheared gneiss much later, in middle Tertiary time. If you look carefully, you may find small reddish-brown garnets in some outcrops, a mineral indicating metamorphism.

The other side of the canyon displays a prominent band of dark rock with white layers. You can get a good close-up view of this rock in outcrops right along the trail. This is sheared Oracle granite. The dark color comes from ground-up biotite; the white layers are rocks that intruded the granite when it was formed in Eocene time. Looking at the outcrop across the canyon with binoculars and examining the one along the trail, you can see that the layers are folded into S and Z shapes of various sizes. These toothpaste-like folds give you a feeling for how intensely this rock has been sheared and deformed.

The trail reaches a high point at a little saddle. From here, you can see that Sabino Canyon intersects a cross valley in which lie the East and West Forks of Sabino Canyon. This cross valley is along the Romero Pass high-angle fault zone, whose movement is up to the south. Most of the mountain face north of the fault consists of a sill of Eocene granite, similar to what you have been walking through.

The trail gradually works its way down into the valley. At the bottom, about 2.5 miles from the trailhead, a trail junction sign is nearly buried by boulders that came out of a nearby canyon in 1999 during a cloudburst. Does this give you the feeling that flash floods are not to be trifled with?

Folding in gneiss of the lower plate

The trail then heads west up the cross valley in open grassland country dotted with pinyon and juniper. The nearby creek is perennial and has many delightful pools. The water supports a rich riparian vegetation. The Romero Pass fault is not easily visible along the trail, but you can deduce its location from fractures in the rocks that are coated with a smooth reddish material (*slickensides*). Slickensides are formed when rocks grind past each other on a fault.

Eventually, the trail crosses the creek, goes through some open grassy areas, then begins to climb to the left (south), about 1.5 miles from the last trail junction. At this point, watch for a track going right, toward the creek. This track leads to Hutches Pool, which is a little upstream from a sandy area. This bedrock pool is an excellent swimming hole. Please be considerate of this place, which gets heavy use.

MILLER PEAK TRAIL

Hike 38

This hike through many vegetation zones displays the effects of subduction on an ancient continental margin and climbs to an isolated peak with spectacular views in all directions, including into Mexico.

LOCATION ■ Coronado National Memorial and Miller Peak Wilderness, Coronado National Forest

DISTANCE ■ 5.3 miles one way

ELEVATION ■ 6580 to 9466 feet

DIFFICULTY ■ Moderately strenuous

TOPOGRAPHIC MAPS ■ Miller Peak, AZ, 1:24,000; Montezuma Pass, AZ–Sonora, 1:24,000; Fort Huachuca, AZ, 1:100,000; Nogales, AZ–Sonora, 1:100,000

GEOLOGIC MAPS ■ 36

PRECAUTIONS ■ Snow and cold in winter, lightning in summer

INFORMATION ■ Coronado National Memorial

Landscape and Geology: Starting in late Triassic time, a *subduction zone* developed off the ancient continent margin to the southwest of this region (see figure 6). The dense crust of the oceanic plate was dragged under the more buoyant crust of the North American continent. Once at great depth, the dragged-down oceanic crust was heated enough to melt, and the resulting magma rose to the surface in the form of volcanoes and underlying *plutons*. Some of the magma was silica-rich. Its eruption produced great volcanoes, many with calderas. The Huachuca Mountains probably were one such volcano. Some of the magma cooled and solidified below the surface, forming intrusions. Mineral-enriched fluids heated by the magma altered rocks through which they passed and produced mineral deposits.

Blocks falling off the caldera walls into the volcanic material accumulating on the caldera floor may account for the strange exotic blocks of limestone that are conspicuous along this hike. Volcanic ash blown into the atmosphere during eruptions such as those recorded in the rocks of the Huachuca Mountains may be one source of the *bentonite* (a clay derived from weathering of volcanic ash) found in the Triassic Chinle Formation, far to the north on the Colorado Plateau (Hike 9).

The original configuration of the caldera has been destroyed by *thrust faults* of late Mesozoic age. These faults are the product of compressive forces generated by the collision of the plates. The caldera was destroyed even more in Tertiary time when movement on high-angle normal faults created the present Basin and Range Province.

Trail Guide: Take Arizona Highway 92 south from Sierra Vista. After about 20 miles, turn south onto Coronado Memorial Road. Continue beyond the delightful, if small, visitor center at 5 miles. The road soon becomes a winding mountain road unsuitable for long vehicles such as motorhomes. Park at Montezuma Pass Overlook, where there are toilets and trash cans. The trail starts on the north side of the road across from the parking lot.

This is the Crest Trail, part of the Arizona Trail System. Pets must be on leashes within the national memorial. Take along your binoculars and the geologic map to help decipher the complex but fascinating geology of this place.

The rock in the cuts at the parking lot and along the beginning of the trail is the Glance Conglomerate of Cretaceous age. Its *clasts* (fragments included in the rock) are composed mostly of upper Paleozoic sedimentary rocks, the Jurassic Huachuca quartz monzonite (a granite-like igneous rock), and silica-rich volcanic rocks, all of which are present in the Huachuca Mountains. This conglomerate tells us that both the volcanic rocks of the Huachuca caldera complex and the underlying (intrusive) plutonic rocks were being eroded vigorously by early Cretaceous time. Thus, the area of the caldera must have already been deformed and uplifted by then.

Just beyond on the trail is another conglomerate that contains fragments of purplish *andesite*, a fine-grained basalt-like volcanic rock. After it come flows of the andesite itself. This is a messy, altered rock that is hard to identify. A conspicuous light-gray block near the trail is one of the exotic masses of limestone within the andesite.

At about one-half mile from the start, the trail reaches a saddle after a few switchbacks, near another large block of limestone. You have crossed one of the many northwest-trending high-angle faults cut into the Jurassic and Triassic Huachuca volcanics, which are composed of weathered silica-rich tuffs and lavas. This is a light-colored rock with a pinkish cast, quite different from the andesite. This unit is believed to have been deposited within a caldera,

Cross bedding in the Morita Formation

with the limestone blocks falling off the walls of the caldera into the lava and tuff accumulating on its floor. The blocks within the andesite may reflect a similar but earlier event.

Once past the limestone block, you cross a second saddle and then a gully. The gully is along another fault, which brings a new formation in contact with the volcanics. This is the Morita Formation of Cretaceous age, composed of well-bedded reddish siltstone and mudstone and pinkish-gray sandstone with fluvial cross bedding (see figure 12). The Morita is exposed all along the grassy nose ahead. This unit is younger than the Glance and contains no exotic blocks. Its fine grain size and thin beds tells you it was deposited in low-energy water. Evidently, the unrest associated with formation of the caldera and its subsequent uplift and erosion (recorded in the Glance) were over by the time the Morita was laid down. As we shall soon see, this was just a temporary respite. Once you are well beyond the nose, take a look at the low-angle cross bedding in an outcrop just left of the trail and before a major gully.

At the gully, the trail crosses yet another fault that brings you back into limestone blocks within the Huachuca volcanics, then switchbacks near several *adits* (miners' pits) in the limestone where it is stained with copper. In the limestone, you can see large crystals that flash in the sun and much shearing and folding. The crystals are the mineral *calcite* (calcium carbonate), and the rock is *marble*, metamorphosed limestone.

The reason for the metamorphism here is visible just before the last mine dump, where you encounter a medium-grained *equigranular* plutonic rock, meaning the crystals are all the same size. Look at this intrusive igneous rock with your hand lens. The glassy crystals are quartz, the white opaque ones are plagioclase feldspar, and the pinkish ones orthoclase feldspar. This is a dike of the Jurassic Huachuca quartz monzonite. You cross another similar dike a little farther along the trail. This rock was probably made by the same magma that produced the Huachuca volcanics, but in this case it cooled at depth instead of coming to the surface.

Hot, mineral-rich fluids associated with these intrusive rocks altered and mineralized the limestone, as you can see from the blue and green copper colors in the adits.

You crest the ridge a little less than 2 miles from the trailhead and about 1000 feet higher. Catch your breath and enjoy your first view of Miller Peak. Beyond this point, you contour along a ridge, crossing several fault blocks of Morita, Huachuca volcanics, and Huachuca quartz monzonite. You should be able to recognize these units by now.

The trail eventually climbs onto the ridge along gentle terrain produced by the easily eroded Morita Formation. The imposing pinnacles of limestone in this area are within the Huachuca volcanics.

Take advantage of the good viewpoint at 2.5 miles to look north across Lutz

View from Miller Peak, looking southeast across the San Pedro River valley and the south end of the Mule Mountains into Mexico

Canyon to the east ridge of Miller Peak. This is a good place to work out some of the complex structure of this area.

Notice that the lower part of the far slope has few outcrops, whereas the upper part has many. There is a reason for this: the lower part is Huachuca quartz monzonite, whereas the upper part is a *thrust plate* (a sheet of rock above a low-angle thrust fault) that brings the Huachuca volcanics over the monzonite. This sheet or plate forms the top of Miller Peak. Thrusts are formed by compressive forces active during mountain-building events. Note that the "plates" we are talking about here are not the crustal plates of plate tectonics but rather smaller thinner ones that involve only a tiny part of the crust.

You may also discover that the eastern part of the same ridge looks different from the rest of the ridge because it has many rugged outcrops of rock that look like limestone. This is limestone in a thrust plate that rode over both the quartz monzonite and the plate of Huachuca volcanics. The plates or sheets are stacked on top of one another, and the limestone plate is the youngest.

Movement along these thrust sheets occurred in latest Mesozoic time and were part of the Laramide orogeny. This was a great mountain-building event associated with the collision of plates.

The final climb to the peak is in beautiful stands of cool-climate trees, including aspen. These are refugees that, during the cooler and wetter ice ages, lived at much lower elevations. If the climate gets any warmer, they will all disappear because there will be no higher ground to which to retreat.

You climb through rugged outcrops of quartz monzonite that look like granite—this might as well be the Sierra Nevada. The outcrops end at the top of the aspen grove and only a little below the summit: you have crossed the thrust fault and are now in the thrust plate of Huachuca volcanics. The very top of the peak is a limestone mass within these volcanics.

The view from the top at 5.3 miles is well worth the climb. To the south you see the ranges in Mexico and the mighty plume of smoke and general pollution from the Canaanea copper mine. To the west are the Patagonia Mountains. To the northwest are the tooth of Baboquivari Peak, the distinctive pyramid of Mount Wrightson in the Santa Ritas, and the headwaters of the Santa Cruz River in the San Rafael Valley. To the north, you can see the great domes of the Santa Catalinas and the Rincons near Tucson, and closer at hand, the Whetstones with their tilted Paleozoic strata and the suburban sprawl of Sierra Vista.

The Pinalenos are the distant hump on the skyline to the northeast. The Dragoons are closer at hand in the same general direction, and behind them you can just make out the double peaks of the Dos Cabezas. To the east, you see the broad valley of the San Pedro River, then the Mule Mountains, and in the distance, the broad mass of the Chiricahuas. Views like these, 100 miles in all directions, do not come along every day.

MONTE VISTA
LOOKOUT TRAIL

Hike 39

This shaded mountain hike within the Turkey Creek caldera leads to a superb alpine view of the rugged Chiricahua Mountains and surrounding basin and range country.

LOCATION ■ Chiricahua Wilderness, Coronado National Forest

DISTANCE ■ About 4 miles one way

ELEVATION ■ 6640 to 9355 feet

DIFFICULTY ■ Moderately strenuous

TOPOGRAPHIC MAPS ■ Chiricahua Peak, AZ, 1:24,000; Willcox, AZ, 1:100,000; Chiricahua Peak, AZ, 1:100,000

GEOLOGIC MAPS ■ 31 and 32

PRECAUTIONS ■ Likely to be impassable due to snow from December to March. Watch for lightning in summer.

INFORMATION ■ Coronado National Forest, Douglas Ranger District 3081

Landscape and Geology: The Chiricahua Mountains are the faulted and eroded remnant of an enormous volcano that formed here about 26 million years ago (Oligocene time). The original shape of the volcano is no longer visible because of faulting and erosion, but the history and configuration of the volcano can be reconstructed by carefully examining the rocks that it produced.

You can find a sketch of the history of the volcano in Hike 34 (Heart of Rocks–Echo Canyon). Also, USGS Map I-2541 (geologic map 31 at the back of the book) is a truly excellent overview and can be purchased at the visitor center.

The heart of the Chiricahua volcano is Turkey Creek *caldera*, a circular depression 12 miles in diameter that was the source of the rhyolite ash-flow tuff so characteristic of Chiricahua National Monument. *Ash-flow tuff* is the solidified froth of silica-rich lava that flowed at great speed out of the volcano. The caldera formed because eruption of an enormous volume of tuff left the roof of the magma chamber unsupported, causing it to collapse.

Not long after the collapse, more material from the magma chamber intruded the caldera floor, bowing it up into a *resurgent dome*, so called because the renewed emplacement of magma puffed up the volcano again. This time, the magma had the composition of *dacite*, less rich in silica than rhyolite. Some of the dacite also wormed its way along the faults at the caldera's edge and vented to the surface, accumulating mostly in the moat between the dome and the caldera wall. A little later, rhyolite lava rose to the surface, also forming flows within the moat.

The dacite and rhyolite are more resistant to erosion than other rocks, so they now form high ground, whereas the formerly higher but less resistant rocks of the caldera rim have been worn down to a level lower than the rhyolite and

View southeast from the Monte Vista Lookout

dacite. It is mostly the high ground that allows us to reconstruct where the caldera wall used to be.

Trail Guide: Exit from Interstate 10 south onto US 191, then take AZ 181 eastward to a junction with the dirt Turkey Creek road. Follow this road about 10.6 miles to its end at the trailhead for Morse Canyon Trail. Park in the lot, which provides no facilities. This excellent trail climbs steeply up the well-wooded north slope of the Johnson Peak–Monte Vista Peak complex and crests out on a saddle near Johnson Peak. Trees along the trail include Douglas fir, ponderosa pine, and other three-needle pines.

The trailhead and most of the Turkey Creek road are in the dacite of the resurgent dome, but this rock is not exposed at the trailhead. The large boulders here are part of *colluvium* that may have formed under near-glacial conditions during the last ice age. Colluvium is sediment and rocks that mantle a slope.

After crossing the creek and going beyond the first major switchback at one-half mile, you start walking on the *intracaldera* ash-flow tuff, which accumulated inside the caldera as it was collapsing. With the aid of a hand lens, you can see glassy rounded quartz crystals, elongated crystals of the feldspar *sanidine* (showing a play of colors), and yellowish fibrous clots of squashed *pumice* (chilled glass froth).

At Johnson Saddle (at about 2.5 miles), turn left at the trail junction toward Monte Vista Peak. The saddle is underlain by the rhyolite that flowed into the moat. This unexciting rock is medium gray and fine-grained and contains a few crystals of feldspar and rounded quartz, as well as small amounts of fine dark minerals. Exciting or not, this rock has the virtue of being so hard to erode that it forms much of the high ground of the Chiricahua crest in this area. Since the rhyolite flowed into the moat near the walls of the caldera, we can use the outcrops of the rhyolite, that is, the Chiricahua crest, to approximate the boundary of the ancient caldera.

At about 3.5 miles, turn right at the trail junction to Monte Vista Peak. The peak is made of a rhyolite tuff that contains crystals of quartz, feldspar, sanidine, minor dark minerals, and lots of squashed pumice.

The view from the top at about 4 miles is extensive, especially from the fire tower. The rugged mountains to the north are inside the Turkey Creek caldera. To the west you see the flats of Sulphur Springs Valley, backed by the Dragoon Mountains. The Chiricahua volcano once extended into these flats, but that part has been dropped down by basin and range faulting. The Swisshelm Mountains are in the distance to the southwest.

Turkey Mountain, about 2 miles in the middle distance to the southwest, is near the only place where the ancient structural boundary of Turkey Creek caldera is exposed. The low-lying country south of the steep south face of Turkey Mountain is underlain by easily eroded caldera wall rock of Cretaceous age, whereas Turkey Mountain and the country to its north are underlain by intracaldera tuff. The boundary of the caldera is between the two. This is a fine example of *topographic inversion*: the originally low area (caldera floor) is now high, whereas the originally high area (caldera rim) is now low. The inversion has come about because of the different resistance to erosion of fill versus wall.

In all other places, the caldera boundary is buried by the rhyolite and dacite that flowed out along it. You can still locate the ancient boundary approximately on the basis of topography: the resistant rhyolite and dacite now form

The Monte Vista Lookout

a high ridge just inward from the caldera boundary. The high ridge includes Raspberry Peak, Chiricahua Peak, and Flys Peak, all east and northeast of Montevista Peak.

MOUNT WRIGHTSON TRAIL

Hike 40

Rocks from a Mesozoic subduction zone are visible as you hike through lush forests to formidable alpine crags, then to a small meadow atop an isolated peak with a view of the world.

LOCATION ■ Mount Wrightson Wilderness, Coronado National Forest

DISTANCE ■ 13 miles round trip

ELEVATION ■ 5400 to 9453 feet

DIFFICULTY ■ Moderately strenuous

TOPOGRAPHIC MAPS ■ Mount Wrightson, AZ, 1:24,000; Fort Huachuca, AZ, 1:100,000

GEOLOGIC MAPS ■ 37

PRECAUTIONS ■ Avoid hiking in winter; snow and ice make some parts impassable or too slippery for safety.

INFORMATION ■ Coronado National Forest, Nogales Ranger District

Landscape and Geology: The Santa Rita Mountains are part of a zone of abundant plutonic and volcanic rocks of Mesozoic age, many of which are associated with mineralization responsible for Arizona's mining industry. All are the result of a persistent subduction zone that developed off the southwest margin of the continent at the end of Triassic time and lasted for about 150 million years to the beginning of the Cenozoic.

At the subduction zone, dense oceanic crust was dragged down under the continent, where it was heated and melted. This materal then rose to the surface in the form of magma to produce volcanoes and the plutons under them (see figure 6). The volcanoes were mostly in the form of an offshore island arc, as is the case today with the Japanese Archipelago and the Aleutian Islands.

Two distinct events are recorded in the Santa Ritas. The older Triassic to Jurassic event (210–180 million years ago) produced the Mount Wrightson Formation, a collection of rhyolitic-through-andesitic flows and welded *tuffs* (volcanic ash deposits) that locally contain interbeds of sedimentary rocks. One of these, a cross-bedded *eolian* (windblown) sandstone, may be the same age as similar well-known eolian sandstones of the Colorado Plateau.

The younger event happened some 69 million years ago in latest Cretaceous time and produced a series of volcanic and plutonic rocks similar to those of the first event. Only the plutonic rocks of this event—the Madera Canyon granodiorite and the Josephine Canyon diorite—are exposed along the trail.

Mount Wrightson's summit, composed of the Mount Wrightson Formation

Geologists have come to realize that rock suites of the kind just described may be related to *calderas*, huge craters produced by volcanic eruption and subsequent collapse. The magma is the product of subduction. The volcanic rocks, especially the welded tuffs, are the part of the magma that reached the surface in or near the caldera. The plutonic rocks represent that portion of the magma that cooled and solidified at depth under the caldera. The mineralization so widespread in the Tucson area is associated with these magmatic events, especially the Cretaceous one. Hot, mineral-rich fluids derived from the magma altered the rocks and enriched them in valuable minerals. In places, the fluids also altered volcanic rocks by adding silica (SiO_2), making them very hard. We can see the result of this in the Wrightson Formation, the very hard middle member of which forms the impressive summit crags and cliffs of Mount Wrightson and is responsible for the mountain's lofty height.

Trail Guide: Exit from Interstate 19 at Exit 63. Follow the brown signs for Madera Canyon Recreation Area. Go about 15 miles on a paved road to the parking lot at the end of the road in Madera Canyon. The recreation area includes a campground.

The route followed here begins up the gentle grade of the Super Trail. It starts by climbing the north slope of the mountain through lush woods of alligator juniper, live oak, pine, madrone, sycamore in the washes, and Douglas fir at higher elevations. The trail is in the Madera Canyon granodiorite, part of a Cretaceous pluton. This is a medium- to coarse-grained *equigranular* (crystals are all the same size) granitic rock. Your hand lens can show you glassy quartz, white to pink feldspar, black shiny *biotite* mica in "books," and small amounts of the black mineral *hornblende* with a satin sheen. In places, the rock weathers to yellow and forms a sandy soil called *grus* that makes for easy walking.

You can usually find drinking water at Sprung Spring at 3.5 miles. Near here, you start walking on the Josephine Canyon quartz diorite, another Cretaceous plutonic rock. You won't see much, though, because this is a chilled fine-grained contact zone with poor exposures.

At Josephine Saddle, about 1000 feet beyond the spring, you come to several trail intersections. Keep bearing left and follow the Old Baldy Trail to Mount Wrightson.

Shortly after the last of these junctions, you enter a new and distinctly different rock type, consisting of brownish gray to reddish fine-grained igneous rocks. Some have boxy crystals of feldspar, others have flow banding, while others have wormy features that look like collapsed cavities. These are dacite, latite, and rhyolite lava flows and ash-flow tuffs of the Triassic and Jurassic Mount Wrightson Formation, in which the trail remains all the way to the summit. These rocks were probably deposited in or near a volcanic caldera about 180 million years ago. Then, 100 million years later, they were intruded by the granodiorite and quartz diorite through which you have been walking. This intrusion altered, recrystallized, and silicified them (hardened them with silica). These processes make the rocks difficult to identify, but the silicification makes the rocks hard, giving rise to the rugged mountain scenery ahead.

The trail is now in an open country of grass, ferns, deciduous oaks, and pines. Douglas firs nestle in the summit crags, which are made picturesque by steep jointing. Bellows Spring generally has water.

The next task is to climb up through a notch in a cliff made by the Mount Wrightson Formation. At 5.5 miles from the trailhead, the ridge on top rewards you with nice logs on which to rest.

When you are ready to continue, keep right at the next two trail junctions. After rounding a nose beyond the second junction, you may notice a prominent outcrop of a new kind of rock right across the trail. This is orange-yellow cross-bedded sandstone, with quartz grains that are fine, well rounded, and all the same size. The cross bedding is steep and parallel (see figure 12). These features tell you that these are ancient sand dunes. This is the eolian sandstone within the Mount Wrightson Formation.

The trail then switchbacks to the summit through and over cliffs of the Mount Wrightson Formation. Watch your footing—a few spots are tricky. At about 6.5 miles, the surprisingly small top of Mount Wrightson sports a meadow and the remnants of an old lookout. The views are exceptional, even in this country of exceptional views. This isolated summit can also be very windy—don't get blown off!

Far to the east is the large hump of the Chiricahuas (Hikes 34 and 39); the Huachucas (Hike 38) are to the southeast, and the Patagonias to the south. To the southwest across the broad valley of the Santa Cruz River, you can see the

Atascosa Mountains (Hike 28) and the tooth shape of Baboquivari to the west. Mount Hopkins Observatory is in the middle distance in this direction. To the north, the rounded humps of the Catalinas (Hike 37) and Rincons rise above the Tucson basin; the Whetstones complete the picture in the middle distance to the northeast. Now aren't you glad you struggled up here?

On the return trip, keep right at the first trail junction and follow the Super Trail down to Josephine Saddle. You can make great time on this even-graded trail on the south side of the mountain. This trail is in chaparral country, affording fine views to the south but little shade. There are good outcrops of the Mount Wrightson Formation all along the trail.

Once on the southwest side of the mountain, you go through a zone of dark-gray, fine-grained rock with large feldspar crystals. This is the Mount Wrightson Formation here altered by *contact metamorphism* (heating and pressure along a narrow zone) produced by intrusion of the nearby Josephine Canyon quartz diorite. You encounter this diorite in the switchbacks as you descend, where it is finely crystalline, medium gray, with conspicuous dark minerals.

At Josephine Saddle, follow the Old Baldy Trail all the way back to the parking lot. Once you drop off the saddle, this trail is in the Madera Canyon granodiorite.

View from Mount Wrightson, looking west. You can see the Mount Hopkins Observatory, the Santa Cruz valley, and Baboquivari Peak. The Mount Wrightson Foundation is underfoot.

SYCAMORE CANYON TRAIL

Hike 41

*If you are not too distracted by the excellent swimming holes,
lush riparian vegetation, and interesting birds, this short hike is
a great place to examine Tertiary rhyolite flows and tuffs.*

LOCATION ■ Pajarita Wilderness, Coronado National Forest

DISTANCE ■ About 2.5 miles one way

ELEVATION ■ 4000 to 3750 feet

DIFFICULTY ■ Moderate

TOPOGRAPHIC MAPS ■ Ruby, AZ, 1:24,000; Atascosa Mountains, AZ–Sonora,
1:100,000

GEOLOGIC MAPS ■ 25

PRECAUTIONS ■ Watch out for extreme heat and flash floods in summer in this
remote area.

INFORMATION ■ Coronado National Forest, Nogales Ranger District

Landscape and Geology: This rugged canyon is carved into rhyolite flows
and tuffs of Miocene age. The scenery of Sycamore Canyon is enhanced by
the weathering characteristics of the rocks, which result in pinnacles along
the sides of the canyon and smooth water-polished rock in the streambed.

The rocks along the canyon are the same age as those of the Atascosa
Mountains to the northeast (Hike 28). They are present here at low elevation
within a *graben*—a zone dropped down relative to its surroundings by two faults
along its sides. The faults strike northward, and the western one passes near
the old mining area of Ruby.

Trail Guide: Turn west off Interstate 19 at Exit 12, the Peña Blanca/Ruby Road,
AZ 289. Follow the road 9 miles west to Peña Blanca Recreation Area where the
pavement ends and the road becomes the Arivaca–Ruby Road, FR 39. Continue
about 9.5 miles to Sycamore Canyon, where road FR 218 splits off to the south
and leads in a few hundred yards to the trailhead for the Sycamore Canyon
Trail, #40. Park at the trailhead parking lot, which has no facilities. The trail
can be followed as far as the Mexican border, about 6 miles away, but the most
interesting and scenic parts are in the first 2.5 miles or so, the part logged here.

The remnants of an adobe wall a short distance down the trail mark the site
of an old ranch that was active briefly in the 1880s. The ranchers were driven
off by Native American attacks in 1886. The rounded hills here are developed
on late Cenozoic sedimentary basin fill that supports live oaks and grassland.
The trail soon enters the wash, where it becomes indistinct. Follow whatever
track you can find or find your own path, but stay generally along the wash.

The first outcrops you come to are of a dark, fine-grained sheeted igneous rock
with no visible quartz—probably a basalt. From here on down, the rocks are rhyolite flows (silica-rich lava), tuffs (volcanic ash), and volcanic sediments.

Tuffs and flows in Sycamore Canyon

At first, the canyon walls are made up of unbedded horizontal flows of rhyolite weathered to rounded shapes. The yellow-white color shows that the rock has been *devitrified*, meaning that the glass that originally formed the rock (which was caused by rapid cooling) has been altered by the growth of fine crystals.

Some of the rhyolite forms irregular, gnarled outcrops. This is *flow breccia*, formed when chunks of partially solidified rock at the surface of the lava flow is broken up and incorporated within the still-flowing interior.

You can get a good look at features typical of rhyolite flows by carefully examining the water-polished rock in the bed of the stream. You can see *flow banding*, produced when the rhyolite lava is still oozing like taffy. Notice the vugs filled with the bluish-white mineral *chalcedony* (microcrystalline quartz) and the spherical cavities filled with needle-like quartz and feldspar crystals growing outward from the center, appropriately named *spherulites*. Also note the bubble-like masses with concentric shells a few hundred feet upstream from a conspicuous pinnacle on the left side of the wash. These features are caused by gases and fluids trapped within the cooling lava.

Beyond the pinnacle and an open stretch, at about 1 mile from the trailhead, you must climb over a spur on the left, using a rough path that starts just left of an obvious camping spot under an overhang. At high water, you must use this route. At low water, you can instead go down the wash a few hundred feet to where flow breccia forms a dam across the river. You can get by the lovely swimming hole below the dam by making your way on the right.

If you have gone over the spur, work your way back down to the canyon floor in about 500 feet. Follow the obvious way down. The canyon narrows a short distance beyond this point, in an area of steeply dipping well-bedded rocks that contain pebbles in places. The pebbly layers are tuffaceous sediments and the fine-grained ones are *air-fall tuffs*, the kind of tuff made by volcanic ash settling out of the sky during an eruption. Here, you can see at close range how these well-bedded pebbly rocks differ from rhyolite lava flows.

At 1.3 miles, the water-worn and rounded rocks form a picturesque slick-rock slot with water pools at the bottom. This is one of the most interesting and photogenic parts of the canyon. Be careful as you walk through this narrow part of the canyon. Dogs are likely to have trouble finding their footing on the steep, slick rock surfaces and may refuse to go farther.

You may notice while walking that the narrow parts of the canyon contain almost no river gravel, whereas the wider parts are full of stream debris. This has to do with the velocity of the water. A stream in flood flows very rapidly through narrow places. The speed greatly increases the energy of the flowing water, enabling it to move any debris it encounters. In the wider reaches, however, the speed of the water slackens and so does its energy. Thus, the water

Flow bonding in rhyolite (Sycamore Canyon)

can no longer move sediment and drops what it had picked up in the narrows.

Beyond the narrows, you discover a wider canyon and many sycamore trees. These attractive plants are common along flowing streams in Arizona.

Water flows from a narrow canyon entering the main wash from the east a few hundred feet downstream from the narrows. The much wider Penasco Canyon, which also enters from the east about one-half mile from the narrows, has no water in it.

The dark glassy material visible on the left just upstream from the confluence with Penasco Canyon is volcanic glass formed by rapid cooling at the base of a lava flow.

Continue about one-third mile downstream from Penasco Canyon. In this stretch, you see gently dipping ash-flow tuffs, which form thick beds with no internal layering, and well-bedded air-fall tuffs and tuffaceous sediments. This is a good place to see the difference between these kinds of deposits. You may be lucky and see rare birds here. This is also a good place to turn around.

Glossary

aa lava—volcanic lava flow having a rough, jagged, clinkery surface

aggradation—building up of a river's bed through deposition of sediments carried by the river

air-fall tuff—well-bedded sedimentary rock composed of volcanic ash that fell showerlike from the sky during a volcanic eruption

alluvial fan—thick sloping mass of loose rock shaped like a fan and deposited by a stream where it comes out of a narrow mountain valley onto a plain or basin

alluvium—unconsolidated sedimentary detritus deposited in recent geologic time by running water in the bed or floodplain of a stream, in a delta, or as a fan or pediment at the foot of a mountain slope

amphibole—group of common silicates; part of the "dark minerals" containing iron, magnesium, calcium, and sodium

andesite—dark-colored, fine-grained volcanic rock that is the extrusive equivalent of diorite; may contain crystals of sodium-rich plagioclase and dark minerals

angle of repose—maximum angle from the horizontal for a slope on which loose material such as sand stays without sliding

angular—said of a sedimentary particle that has not been affected by abrasion and that retains its original shape, with sharp edges and angles

angular unconformity—type of unconformity (gap in the geologic record) in which strata above and below it are not parallel

anticline—convex upward (arch-shaped) structural fold whose core contains older rocks

arkose—feldspar-rich sandstone, typically reddish, composed of the products of disintegration of granite

arroyo—small, flat-floored, steep-walled channel or gully of an ephemeral or intermittent stream in arid regions

ash—fine particulate material ejected by a volcano

ash-flow tuff—consolidated deposit of volcanic ash that erupted from a volcano along with great quantities of gases and traveled down the flanks of the volcano

attitude—position of a structural surface such as bedding relative to the horizontal, expressed by measurement of its strike and dip

augen—large mineral grains or aggregates in schist and gneiss that have a lens-shaped, eye-like form

augite—common mineral of the pyroxene group, generally black or dark green

badlands—intricate topography carved by erosion into weak rocks

bajada—broad, continuous, thick alluvial slope extending from the base of a mountain range into a nearby basin, formed by the lateral joining of many alluvial fans, giving it an undulating surface

basalt—dark-colored, silica-poor volcanic rock composed of calcium-rich plagioclase and pyroxene; occurs mostly as lava flows but also as shallow intrusive masses such as dikes

basement—foundation of igneous and metamorphic rocks below the lowest sedimentary rock in any given area

base surge—ring-shaped cloud of gas and suspended solid debris that moves radially outward at high velocity from a volcanic explosion

basin fill—material deposited in a topographic low or basin

basin and range—said of structure or terrain dominated by generally parallel fault-block mountains separated by broad alluvium-filled downdropped basins

batholith—large plutonic mass that covers an area of more than 40 square miles

bedding—arrangement of sedimentary rocks in beds or layers; also the characteristics of the pattern of beds

bench—horizontal tread-like surface produced by erosion or by a resistant layer

bentonite—clay rich in the mineral montmorillonite, produced by alteration of volcanic material such as tuff or volcanic ash; swells greatly when wet

biotite—dark mica, a common silicate mineral with a sheet crystal structure tending to break into flakes; contains iron, magnesium, aluminum, and potassium

block lava—basalt lava with a rough surface composed of angular blocks

bolson—flat-floored alluvium-filled desert basin into which drainage from the surrounding mountains empties

bomb—rounded mass of lava larger than about 2.5 inches in size ejected from a volcano while still viscous and shaped during flight

brachiopod—fossil marine mollusk in which the upper and lower valves (shells) have different shapes

breccia—coarse-grained clastic rock composed of angular broken rock fragments held together by a mineral cement or fine-grained matrix

brittle—said of a rock or style of deformation characterized by fracturing rather than flowing like taffy

calcite—common mineral composed of calcium carbonate ($CaCO_3$)that is the main constituent of limestone and a common cement of sandstone

caldera—large, basin-shaped, roughly circular volcanic depression created by collapse of a volcano after a great eruption

capture—process by which the headwaters of a more energetic stream divert the water and "pirate" the drainage basin of a less energetic one

carbonate—common rock-forming compound that contains carbon and oxygen (CO_3), such as calcite ($CaCO_3$); another name for limestone and dolomite

cavernous zone—part of a welded tuff that has many cavities

cement—mineral material, usually chemically precipitated, that occurs in the spaces between individual grains of a consolidated sedimentary rock, binding the grains together

Cenozoic—era of geologic time between about 65 million years ago and the present characterized by the evolution and abundance of mammals, birds, and flowering plants

chatoyance—property of certain minerals in reflected light to produce a play of light or color

chemical rock—sedimentary rock composed of material formed directly by chemical precipitation from a solution, such as rock salt

chert—hard, dense sedimentary rock composed of finely crystalline silica

chevron fold—structural fold in a zig-zag shape with sharp crests

chlorite—greenish, platy, mica-like aluminum-rich silicate mineral containing iron and magnesium

cienega—marshy meadow made wet by springs and having abundant vegetation

cinder cone—conical hill formed by the accumulation of mostly basaltic material ejected from a central vent marked by a crater

cirque—deep, steep-walled half-bowl located high on the side of a mountain, usually at the head of a glacial valley, and produced by the erosive activity of a mountain glacier

clast—individual constituent grain or fragment of a sedimentary rock produced by the mechanical disintegration of a larger rock mass; piece or chunk of rock such as a pebble

coarse-grained—said of a crystalline or sedimentary rock in which the grains are larger than 0.2 inch

colluvium—sheetlike body of angular and unsorted debris on a slope

columnar jointing—parallel, prismatic columns, generally polygonal in cross section, formed as a result of contraction during cooling of basaltic flows

composite volcano—steep-sided volcano constructed of alternating layers of viscous lava and fragmented volcanic material, along with dikes and sills; also called stratovolcano

concretion—hard, compact, typically spherical mass in a rock that is better cemented than the surrounding rock and erodes out

contact metamorphism—type of metamorphism that occurs in country rock near the margin of an intrusive mass due to heating, fluids emanating from the intrusion, and deformation from emplacement of the intrusive mass

continental shelf—that part of the continental margin that is between the shoreline and the continental slope, is nearly flat, and has a water depth less than about 650 feet

country rock—original surrounding rock that is intruded by an igneous mass

crater—general term for basin-like rimmed depression created by a volanic eruption or explosion, or by meteor impact

cropping out—said of bedrock that is exposed at the surface

cross bed—bedding in sandstone inclined at an angle to the main planes of stratification and caused by movement of sand by wind or water

crust—outermost layer or shell of the Earth ranging in thickness from about 5 to 30 miles and composed of more brittle, less dense material than the underlying mantle

dacite—fine-grained volcanic rock with more quartz than andesite, and calcium-poor plagioclase feldspar, commonly containing visible crystals; extrusive equivalent of granodiorite

dark minerals—dark-colored minerals rich in iron, magnesium, sodium, and calcium

detachment fault—low-angle fault that separates blocks of rock that have deformed in different and independent fashions

devitrified—said of rock in which the original volcanic glass has been converted to finely crystalline material

diabase— medium-grained intrusive rock consisting of lath-shaped plagioclase crystals enclosed in dark pyroxene crystals

diatreme—crater formed by a volcanic explosion and filled with broken-up rock, including tuff from the volcano

dike—tabular igneous intrusion that cuts across the bedding or foliation of the country rock (rock being intruded)

diorite—quartz-poor igneous rock with abundant dark minerals and sodium-rich plagioclase; intrusive equivalent of andesite

dip—angle between a structural surface such as bedding or a fault plane and the horizontal, measured perpendicular to strike; a surface with zero dip is horizontal and one with 90° dip is vertical

dip-slip fault—fault on which the movement is parallel to the dip

discharge—rate at which a river flows past a specific place at any given moment; amount of water flowing in a river or stream

dolomite—common mineral that is a carbonate, like calcite, but contains magnesium in addition to calcium; also, a sedimentary rock containing at least 50 percent of the mineral dolomite

dome—steep-sided, rounded extrusion of highly viscous lava squeezed out from a volcano, forming a dome-shaped or bulbous mass of congealed lava around the vent; also, a circular uplift or anticlinal structure in which the rocks dip away in all directions

dune—hill or ridge formed by loose, windblown sand, capable of movement from place to place

eolian—material moved and deposited by the wind

equigranular—said of a rock whose grains are all of roughly the same size

erosional unconformity—type of unconformity (gap in the geologic record) marked by an erosional surface that separates older rocks that have been subjected to erosion from younger sediments that cover them

exfoliation—form of weathering in which concentric shells of rock are successively loosened and separated from a block, tending to produce rounded outcrop surfaces

extension—increase in length in the Earth's crust resulting from structural pulling apart, as occurred in the Basin and Range Province

extrusive—type of igneous rock created by magma erupting onto the surface of the earth; equivalent to "volcanic"

fanglomerate—sedimentary rock consisting of fragments of all sizes, deposited in an alluvial fan, and later cemented into rock

fault—fracture or zone of fracture in the Earth's crust along which there has been displacement or movement of the sides relative to one another

fault-block range—mountain range made up of a structural block between two bounding faults at the margins of the range

feldspar—group of silicate minerals that contain aluminum, potassium, sodium, and calcium, the most common rock-forming minerals

fiamme—dark glassy lenses, 0.5 inch to a few inches in size, formed by the collapse of pumice fragments in welded tuffs

fine-grained—type of crystalline or sedimentary rock that has grains too small to be seen easily by the unaided eye

flow—liquid lava issuing and moving away from a vent at the surface; also, the solidified body of rock formed in this way

flow banding—banding produced by differences in color, minerals, or grain size in a rock such as rhyolite when it was flowing as a lava

flow breccia—lava flow containing broken fragments of rocks incorporated when lava is flowing; cooling crust breaks and is incorporated in the still-hot and moving interior of the flow

fold—bend of a planar structure, such as bedding or foliation, caused by deformation

foliation—planar arrangement of features in a rock, especially, the planar structure that results from the flattening of grains in a metamorphic rock

fossiliferous—type of sedimentary rock that contains abundant fossils

frosted—sand grains that look like frosted glass

fumarole—volcanic or geothermal vent from which gas and vapor are emitted

gabbro—dark plutonic rock, often coarse-grained, with calcium-rich plagioclase and pyroxene; intrusive equivalent of basalt

geologic province—extensive region characterized throughout by similar geologic history and features

geomorphology—science that treats the general configuration of the Earth's surface; also the classification, description, nature, origin, and development of present-day landforms

glacier—large mass of ice formed on land by the compaction and recrystallization of snow, surviving from year to year, and moving under its own weight

glass—amorphous (noncrystalline) product of rapid cooling of a magma in which crystals do not have time to grow

gneiss—foliated metamorphic rock consisting of alternating folded layers of light-colored minerals with dark-colored platy or flaky ones

gouge—soft, uncemented clayey rock material resulting from grinding along a fault

graben—down-dropped block between two approximately parallel faults

gradient—angle between the slope of a stream or river and the horizontal

granite—crystalline medium- to coarse-grained plutonic rock with abundant quartz; intrusive equivalent of rhyolite

granodiorite—coarse-grained plutonic rock intermediate in character between granite and diorite, containing quartz, plagioclase, potassium feldspar, and the dark minerals biotite and hornblende

groundmass—finer-grained material between visible crystals of a porphyritic igneous rock

grus—coarse, quartz-rich sandy soil with angular fragments, formed by in-place disintegration of granite

high-angle fault—fault with a dip greater than 45°

Holocene Epoch—interval of geologic time between the present and the end of the ice age, or Pleistocene; the last 10,000 years

hornfels—nondescript fine-grained rock produced by contact metamorphism

hydrothermal—of or pertaining to the action of hot water or to the product of this action, such as a mineral deposit precipitated from a hot water solution

igneous—type of rock or mineral solidified from molten underground magma or from lava

incision—process by which a downward-eroding stream deepens and entrenches its channel, producing a narrow, steep-walled valley

induration—hardening of rock by heat, pressure, or the introduction of cementing material

integrated drainage—system of interconnected streams and washes developed by coalescence across mountains and ridges of many formerly separate drainage basins

interior drainage—surface drainage that does not reach the sea but ends in a closed basin within a land mass, such as Death Valley

inverted topography—topography that is the inverse of geologic structure, such as a valley that occupies a structural dome or anticline

island arc—curved chain of islands associated with a subduction zone and rising from the deep sea floor near a continent

joint—surface of fracture or parting in a rock along which no displacement or movement takes place

karst—type of topography formed on limestone and other soluble rocks by chemical solution, characterized by sinkholes, caves, and underground drainage

laccolith—shallow igneous mass that has intruded strata, bowing the overlying beds into a dome

lahar—mudflow composed chiefly of volcanic debris on the flanks of a volcano

Laramide orogeny—major mountain-building event typically recorded in the Rocky Mountain area, which extended from late Cretacous into early Tertiary time, accompanied by emplacement of plutons, volcanism, and mineralization

latite—porphyritic volcanic rock with little quartz in which the visible crystals are plagioclase and potassium feldspar

lava dome—dome-shaped mass of viscous lava, generally silica-rich, that was forced to the surface by the pressure of the lava and solidified over or near the vent

limestone—sedimentary rock composed mainly of calcite (calcium carbonate, $CaCO_3$) and commonly formed by shells of fossil marine organisms

loess—blanket deposit of silt, generally covering wide areas

low-angle fault—fault that dips less than 45°

lower plate—block beneath a detachment fault in a metamorphic core complex, deformed in a nonbrittle, taffy-like way

mafic—dark-colored rock rich in dark minerals, those containing iron and magnesium

magma—mobile molten rock within the interior of the Earth that can intrude other rocks below the surface or vent to the surface, becoming lava

magma chamber—reservoir of magma in the crust at a depth of a few miles to tens of miles from which volcanic materials are derived

mantle—zone of the Earth's interior below the crust and above the core

marble—metamorphic rock consisting of fine- to coarse-grained recrystallized calcite or dolomite, usually with a sugary texture; metamorphosed limestone

matrix—finer-grained sediment filling the space between coarser fragments in a sedimentary rock

Mesozoic Era—geologic time between the Paleozoic and the Cenozoic, between about 250 and 65 million years ago, when reptiles flourished

metamorphic core complex—three-fold geologic entity created by crustal extension in which an "upper plate" has deformed in brittle fashion along many faults, a lower plate of gneiss has deformed in plastic fashion, and a detachment fault separates the two and marks the transition from plastic to brittle deformation

metamorphic rock—rock derived from any preexisting rock through changes in temperature, pressure, stress, or chemical environment in which the rock is not melted

metaquartzite—hard, durable metamorphic rock formed by recrystallization of original quartz sandstone through metamorphic processes

microcrystalline—said of the texture of a rock consisting of crystals so fine that they can be seen only under a microscope

mineral—inorganic element or compound having an orderly internal structure and characteristic chemical composition, crystal form, and physical properties

mineralogy—study of the properties of minerals, including their formation, occurrence, properties, composition, and classification

monocline—simple structural bend or fold in which a middle segment with a steeper dip is between two segments that are relatively flat

moraine—mound or ridge of unsorted glacial sediment, predominantly till, deposited by the direct action of a glacier

morphology—shape, form, and surface characteristics of an object or landscape

muscovite—colorless to yellow or pale brown potassium-bearing mica

neck—vertical pipe-like intrusion consisting of lava solidified in the vent of a volcano

normal fault—fault in which the block above the fault plane has moved relatively down with respect to the other block, in the "normal" sense

obsidian—black to dark-colored volcanic glass of rhyolitic composition

olivine—olive-green glassy silicate that is one of the "dark minerals" containing iron and magnesium; common constituent of basalt

ophitic—texture of igneous rocks such as diabase in which light-colored lath-shaped crystals of plagioclase are enclosed in dark crystals of pyroxene

orogeny—tectonic deformational event in the Earth's crust responsible for building mountains

orthoclase—type of feldspar (aluminum silicate) that contains potassium

Paleozoic Era—geologic time between the Proterozoic (Precambrian) and the Mesozoic, about 550 to 250 million years ago; when life forms became abundant and varied on Earth

pediment—broad, gently sloping, undulating, rock-floored erosion surface developed by running water in arid regions at the foot of a mountain front, mantled by a thin veneer of sediment that covers bedrock

pegmatite—exceptionally coarse-grained igneous rock, generally the same composition as granite, usually in dikes, lenses, and veins

period—unit of standard geologic time, such as the Jurassic Period; several periods are grouped into eras

petrology—study of the composition and origin of rocks

pillow—blob-shaped masses of lava closely fitted into one another and produced by lava flow or magma extrusion under water

piracy—process by which the headwaters of a more energetic stream divert the water and capture the drainage basin of a less energetic one

plagioclase—type of feldspar (aluminum silicate) that contains calcium and sodium

plate tectonics— science of the movement and interaction of the great plates into which the Earth's crust is divided

playa—flat-floored area occupied at times by an ephemeral lake

plug—vertical pipelike body of congealed lava filling the conduit of a former volcanic vent

pluton—general term for an igneous intrusion formed at depth by crystallization and solidification of magma

porphyritic—said of the texture of an igneous rock in which larger crystals are set in a finer-grained background, or groundmass

Precambrian—time before the beginning of the Cambrian Period, before about 550 million years ago and before the explosion of life on Earth

Proterozoic—that part of Precambrian time between about 2500 and 550 million years ago

pumice—light-colored, frothy glassy rock, typically of rhyolitic composition

pyroclastic—clastic or fragmental rock material such as cinders formed by explosive ejection from a volcanic vent

pyroxene—group of common silicate minerals, part of the "dark minerals" containing iron, magnesium, and calcium

quartz—one of the most common rock-forming minerals on Earth, composed of silicon dioxide (SiO_2)

quartz diorite—medium- to coarse-grained plutonic rock containing quartz and sodium-rich plagioclase;intrusive equivalent of dacite

quartzite—hard, well-indurated sedimentary or metamorphic rock composed of quartz grains cemented with silica

recessional moraine—end or lateral moraine built during a temporary pause in the final retreat of a glacier, composed of unsorted debris carried by the ice

resurgent dome—dome-shaped mass caused by the emplacement of new magma into the floor of a collapsed caldera

reverse fault—fault in which the block above the fault plane has moved relatively up with respect to the other block, in the "reverse" sense

rhyolite—volcanic rock high in silica, commonly with flow banding and crystals of quartz and potassium feldspar; extrusive equivalent of granite

rim—border, margin, edge, or face of a landform such as the curved brim surrounding the top part of a crater or caldera

ripple marks—ripple-shaped ridges and troughs preserved on bedding planes produced by wave action, currents, or wind on unconsolidated sediment

rock avalanche—very rapid, avalanche-like downslope movement of rock fragments

roof pendant—downward projection of country rock into an igneous intrusion at or near the top of the intrusion

rounding—degree to which the edges of a particle have been worn off, leaving a shape that approaches a sphere or ellipsoid

sandstone—medium-grained clastic sedimentary rock composed of sand-sized fragments and bonded by a cementing mineral such as calcite

sanidine—high-temperature potassium-bearing feldspar, common in rhyolite and rhyolitic welded tuff; typically glassy, with plays of light and color

schist—strongly foliated (banded) metamorphic rock that splits into flakes or slabs because of abundant parallel platy minerals such as mica

scree—broken rock fragments on a steep slope, generally below a cliff; also called talus

sedimentary rock—type of rock resulting from the consolidation of loose sediment such as clay, silt, sand, or gravel that has accumulated in layers

shield volcano—type of volcano that has the shape of a broad, flattened dome built of flows of fluid, usually basaltic lava

silica—common rock-forming compound, SiO_2, of which quartz is the most common form

silicate—group of minerals that contain silica in the form SiO_4; most common constituents of rocks

silicification—introduction of or replacement by silica in a rock

sill—nearly horizontal, tabular igneous intrusion that parallels the bedding or layering of the surrounding rocks

slate—fine-grained metamorphic rock, formed from shale, that can be split into slabs and thin plates

slickenside—polished and striated surface resulting from movement and friction along a fault plane

slickrock—colloquial term used on the Colorado Plateau to denote areas where bedrock (generally sandstone) is at the surface without being covered by alluvium

sorting—degree to which particles (clasts) in a sedimentary rock are of the same size

spheroidal weathering—form of weathering in which concentric shells of decayed rock are successively loosened and separated from a block, tending to produce rounded boulders

spherulite—rounded or spherical mass of needle-shaped crystals that radiate outward from a central point, most often composed of feldspar

stock—plutonic (intrusive) igneous mass that is less than 40 square miles in surface exposure area

stratigraphy—science and study of the properties of sedimentary rock layers (strata), including succession, age relations, form, distribution, composition, and fossil content

stratovolcano—steep-sided volcano composed of alternating layers of lava and fragmental material such as cinders and ash, with abundant dikes; also called a composite volcano

strike—direction of a horizontal line drawn on a structural surface such as bedding or a fault plane

strike ridge—ridge developed parallel to strike on a resistant rock layer

strike valley—valley eroded in, and parallel to the strike of, weak strata

stromatolite—fossil wavy layers in a sedimentary rock produced by the trapping of sediment by sticky microorganisms such as algae in a shallow sea

structure—general disposition, attitude, arrangement, and relative position of rock masses in the Earth's crust, including faults and folds

structural geology—branch of geology that deals with the form, arrangement, and internal structure of rocks and the processes by which the structure was formed

structural high—area where rocks are structurally higher than the same rocks in surrounding areas

subduction—plate tectonic process by which one crustal plate slides under another, usually an oceanic plate beneath continental crust

syncline—convex-upward (U-shaped) structural fold whose core contains the stratigraphically youngest rocks

tabular—type of feature in which two dimensions are much greater than the third, that is, thin compared to its extent

talus—broken rock fragments on a steep slope, generally below a cliff; also called scree

tectonics—study of the mutual relationships, origin, and historical evolution of structural and deformational features of the outer part of the Earth, seen at the broad scale

terminal moraine—accumulation of unsorted glacier sediment (till) forming an arc-shaped ridge across a valley and marking the farthest advance of a valley glacier

terrace—long, narrow, level or gently inclined surface, usually marking a former position of a river floodplain or a lake bed

texture—size, shape, and arrangement of constituent particles in a sedimentary rock or the crystallinity, granularity, and arrangement of minerals in an igneous rock

through-flowing drainage—system of interconnected rivers, streams, and washes that ultimately reach the sea

thrust fault—fault with a dip of 45° or less on which the block or plate above the fault has moved up, or has been thrust over, the one below

till—unsorted and unstratified material deposited directly by a glacier without reworking by water; consists of a mixture of clay, silt, sand, gravel, and boulders of any size

topographic inversion—process by which areas that originally were relatively low become higher than the formerly higher surroundings through preferential erosion, typically because the former low areas were shielded by a hard-to-erode cap such as basalt

tuff—general term for consolidated pyroclastic igneous rocks

tuff breccia—chaotic rock containing volcanic fragments of all sizes, as well as material wrenched from the walls of the vent

unconformity—break or gap in the geologic record representing rocks that are missing from the sequence

unsorted—said of sediment containing particles of all sizes, such as till

upper plate—plate or block of rock above a low-angle fault in a metamorphic core complex

volcanic ash—fine material (less than about $1/16$ of an inch), usually basaltic, ejected by a cinder cone or other volcanic vent

volcanic rock—generally fine-grained or glassy igneous rock, such as basalt, produced by rapid cooling of magma at or near the surface of the Earth

water table—below-ground level below which rocks or alluvium are saturated with water; top of groundwater level

welded tuff—volcanic rock rich in glass produced by the welding of hot, gas-charged silica-rich lava such as rhyolite

well rounded—said of a sedimentary particle whose original edges and corners have been removed by abrasion through sedimentary transport to form a rounded shape

Geologic Map List

PART 1—COLORADO PLATEAU

1. Geologic map of the eastern part of the Grand Canyon National Park and vicinity, P. W. Huntoon et al., *Grand Canyon Natural History*, Grand Canyon, Arizona (1986), 1:62,500.
2. Geology of the Lees Ferry area, Coconino County, Arizona, D. A. Phoenix, *USGS Bulletin 1137* (1963), 1:24,000.
3. Photogeologic map of the Lees Ferry SE quadrangle, Coconino County, Arizona, K. McQueen, *USGS Miscellaneous Investigations Map I-169* (1956), 1:24,000.
4. Geologic map of the Pine 7.5' quadrangle, Coconino and Gila Counties, Arizona, M. K. Weisman and G. W. Weir, *USGS Miscellaneous Field Studies Map MF-2123* (1990), 1:24,000.
5. Geology of the Clarkdale quadrangle, Arizona, R. E. Lehner, *USGS Bulletin 1021-N* (1958), 1:48,000.
6. No detailed geologic map is available, other than in a hard-to-get thesis. However, an informative guide with generalized maps is available. Guide with generalized maps: The mouth of the Grand Canyon and edge of the Colorado Plateau in the Upper Lake Mead area, Arizona, I. Lucchitta, *GSA Centennial Field Guide—Rocky Mountain Section*, Guide No. 82 (1987): 365–370.
7. Geologic map of the Sedona 30' x 60' quadrangle, Yavapai and Coconino Counties, Arizona, G. W. Weir et al., *USGS Miscellaneous Investigations Series Map I-1896* (1989), 1:100,000. Also refer to: R.F. Holm and R.A. Cloud, "Regional significance of recurrent faulting and intracanyon volcanism at Oak Creek Canyon, southern Colorado Plateau, Arizona," *Geology 18* (1990): 1014–1017.
8. Geology and uranium–vanadium deposits of the Monument Valley area, Apache and Navajo Counties, Arizona, I. J. Witkind and R. E. Thaden, *USGS Bulletin 1103* (1963), 1:24,000, 1:31,680, 1:62,500.
9. Stratigraphy of the Chinle and Moenkopi Formations, Navajo and Hopi Indian Reservations, Arizona, New Mexico, and Utah, C. A. Repenning et al., *USGS Professional Paper 521-B* (1969), 1:500,000.
10. You don't really need a geologic map for this walk, and no detailed map is available. Regional hydrogeology of the Navajo and Hopi Indian Reservations, Arizona, New Mexico, and Utah, M. E. Cooley et al., *USGS Professional Paper 531-A* (1969), 1:125,000.

11. Magmatism associated with lithospheric extension: middle to late Cenozoic magmatism of the southeastern Colorado Plateau and central Rio Grande rift, New Mexico and Arizona, W. S. Baldridge et al., in "Field excursions to volcanic terranes in the western United States, Volume I: Southern Rocky Mountain Region," *New Mexico Institute of Mining and Technology Memoir 46* (1989) (no map scale given).

12. Geologic map of the eastern San Francisco volcanic field, Arizona, R. B. Moore and E. W. Wolfe, *USGS Miscellaneous Investigations Map I-953* (1976), 1:50,000.

13. Geologic map of San Francisco Mountain, Elden Mountain, Dry Lake Hills, Coconino County, Arizona, R. F. Holm, *USGS Miscellaneous Investigations Map I-1663* (1988), 1:24,000.

14. Geologic map of the central part of the San Francisco Volcanic Field, north-central Arizona, E. W. Wolfe et al., *USGS Miscellaneous Field Studies Map MF-1959* (1987), 1:50,000.

15. Geologic map of the northwest part of the San Francisco Volcanic Field, north-central Arizona, E. W. Wolfe et al., *USGS Miscellaneous Field Studies Map MF-1957* (1987), 1:50,000.

16. Geologic map of the SP Mountain part of the San Francisco Volcanic Field, north-central Arizona, G. E. Ulrich and N. E. Bailey, *USGS Miscellaneous Field Studies Map MF-1956* (1987), 1:50,000.

17. Geologic map of Vulcans Throne and vicinity, western Grand Canyon, Arizona, G. H. Billingsley and P. W. Huntoon, *Grand Canyon Natural History Association, Grand Canyon, Arizona* (1983), 1:48,000.

18. Breccia-pipe and geologic map of the northeastern part of the Hualapai Indian Reservation and vicinity, Arizona, K. J. Wenrich, *USGS Miscellaneous Investigation Series, I-2440,* 1:48,000.

PART 2 — ARIZONA TRANSITION ZONE

19. Geologic map of the Sierra Ancha Wilderness and Salome study area, Gila County, Arizona, J. R. Bergquist et al., *USGS Miscellaneous Field Studies Map MF-1162-A* (1981), 1:48,000.

20. Geologic map and balanced cross-section of the northern Mazatzal Mountains, central Arizona, D. D. Puls, *Arizona Geological Survey Contributed Map 91-B* (1985), 1:10,000.

21. Geologic map of the Mingus Mountain Quadrangle, Yavapai County, Arizona, C. A. Anderson and S. C. Creasey, *USGS Geologic Quadrangle Map GQ-715* (1967), 1:62,500.

22. Geologic map of Florence Junction and the southern portion of the Weavers Needle 7.5' quadrangles, Pinal County, Arizona, C. A. Ferguson and S. J. Skotnicki, *Arizona Geological Survey Open-File Report 95-10* (1995), 1:24,000.

23. Geology of the Globe copper district, Arizona, F.L. Ransome, *USGS Professional Paper 12* (1903), 1:12,000, 1:62,500.

PART 3—BASIN AND RANGE PROVINCE

24. Geologic map of the Brandenburg Mountain quadrangle, Pinal County, Arizona, M. H. Krieger, *USGS Geologic Quadrangle Map GQ-668* (1968), 1:24,000.

25. Mineral resource potential and geology of Coronado National Forest, southeastern Arizona and southwestern New Mexico, E. A. Du Bray, ed., *USGS Bulletin 2083A-K* (1996).

26. Geologic map of the Centennial Wash quadrangle, Mohave and La Paz Counties, Arizona, I. Lucchitta and N. H. Suneson, *USGS Geologic Quadrangle Map GQ-1718* (1994), 1:24,000.

27. Geologic map and cross sections of the Dragoon Mountains, southeastern Arizona, H. Drewes, *USGS Miscellaneous Field Studies Map I-1662* (1987), 1:24,000.

28. Reconnaissance geologic map of the Mount Ajo and part of the Pisinimo quadrangles, Pima County, Arizona, R. M. Tosdal et al., *USGS Miscellaneous Field Studies Map MF-1820* (1986), 1:62,500.

29. Interpretative geologic map of Mount Ajo quadrangle, Organ Pipe National Monument, Arizona, J. L. Brown, *USGS Open-File Report 92-23* (1992), 1:24,000.

30. Geologic map and sections of the Bowie Mountain North quadrangle, Cochise County, Arizona, H. Drewes, *USGS Miscellaneous Investigations Map I-1492* (1981), 1:24,000.

31. Interpretative map and guide to the volcanic geology of Chiricahua National Monument and vicinity, Cochise County, Arizona, J. S. Pallister and E. A. du Bray, *USGS Miscellaneous Investigations Map I-2541* (1997), 1:24,000.

32. Geologic map of the Chiricahua Peak quadrangle, Cochise County, Arizona, E. A. du Bray and J. S. Pallister, *USGS Geologic Quadrangle Map GQ-1733* (1994), 1:24,000.

33. Geologic map of the Tucson Mountains caldera, southern Arizona, P. W. Lipman, *USGS Miscellaneous Investigations Map I-2205* (1993), 1:24,000.

34. Reconnaissance geologic map of the Picacho Mountains, Arizona, W. E. Yeend, *USGS Miscellaneous Field Studies Map MF-778* (1976), 1:62,500.

35. Geology and mineral resources of the Santa Catalina Mountains, southeastern Arizona: A cross sectional approach, E. R. Force, *University of Arizona, Center for Mineral Resources, Monographs in Mineral Resource Science No. 1*, 1:12,000, 1:48,000.

36. Geologic map of the Huachuca and Mustang Mountains, southeastern Arizona, P. T. Hayes and R. B. Raup, *USGS Miscellaneous Investigations Map I-509* (1968), 1:48,000.

37. Geologic map of the Mount Wrightson quadrangle, southeast of Tucson, Santa Cruz and Pima Counties, Arizona, H. Drewes, *USGS Miscellaneous Investigations Map I-614* (1971), 1:48,000.

Suggested Reading

ARIZONA GEOLOGY

Beus, S. S., and M. Morales, eds. *Grand Canyon Geology*. New York: Oxford University Press, 1990. The best summary of the geology of the Grand Canyon written in a reasonably comprehensible way for the interested nongeologist.

Chronic, H. *Roadside Geology of Arizona*. Missoula, Mont: Mountain Press Publishing Company, 1983. An informative guide to the geology of the state as seen from the highway, intended for the layperson.

Duffield, W. A. *Volcanoes of Northern Arizona*. Grand Canyon, Ariz.: Grand Canyon Association, 1997. A very readable, lucid, and wonderfully illustrated guide to the "sleeping giants of the Grand Canyon region."

Jenney, J. P., and S. J. Reynolds, eds. "Geologic Evolution of Arizona." *Arizona Geologic Society Digest* 17 (1989). The most comprehensive summary of Arizona geology but intended for the specialist.

Smiley, T. L., J. D. Nations, T. L. Pewe, and J. P. Schafer, eds. *Landscapes of Arizona*. Lanham, Md.: University Press of America, 1984. The evolution of Arizona's landscape written for the nongeologist. It contains many fine photographs, but may be hard to find.

GENERAL GEOLOGY AND TEXTBOOKS

Hamblin, W. K., and E. H. Christiansen. *Earth's Dynamic Systems*. Upper Saddle River, N.J.: Prentice Hall, 2001. A good introductory textbook distinguished by excellent illustrations.

McPhee, J. A. *Rising from the Plains*. New York: Farrar, Straus, Giroux, 1986. Few authors match John McPhee in capturing the excitement of geology for the layperson. Here is his account of the formation of the Rocky Mountains.

McPhee, J. A. *Basin and Range*. New York: Farrar, Straus, Giroux, 1981. The inimitable McPhee describes the geology of the Basin and Range Province.

Pielou, E. C. *After the Ice Age*. Chicago: The University of Chicago Press, 1991. An account of the waxing and waning of ice sheets during the ice ages and of life's response to these changes.

Thomson, G. R., and J. Turk. *Modern Physical Geology*. Fort Worth, Tex.: Saunders College Publishing, 1997. A great introductory textbook with wonderful illustrations.

Wicander R., and J. S. Monroe. *Essentials of Geology*. Belmont, Calif.: West/ Wadsworth, 1999. A fine introductory textbook.

HIKING GUIDEBOOKS

Mangum, R. K., and S. G. Mangum. *Flagstaff Hikes.* Flagstaff, Ariz.: Hexagon Press, 1998. A comprehensive collection of hikes in the Flagstaff area.

Mangum, R. K., and S. G. Mangum. *Sedona Hikes.* Flagstaff, Ariz: Hexagon Press, 2000. A comprehensive collection of hikes in the Sedona area.

Mazel, D. *Arizona Trails.* Berkeley, Calif.: Wilderness Press, 1992. A guide to trails in much of the state.

Molvar, E. *Hiking Arizona's Cactus Country.* Helena, Mont.: Falcon Press, 1995. Good for the southern part of the state.

Warren, S. S. *100 Classic Hikes in Arizona.* Seattle: The Mountaineers Books, 2000. A good basic hiking book.

Addresses and Contact Information

Apache–Sitgreaves National Forest
Springerville Ranger District
P.O. Box 760
Springerville, AZ 85938
Phone (520) 333-4372
www.fs.fed.us/r3/asnf/

Arizona State Parks
1300 West Washington
Phoenix, AZ 85007
Phone (602) 542-4174
www.pr.state.az.us/park

Bureau of Land Management
Kingman Field Office
2475 Beverly Avenue
Kingman, AZ 86401-3629
Phone (520) 692-4400
www.az.blm.gov/kfo/index.htm

Bureau of Land Management
Safford Field Office
711 14th Avenue
Safford, AZ 85546-3321
Phone (520) 348-4400
www.az.blm.gov/sfo/index.htm

Canyon de Chelly National Monument
Superintendent
P.O. Box 588
Chinle, AZ 86503
Phone (520) 674-5500
www.nps.gov/cach/

Chiricahua National Monument
Superintendent
HCR 2, Box 6500
Willcox, AZ 85643-9737
Phone (520) 824-3560
www.nps.gov/chir/

Coconino National Forest
Peaks Ranger District
5075 North Highway 89
Flagstaff, AZ 86004
Phone (520) 526-0866
www.fs.fed.us/r3/coconino/

Coconino National Forest
Sedona Ranger District
P.O. Box 300
250 Brewer Road
Sedona, AZ 86339-0330
Phone (520) 282-4119
www.fs.fed.us/r3/coconino/

Coronado National Forest
Douglas Ranger District
3081 North Leslie Canyon Road
Douglas, AZ 85607
Phone (520) 364-3468
www.fs.fed.us/r3/coronado/douglas
/index.html

Coronado National Forest
Nogales Ranger District
303 Old Tucson Road
Nogales, AZ 85621
Phone (520) 281-2296
www.fs.fed.us/r3/coronado/nrd
/nogo.htm

Coronado National Forest
Santa Catalina Ranger District
5700 North Sabino Canyon Road
Tucson, AZ 85750
Phone (520) 749-8700
www.fs.fed.us/r3/coronado/scrd/

Coronado National Memorial
4101 East Montezuma Canyon Road
Hereford, AZ 85615
Phone (520) 366-5515
www.nps.gov/coro/

Fort Bowie National Historic Site
Superintendent
HCR 2, Box 6500
Willcox, AZ 85643-9737
If disabled, phone (520) 847-2500
www.nps.gov/fobo/

Glen Canyon National
Recreation Area
Superintendent
P.O. Box 1507
Page, AZ 86040-1507
Phone (520) 608-6404
www.nps.gov/glca/

Grand Canyon National Park
P.O. Box 129
Grand Canyon, AZ 86023
Phone (520) 638-7888
www.nps.gov/grca/

Kaibab National Forest
800 South Sixth Street
Williams, AZ 86046
Phone (520) 635-8200
www.fs.fed.us/r3/kai/index.html

Lake Mead National
Recreation Area
601 Nevada Highway
Boulder City, NV 89005
Phone (702) 293-8907
www.nps.gov/lame/

Navajo National Monument
Superintendent
HC-71, Box 3
Tonalea, AZ 86044-9704
Phone (520) 672-2700
www.nps.gov/nava/

Organ Pipe Cactus National
Monument
Route 1, Box 100
Ajo, AZ 85321-9626
Phone (520) 387-6849
www.nps.gov/orpi/

Petrified Forest National Park
Superintendent
P.O. Box 2217
Petrified Forest National Park, AZ
86028
Phone (520) 524-6228
www.nps.gov/pefo

Prescott National Forest
Verde Ranger District
P.O. Box 670
300 East Highway 260
Camp Verde, AZ 86322
Phone (520) 567-4121
www.fs.fed.us/r3/prescott/

Saguaro National Park
3693 South Old Spanish Trail
Tucson, AZ 85730-5601
Phone (520) 733-5158
www.nps.gov/sagu

Tonto National Forest
Globe Ranger District
Route 1, Box 33
Globe, AZ 85501
Phone (520) 402-6200
*www.fs.fed.us/r3/tonto/districts
/districts.htm*

Tonto National Forest
Mesa Ranger District
26 North MacDonald Street
Mesa, AZ 85211-5800
Phone (480) 610-3300
*www.fs.fed.us/r3/tonto/districts
    /districts.htm*

Tonto National Forest
Payson Ranger District
1009 East Highway 260
Payson, AZ 85541
Phone (520) 474-7900
*www.fs.fed.us/r3/tonto/districts
    /districts.htm*

Tonto National Forest
Pleasant Valley Ranger District
P.O. Box 450
Forest Road #63
Young, AZ 85554
Phone (520) 462-4300
*www.fs.fed.us/r3/tonto/districts
    /districts.htm*

Tonto National Forest
Tonto Basin Ranger District
HC02, Box 4800
State Highway 88
Roosevelt, AZ 85545
Phone (520) 467-3200
*www.fs.fed.us/r3/tonto/districts
    /districts.htm*

West Aravaipa Ranger Station
Phone (520) 357-7111
*www.az.blm.gov/sfo/aravaipa
    /aravaipa.htm*

Index

About the Author

Ivo Lucchitta was born in central Europe as the dark clouds of World War II were gathering. In spite of this unpromising beginning, he earned a baccalaureate in classics in Rome, emigrated to the United States in 1956, and received his Bachelor of Science degree in geology at Caltech in 1961 and a Ph.D. in geology at Penn State in 1966. He then signed on with the U.S. Geological Survey in Flagstaff, Arizona.

After working initially on the Apollo program of lunar exploration, he returned to his main love, geological research done in the field. He has worked in many places in the western United States and Alaska and on a variety of topics. One persistent thread throughout his career has been the Grand Canyon and the Colorado River.

In time, his interest in revealing the charms of geology to interested non-specialists has led to a number of writings and to participation in television documentaries. The process continues with this book.

Ivo lives in Flagstaff with his wife, Baerbel, a husky dog, and a piano. His daughter Maya lives among the mists of Seattle.

Raechel Running Photography

THE MOUNTAINEERS, founded in 1906, is a nonprofit outdoor activity and conservation club, whose mission is "to explore, study, preserve, and enjoy the natural beauty of the outdoors . . . ." Based in Seattle, Washington, the club is now the third-largest such organization in the United States, with 15,000 members and five branches throughout Washington State.

The Mountaineers sponsors both classes and year-round outdoor activities in the Pacific Northwest, which include hiking, mountain climbing, ski-touring, snowshoeing, bicycling, camping, kayaking and canoeing, nature study, sailing, and adventure travel. The club's conservation division supports environmental causes through educational activities, sponsoring legislation, and presenting informational programs. All club activities are led by skilled, experienced volunteers, who are dedicated to promoting safe and responsible enjoyment and preservation of the outdoors.

If you would like to participate in these organized outdoor activities or the club's programs, consider a membership in The Mountaineers. For information and an application, write or call The Mountaineers, Club Headquarters, 300 Third Avenue West, Seattle, WA 98119;. 206-284-6310.

The Mountaineers Books, an active, nonprofit publishing program of the club, produces guidebooks, instructional texts, historical works, natural history guides, and works on environmental conservation. All books produced by The Mountaineers fulfill the club's mission.

Send or call for our catalog of more than 450 outdoor titles:

The Mountaineers Books
1001 SW Klickitat Way, Suite 201
Seattle, WA 98134
800-553-4453
mbooks@mountaineersbooks.org
www.mountaineersbooks.org

The Mountaineers Books is proud to be a corporate sponsor of Leave No Trace, whose mission is to promote and inspire responsible outdoor recreation through education, research, and partnerships. The Leave No Trace program is focused specifically on human-powered (non-motorized) recreation.

Leave No Trace strives to educate visitors about the nature of their recreational impacts, as well as offer techniques to prevent and minimize such impacts. Leave No Trace is best understood as an educational and ethical program, not as a set of rules and regulations. For more information, visit *www.lnt.org,* or call 800-332-4100.